Journeys into Night

... when I look around to see how we can win the war I see that there is only one sure path. We have no Continental army which can defeat the German military power. The blockade is broken and Hitler has Asia and probably Africa to draw from. Should he be repulsed here or not try invasion, he will recoil eastward, and we have nothing to stop him. But there is one thing that will bring him back and bring him down, and that is an absolutely devastating, exterminating attack by very heavy bombers from this country upon the Nazi homeland. We must be able to overwhelm them by this means, without which I do not see a way through. (Churchill to Beaverbrook, July 8, 1940)

BY THE SAME AUTHOR

Marching as to War
Hudson

No Moon Tonight
Penguin

All the Green Year
Angus and Robertson

An Afternoon of Time
Angus and Robertson

Take-off to Touchdown
Angus and Robertson

Wrecks and Reputations
Warrnambool Institute Press

Settlers under Sail
Victorian Government Printer

Flight and Time
Neptune

The Long Farewell
Penguin

Journeys into Night

Don Charlwood

For Lila, who, with Ellis, helped an
unknown Australian "get the girl
in the end."

Much love,
Don Charlwood

HUDSON
HAWTHORN

Published by
HUDSON PUBLISHING
6 Muir Street, Hawthorn 3122
Victoria, Australia

First Published 1991
Reprinted 1991

Laserset in 11/14 pt Palatino by the publishers

Printed by Globe Press Pty Ltd
50 Weston Street, Brunswick 3056
Victoria, Australia

Australian C.I.P. data:

Charlwood, D.E. (Donald Ernest), 1915 –   .
  Journeys into Night.

  Includes index
  ISBN 0 949873 37 3

  1. Charlwood, D.E. (Donald Ernest), 1915 –
  – Biography. 2. World War, 1939-1945 – Personal
  narratives, Australian. 3. Novelists, Australian – 20th
  century – Biography. I. Title.

A823.1

Contents

To Geoff Maddern, Arthur Browett and Graham Briggs
– remnant of our crew of fifty years ago –
in remembrance of all those we knew together

Author's Note

In *Marching as to War* I wrote of my upbringing in Victoria between the World Wars and the shaping of our generation as 'children of the British Empire'. Those were days when most of us had grandparents from England, Ireland or Scotland and Australia reckoned herself ninety-eight percent British.

Although we were brought up in an unquestioning era, the older ones among us harboured a horror of war that stemmed from books and films and tales of men who had survived the cataclysmic 'war to end war'. No one, in my memory, was able to explain why the 'Great War' had been fought, nor did we ask too much, since this could have been construed as casting doubt on whether its fearful cost had been worthwhile – a question too painful for our elders to confront.

As related in *Marching as to War*, I went into RAAF aircrew before the entry of Japan into the Second World War and became one of 9000 Australians posted to RAF Bomber Command. Like the aircrew men of Canada, New Zealand, Rhodesia and many other parts of the now-vanished Empire, we saw ourselves as supporting the 'Homeland'.

In those years pilots and navigators trained for about eighteen months; once in Bomber Command, aircrew lives averaged about eighteen weeks. Of course, hundreds survived; some completed fifty, seventy, even a hundred 'operational sorties' over enemy territory. Years afterwards, when I saw a large group of survivors, I found it easy to delude myself, to think that, after all, it had been no more than an exhilarating adventure. In truth, those who survived were the tip of the iceberg of the dead. One has only to consider the replacement rate of the heavy bombers that the men flew; as Lord Cherwell reminded Churchill in 1942, 'We know from experience that we can count on nearly fourteen operational sorties per bomber produced.'* The minimum number of sorties set for a crew flying them was thirty.

My own experience was limited to thirty. I was somewhat older than most – twenty-seven when I began operational flying; perhaps because of this I was more questioning than a lot who were younger.

Early in 1945 I returned to Australia and, like many former aircrew men, became associated with civil flying: I joined the air traffic control branch of the Department of Civil Aviation. Eventually I was to become responsible for the selection and training of men for ATC. This was a piece of good fortune, since my interest all through my Air Force years had been people rather than aeroplanes and technology.

The year I went into ATC I began writing a book about the Bomber Command experience while it was still fresh in mind. My progress was slow – ATC proved a demanding job; also, my wife and I had not only started a family, but had become involved in helping my father-in-law build our home. The book took ten years to complete; I called it *No Moon Tonight*. Often it has been regarded as fiction; certainly in form it resembles a novel, but its contents are factual. When I wrote it, the novel was the form of writing with which I was most familiar.

Even after fifty years the Bomber Command experience still tugs at me – the task we had to do and the price paid in the doing of it. Now it is like looking back on a mountain range crossed in youth – the immediacy of the crossing has passed, but age gives changed viewpoints of the far-off scene. In these pages I have written again of the only group I really knew, travelling with them the long road from training to the end,

---

*   Cherwell to Churchill 30 Mar. 1942, quoted in *The Bombers* by Norman
    Longmate, Century Hutchinson, London, 1983.

utilizing some of their diaries and letters. Inevitably I have gone over several of the happenings related in *No Moon Tonight*; I trust they have borne amplification. These pages trace only a few threads in the tragic tapestry of the Bomber Command war and touch only a few lives among the 125,000 aircrew who served.

For access to letters and diaries I should like to thank my pilot, Mr Geoff Maddern; Mr John Bryant, brother of Max; Prof Elizabeth Webby for her father's letters; Mr. Bruce Webber, brother of Keith; Mrs. J.A.Wood, sister of Bill Charlton; Mr. Don Miller, brother of Colin; and Mrs. Joan Whitelaw, sister of Johnnie Gordon. Also I wish to thank the Literature Board of the Australia Council for a Special Purpose grant that allowed me to travel interstate for research.

Don Charlwood
Templestowe, Victoria 1991

ix

Beginnings

I think it is as well for the man in the street to realize that there is no power on earth that can protect him from being bombed. Whatever people may tell him, the bomber will always get through ... The only defence is in offence, which means that you have to kill more women and children more quickly than the enemy if you want to save yourselves. (Stanley Baldwin, 1932.)

The year war started I was working at Nareen, in a quiet corner of western Victoria. Nareen was no more than a postoffice, a hall with adjoining bluestone supper room, a small granite obelisk to those who had served in the 'Great War' of 1914 – 1918, a Presbyterian church, a tennis court. We no longer even had a store. In the surrounding hills numerous homesteads were scattered, their land watered by reliable streams. It was rolling redgum country, part of Mitchell's *Australia Felix*.

Before Nareen I had been at Frankston High School; I had left there during my Leaving Certificate year to take a fifteen-shilling a week job with a local estate agency and produce market. As I approached eighteen and was due for a rise, I was required to train my own replacement. This was a typical Depression ploy. Once out of work I could find nothing; Melbourne was haunted by spectres of unemployed men, hollow-cheeked and hopeless, many of them survivors of the First World War with families dependent upon them.

I first went to Nareen for a holiday. George Riddoch, a cousin of my mother's, lived there on his property *Burnside*. He and his wife made me so welcome and life there so appealed to me that when they invited me back for the shearing and harvesting of 1934 I went gladly. I remained for seven years.

The Riddochs had an only son, a couple of years my junior, a handsome, quiet, easy-going fellow. Over the years Jim Riddoch became like another young brother, our relationship laconic and easy. We worked together in paddocks and sheds and travelled long distances to dances and films. We both read a great deal and enjoyed the same undemanding classical music.

I already had a compulsion to write and occasionally managed to augment my wages by selling articles and short stories' but most of my output went into long letters home. Our family life at Frankston had always been close-knit, each of us full of lively talk about our doings. I was the eldest by three and a half years in a family of four sons. My parents were dismayed when I remained on at *Burnside* year after year instead of seeking a job in the city. I undoubtedly added to their despair through letters sharing my delight in country life. This letter-writing habit I was to take with me to war, sharing more of Bomber Command than it was kind to share.

In the *Burnside* years I also walked a great deal, mostly in the valley of the Wando, taking photographs that occasionally were published. Four or five times I went on longer walks, going for a week at a time into the Grampians, reeling off days of twenty and twenty-five miles. I did not walk alone from choice; it was just that I knew no other walking enthusiast. I mention these walks and my writing because, in Britain the two pastimes became an outlet to me – a therapy even.

All through the thirties our generation had felt the resurgence of Germany, especially the threat to 'the Homeland.' When the Nazis overran the Low Countries in 1940 and France fell, we saw that the new weapon was terror from the air; the Nazis were exulting in unopposed use of it, their Stukas dive-bombing roads jammed with fleeing refugees. When we went to the pictures at Casterton the screen was filled with their victorious troops, goosestepping shoulder to shoulder past Hitler, helmets gleaming, bayonets fixed. We sensed a great evil, as close to England as Casterton was to Nareen.

Aircrew was Jim's idea. Quite apart from being attracted to flying, he shrank, as I did, from trenches and bayonet charges and barbed wire. He was intent upon being a pilot – as nearly everyone was. I had no interest at all in learning to fly, but was attracted to navigation. We hoped to crew together.

The rate of rejection turned out to be extremely high, nevertheless, three of us from Nareen were accepted. Claude Austin, in every way a giant of a man, was a member of a well-known Western District family, in his youth an all-round athlete. He was much over the age limit, a comfortably-placed grazier, married and a father. He managed to have his age accepted as thirty-two, the upper limit. Jim was twenty-two, I twenty-four. All over Australia, Canada, New Zealand, Rhodesia, South Africa trickles of men began flowing into streams; ultimately the streams became a great river that at last reached England.

We were told that our time on the Reserve would run into months, that while we waited we must learn the morse code at our nearest postoffice and do a course of training known as 'the Twenty-one Lessons' to ensure that we would be able to cope with the theoretical work of initial training. Since the Nareen postoffice was only a telephone exchange and a mail point, we began driving eighteen miles two or three nights a week to Coleraine. There Bert Treloar, the local telegraphist, became our instructor. There were hundreds like him, co-opted from postoffice staffs around Australia. One thing we could not decently confess to him: the incessant *dah-dits* of the code drove us to distraction; we resolved never to be categorized as wireless operators, since the wretched code was part of a W.Op's daily life.

Reservists who lived in towns were able to do the 21 Lessons at evening classes conducted by schoolteachers; youngsters straight from school or university scarcely needed help at all. In our cases, Jim had been away from school five years; I eight; Claude fifteen or sixteen. No tuition was available to us; we did the course by correspondence and helped each other out.

The lessons proved extraordinarily well-arranged. They had been devised in Melbourne by Dr. F.J.D. Syer of University High School, who had built onto an existing RAF course. In my case subjects that had been the despair of my schooldays began to lose their mystery and I became buoyed with the hope that I might measure up to becoming an observer. An observer's main task, we understood, was navigation. If I had to go to war, then let it be this.

We knew that aircrew posted to England could be sent to serve in one of three Commands: Fighter Command, Coastal Command or Bomber Command. Fighter Command was the goal of thousands of young innocents just out of school. Eager to emulate the Spitfire and Hurricane pilots seen on British newsreels, they rushed lemming-like toward their goal. It was a career relatively few of them realized. Of the 26,000 aircrew Australia had promised Britain by March 1943, only 10,400 could be pilots. The great majority of men would be sent to Bomber Command – and not necessarily as pilots – to tasks demanding endurance and patience rather than dash.

Coastal Command involved protection of sea lanes against U-boats. This was my own preference, as it seemed to me that Bomber Command's task of attacking military objectives inside Germany would inevitably involve taking civilian lives.

We knew nothing at all of comparative survival rates between Commands, nor did we know where our training would take place. Some aircrew trained in Australia, others in Rhodesia, but the great majority were sent to Canada which had become the centre of the British Empire Air Training Scheme – a scheme so well standardized that men from a variety of countries were able to come together as crews at the end of training. For pilots and observers, training was reckoned to cost 10,000 pounds sterling, a sum beyond our comprehension – nor could we understand where such money was coming from after so long a depression.

We were about halfway through the 21 Lessons when the Nazis began bombing London. On an ABC news commentary on September 11 H.D. Black highlighted its indiscriminate nature:

> *Hitler has launched his total offensive at non-military objectives – hospitals, humble workers' dwellings, homes for the aged ... his bombers are attacking without scruple or shred of mercy the one great non-material factor against him – the morale of the people of England.*

By the time shearing began Jim and I were considering such incongruous subjects as relative velocity, lift and drag, point of no return. We chanted formulae to each other as we skirted fleeces and swung at the long arm of the wool press. RAAF headquarters in the cities were being pestered daily by youngsters eager to start training; as a result, many of us in remote places were left longer on the Reserve.

After seven months Claude and Jim were called up to start on No. 10 Initial Training Course; unaccountably I was left behind. It was our first indication that crewing together might not prove easy. Jim was posted to Bradfield Park, on the northern outskirts of Sydney. The aspirations of the entire Victorian contingent were dealt an unforeseen blow: all were to train as wireless operators. Claude was sent to Somers, south of Melbourne. I received a hastily-written note from him:

*We are AC2s, the lowest form of life; we salute everybody; we run
every time we hear an order ...*

Before long he was categorized 'observer' and sent to Mt.
Gambier for navigation training.

Alone at Nareen I no longer went to Coleraine to practise
morse code, but took it over the telephone, walking a mile or
so to a homestead where a table phone allowed easier tran-
scription than our wall phone. As I walked home between
familiar hills, I heard little more than nocturnal carollings of
magpies and the occasional bleating of sheep from their
camps along the creek. But once or twice I heard a plane
overhead and saw its shape moving across the stars. These, I
knew, were Ansons from Mt. Gambier. I wondered vaguely if
Claude were up there. I had no real notion of his tasks, or even
of his bodily sensations. As I looked up I sensed the contrast
between Nareen life and the life the Ansons represented. They
spoke of Canada, England, Germany.

In April 1941 Jim's contingent was posted to Canada; I was
still not even called up. He came home on final leave. As I sat
in the audience at a farewell we had expected to share, I felt a
gulf between us for the first time. Next day his parents left for
Sydney to see him off. My only consolation now was that I, too,
might get to Canada, that even yet we might crew together.

In a homestead silent and empty I had an odd experience.
In the *Weekly Times* I read an article by a member of the first
course of Australian observers to train in Edmonton, Alberta.
He wrote of lights from Christmas trees shining from house
windows onto snow and of the extraordinary hospitality of
the people. A conviction settled on me as I read that I, too, was
destined to go to Edmonton. Although pre-disposed to Canada,
this did not account for the strength of my conviction. It
turned out to be a remarkably accurate hunch with consequences beyond all imagining.

In May 1941, after eleven months on the reserve, I was called up; my posting was to Somers. By then Jim was in Winnipeg. I sent him a photograph album there, having made up one each for us – snaps of our parents; some interiors of *Burnside*; the Nareen postoffice with Lucy the postmistress wedged beside her small switchboard; Percy our rabbiter, sitting at his cottage fire, his face reflecting the blaze; a truckload of *Burnside* wool about to be driven to Coleraine railway station, the shearers and the rest of us in the foreground. When I look at these photographs now I am struck by their innocence. I find it hard to equate them with scenes of Germany laid waste – a task carried out by thousands like us, mild-mannered, perceptive young men, of higher sensibilities than most, not at all brought up like young Nazis. Germany would soon call us *terrorfliegers*.

1

Postings

… when I look around to see how we can win the war I see that there is only one sure path. We have no Continental army which can defeat the German military power. The blockade is broken and Hitler has Asia and probably Africa to draw from. Should he be repulsed here or not try invasion, he will recoil eastward, and we have nothing to stop him. But there is one thing that will bring him back and bring him down, and that is an absolutely devastating, exterminating attack by very heavy bombers from this country upon the Nazi homeland. We must be able to overwhelm them by this means, without which I do not see a way through. (Churchill to Beaverbrook, July 8, 1940)

Even after fifty years I see us clearly, 210 young men travelling from Melbourne by RAAF buses down the Mornington Peninsula, the date May 23 1941. We are the Victorian intake of No. 15 Course bound for No. 1 Initial Training School, Somers. We range from boys just out of school to a sprinkling of men near the upper age limit. Around me are bank clerks, schoolteachers, a practising solicitor, a couple of Victorian league footballers aged eighteen and nineteen, several young men from remote farms and country towns, a few university students. There is liveliness in the banter; the men are alert and articulate, the younger having about them an infectious excitement. Their parents might think of them as 'decently brought up young men.' Some of the city recruits know each other; they enlisted together and, by persistent asking, have managed to be called up together. I know no one. As we pass through Frankston I find the familiar and the unfamiliar strangely juxtaposed: sitting among strangers, I catch a glimpse

1

of the street where we lived, then of the distant high school, even two people I know, yarning outside the building where my mother was born. I feel severance from a kindly past, yet know that this is good company to be starting with into the unknown.

Though the Somers camp was scarcely twenty miles from Frankston, I had never been there; my boyhood travel had been limited to the distance I could walk out and home in a day.

The camp was by the sea, shut off from its Western Port beach by a belt of teatree and a dark, slow-moving creek. It did not possess aeroplanes; it only prepared us for them. Inside the entrance gate a swarm of trainees greeted us with a mocking cry: 'You'll be sorry!' From their appearance they might have been convicts. All wore shapeless blue boilersuits and berets; they looked like so many ungainly penguins. These boilersuits were dubbed 'goonskins'; they differed only in size and shades of blue. Newcomers' goonskins were navy; unfortunate trainees who were 'scrubbed pilots', sent to Somers for re-mustering, were at the other end of the spectrum: their goonskins were as faded as their spirits. The 'You'll be sorry' followed our buses as they rolled past rows of barracks.

Our course was deposited on the parade ground and formed into ranks, our range of civilian clothes looking all at once absurd. As if to confirm our impression of convict regimentation, we were given our service numbers, digits we would gabble with certainty to the end of our lives. I became 408794. We were split into three 'flights' and handed over to drill sergeants who looked as if they had cut their teeth on bugles. Sergeant Whelan, arms raised from sides, chin in, head back, voice stentorian, marched our flight away for kitting up, assuring us he'd 'make men of us' improbable drongoes though we were. 'Swing those arms! Giddemup! giddemup! giddemup! – tit high!'

2

Laden with kit we marched to rows of unlined huts, each hut with camp beds along its walls, metal beds with folding legs. We sorted ourselves out; I had Cameron of Casterton on one side, Castles of Colac on the other. We exchanged wry grins.

'To the straw heap with those palliasses – at the double!'

As we stuffed straw into the elongated hessian sacks passers-by regarded us with detached amusement, 'You'll be sorry!' One added in a moment of compassion 'When you hear the reveille bell in the morning, hit the floor or the Black Panther'll have you for breakfast.'

That first dawn I heard the bell above rain and wind. As my feet touched the floor, a door burst open and the light was switched on. A red-faced apparition roared, 'You, you, you and you – report to me after parade!'

Soon after daybreak we made our first ludicrous appearance in goonskins. The porkpie hats of smart young city men and the wide brims of squatters' sons were gone; we were reduced to anonymity. Before us stood the officer commanding Somers, Wing Commander the Hon. T.W.White. Tommy, we gathered, was not a bad sort of a bastard; an old Flying Corps bloke; bit pompous, but gave every one a fair go. He spoke in high-flown terms of duty and Empire and keenness, wished us good luck and handed us back to our sergeants.

Within a few day I realized I had never known better company. With Cameron, Castles, Freeman, Good, Kilvington, Lonsdale I drilled on the windswept parade ground, eventually taking my turn to bawl at a squad of my fellows while they showed perverse delight in carrying out wrong orders to the letter, sweeping on like a juggernaut, off the parade ground altogether. I swung on route marches, singing in their company, then half-dozed at a film series on 'Why Aeroplanes Fly'. We were more alert at lectures on venereal diseases, their symp-

3

toms, treatment and the only means of catching them, 'which isn't from a lavatory seat.' Surprisingly we were alert for that dullest of subjects, Air Force Law, this because our lecturer was the lively Mr. Justice Frederick Phillips who appeared before us in the guise of a Squadron Leader with First World War ribbons and the single wing of an observer. He told us he had been 'an animated sandbag' in the Australian Flying Corps; this was when 'observers' did little more than observe. There was much more to it now, he assured us, as observer trainees would soon discover. He was short and lame and jolly – and said to be over fifty, though his eyes were infectiously youthful.

Before the gunnery exam I tramped alone on Somers beach, learning by rote the parts of the Browning machine-gun, as if memorizing a part in a play – how else would I remember such details as 'the rear sear retaining nut and keeper'?

Flt Lt Davis Hughes, later on NSW Minister for Public Works, lectured us in maths and physics with such clarity and skill that I went confidently to the exams – and, on my twenty-sixth birthday, crashed in maths. This was a disaster, as I had already convinced the category-selection board that I was observer material. As a result of the failure I was categorized wireless-operator and posted to Ballarat.

Five of us who had narrowly failed maths were paraded before Sqn Ldr Pratt, the Education Officer. We were a depressed lot. I felt stung by what he had to tell us: we were to be subjected to some kind of test. I presumed the RAAF wanted to avoid recruiting our like again. An IQ paper was put before us. I went at it with uncharacteristic speed and fury. When it was over we were told to wait; each man was called in individually. Pratt seemed unaware that I was bristling with resentment. He sounded distinctly puzzled. 'Charlwood, *I* don't know why you failed that maths paper. You ought to

4

have passed easily. Three of you are in the same situation. I'm recommending that you be made reserve observer trainees. You just *might* be called on. In the meantime, continue getting your clearances to Ballarat.'

Next day mumps broke out in the camp; men went down on all sides. I had had them years before.

'Forget Ballarat. Get yourself cleared for Cootamundra as an observer trainee.'

Cootamundra was not Edmonton, but I gladly set about the clearances. Hurrying from section to section I fell in with a good-looking, melancholy youngster in faded goonskins who had the same posting. His name was Max Bryant; he was aged twenty, an articled law clerk from Cowra. He was smarting and forlorn after being scrubbed as a pilot and was hankering to be given a chance to prove himself as an observer. He so reminded me of my younger brothers that I felt drawn to him in his dejection. As we moved from section to section, I became aware how far removed his attitudes to war and the Air Force were from my own. He was a young crusader who at first scarcely knew what to make of my scepticism. But he seemed to find in me avuncular understanding and from that first day invested me with wisdom I lacked. Max had only just begun to live a man's life. A couple of years earlier he had been dux and captain of Cowra High School.

While we were obtaining clearances to Cootamundra a call erupted for all trainee observers to parade immediately. Four volunteers were required for a contingent soon to leave Sydney for Canada. Max and I stepped forward together; with us were Ted Freeman, a nineteen year-old St. Kilda footballer, inevitably dubbed 'Blue' from a blaze of red hair, and twenty-year old Ron Wheatley, a brown-eyed, quick-thinking Victorian.

I had volunteered because the posting offered prospect of catching up to Jim Riddoch and because of my irrational conviction that I was to go to this unknown place, Edmonton.

5

But once I had made the move I saw it as folly. The previous day my mother had telephoned to tell me my father had been struck by a car and was in hospital in a critical condition. As we left the parade ground for medical examinations before pre-embarkation leave, I felt dismayed at what I had done. A medical officer, anxious to complete our papers, exclaimed, 'Look here; I can't let you go – your blood pressure's too high!' He waved me to a couch. 'Lie there and try to relax.'

After I had rested awhile he reluctantly passed me, still muttering his doubts.

Because of my father's accident my departure for Sydney was delayed until the latest possible time. My final leave remains a blur of contrasting scenes: my father, recognizing me, then drifting back into unconsciousness; my mother, calm and reassuring; a flight to Hamilton* for a Nareen farewell; my speech of thanks in the familiar hall; a hospital goodbye to my father. He was now conscious, but in no state to be told I was leaving. Final farewells to my family at desolate Spencer Street Station. On the train I began a diary:

Today at a quarter to five I snapped the last ties with my old life and set a new course that will lead heaven knows where ...

I had never been to Sydney. When I arrived such heavy rain was falling that I could scarcely discern the bridge I had seen so often on newsreels. The Embarkation Depot at Bradfield Park lay above bushland, wet and fragrant. I looked from face to face in the throng of strange aircrew, but the other three men from Somers were beyond locating. There were numerous pre-embarkation tasks to get done; one was to punch my name, number, religion and blood group on metal identification discs.

---

* This was my first flight, made in Ansett's original Airspeed Envoy, VH–UXM; but my mind was so over-filled that it left few impressions.

'They cut one orf,' said the corporal in charge of hammer and punches, 'an' leave th' other on y' body.'

The punches had become so abraded that my result was barely readable. I imagined a Teutonically-thorough enemy deciphering it scornfully.

Thirty-six hours later we paraded before dawn under arc lights, 378 aircrew, 42 ground staff, all ranked in trade groupings, each group in alphabetical order, our names playing their first part in our destiny – Anglo-Saxon and Gaelic names nearly all of them; a few of German origin. It was announced that the officer commanding our contingent would be Wing Commander Axel Richards, and that we were exceedingly fortunate in that we would be travelling as passengers on the US liner *Monterey*, the first Australians to cross the Pacific on a ship of neutral America. Travelling with us would be the former C.O. of Somers, Wing Commander the Hon. T. W. White, going to England to command the RAAF reception centre at Bournemouth. A padre moved out of the shadows and we joined in singing 'Rock of Ages.' Even now, the memory of those 400 male voices singing so full-heartedly on their native shore, has poignancy in my memory. The padre read then from Paul's *Epistle to the Philippians*, the verses ending:

… *Finally, brethren, whatsoever things are true, whatsoever things are honourable, whatsoever things are just, whatsoever things are pure, whatsoever things are lovely, whatsoever things are of good report; if there be any virtue, and if there be any praise, think on these things.*

Our final hymn was one we would sing at sea many times:

Eternal Father! strong to save,
Whose arm hath bound the restless wave …

In all of this there was bonding with the unknown men

7

beside me, some of whom I would come to know closely, whom I look back on with more than affection.

We moved in darkness to a line of double-decker buses drawn up at the edge of the parade ground, remaining still in our alphabetical order. Dawn was coming with flushed apricot hues, the first bird songs rising from the bush, a fragrance with them that was part of our being. From the upper deck of our bus we saw the sun lift out of the Pacific, 'red with the cold sea mist.' By the time we reached the bridge daylight had come, spring mistiness on the water, sky clear. On the other side of the harbour we climbed through a curious labyrinth of alleyways, crowded with narrow houses, each house oozing age and neglect. 'The Rocks', somebody said. From our upper level we looked into faces of slatternly women, like so many characters from Norman Lindsay's *Bulletin* cartoons. They saluted us cheerfully with mops and brooms, 'Good on y' boys! Good luck!'

Our white ship lay at Mort's Dock, beautiful in the sun, a large American flag painted on her hull. Below her, on the dock, was a line of our kitbags, alphabetically arranged so that each man found the next pair to be his own. Silent and incredulous we filed up the gangway, kitbags over shoulders, directed in nasal accents to two-berth 'staterooms'. So stunned were we in our move from a Spartan RAAF existence to Hollywood that we were scarcely conscious of stepping off our native soil.

I found myself berthed with Colin Cooper, a Brisbane man of about my own age, rubicund and jolly. We were struck speechless by our surroundings; youths of the Depression that we were, we had only seen like of them in films: two portholes, a private toilet, hot and cold water, bedlamps, wardrobes, full-length mirrors. A white-jacketed steward of muddy complexion appeared at our door. 'Gen'lemen, ah shall be looking after yoh stateroom an' lahndry.'

As we stood there, Blue burst in. 'Our toilet has a pale-green seat! *Pale green!* Just come and see it!' He was sharing with a fellow nearly twelve years his senior, who was lying on one of the beds reading a book with complete indifference to his surroundings. This was Johnnie Gordon, schoolteacher, classics scholar, violinist, cricketer.

At 11.00 tugs nosed us out. No one was at the dock to see us off, but as we passed under the bridge we saw thirty or forty people, women, elderly men and a few children, standing close together on the city side, waving to us. Overhead, traffic rumbled about its daily business. There was urgent, painful waving of handkerchiefs and parasols. Occasional *coo-ees* reached us and were answered from the ship; but the group soon fell astern; the harbour broadened; there was mounting seriousness on board as if it had been borne on us that this step was irrevocable. Even before we reached the Heads, the *Monterey*'s routine claimed us with a call for the first sitting for lunch.

I see us at a table for four, brightly set with silver on linen: Bryant, Burrows, Charlton, Charlwood. Max Bryant had already met the others; both were Sydneysiders, both distinctly younger than I was, Burrows, a married man, short, fairish, quick-witted, a cheerful cock to his head; Charlton angular, his hands large and expressive, his demeanor reminding me of an intent young curate.

Unsophisticated products of the Depression that we were, we considered the menu in silence, privately ruling out dish after dish as too expensive. Then someone exclaimed, 'But the Air Force is paying!'

Had the Angel of Death given us some intimation in that lush dining saloon, he would have touched three of four at most of the tables, but his coming was far off and in the meantime, we were to cross the Pacific in luxury and spend seven months getting to know Canada.

By the time we returned to the boat deck the *Monterey* had cleared the coast and the sun was glittering on a blue sea; our broadening wake led back to the Heads. We went aft and lay in deckchairs watching land fall astern. Little was said, but I noticed several men start writing in diaries, a practice most of us kept up assiduously for the rest of our Air Force lives.

By 2 o'clock we could just make out the harbour bridge; by 2.15 it too had gone and only a few blue hills rose above the horizon. By 2.30 even they had vanished and, no matter how our eyes strained, we could see nothing of Australia at all. A cruiser overtook us, flashing on her lamp. Those of us who were awake read the morse: 'Request your course and speed.' We identified her as HMNZS *Achilles*, her name familiar from the Battle of the River Plate. We fell asleep in mild sunshine, bound in luxury for the far-off war.

2

An Invitation

As our forces increase, we intend to pass to a planned attack on civilian morale with the intensity and continuity which are essential if breakdown is to be produced – we believe that if these methods are applied on a vast scale, the whole structure upon which the German forces are based will be destroyed. (British Chiefs of Staff paper for the guidance of the Prime Minister, 31 July 1941)

All night the Tasman pitched us. At breakfast our table steward, middle-aged, bald, portly, sympathised with our discomfort and expressed the hope that we would all come safely home. I doubt that he had ever before attended such unsophisticated travellers. He confided that once the *Monterey* reached San Francisco the crew would claim a 'war risk bonus for carrying foreign belligerents.' We reckoned the risks negligible and being called 'foreigners' rankled. Someone nearby exclaimed, 'Listen Johnnie, we're no more foreigners than you are – we speak English, don't we?'

This puzzled him. He waved plump hands. 'Wa-al, no offence. It's just you ain't citizens of the U-nided States.'

We should hope not! As a Queenslander put it, 'They all *call* themselves Americans, but just look at them – some are Dagoes, some are Chows and that one over there's a bloody Kanaka. And they reckon *we're* foreign!' As for being 'belligerents', the Tasman kept our belligerence at low ebb. I crept sometimes to our cabin, seasickness succeeded by bouts of loneliness. I lay on my bunk, rolling with the ship, listening to creaking timbers, thudding waves, howling wind, finding solace in *The Poets' Way.*

As well as 420 RAAF men the *Monterey* carried homebound American tourists. They were courteous and warmly disposed to us, their ladies even formed a sewing circle for us, nevertheless we regarded them with reservations: they were neutrals; in our eyes their country had failed for the second time in twenty-five years to answer Britain's call.

Within three days we were back among people of our own loyalties. In Auckland scores of New Zealanders were waiting at the docks to take us on car tours and home to dinner. They were back next evening to farewell a contingent of their own aircrew. These chaps wore RAF blue, which to us looked grey – pale contrast with our own deep blue. As the coast faded the Kiwis began a series of morale-boosting hakas on the deck above our cabins. Our small contingent of Anzacs was off to the last of the 'Homeland's' European wars.

The Pacific soon possessed us: the gentle rocking of the ship, the hiss of passing sea, the moist balmy air, all lulled us, casting war out of mind, leading instructors in navigation and morse code to give us up as we drifted into dreams.

When I look now at *Monterey* photographs, I am struck by the cheerful innocence of faces. Most appear free of doubt and distrust. Perhaps it was that all our lives we had accepted the authority of our 'parents, teachers and the law.' The years of depression and impending war do not appear to have marked us.

Each flight of trainees was asked to nominate a spokesman. Among the forty-two observers I knew scarcely half a dozen men, but the rest unanimously voted for a Bundaberg man, 'Tib' Barker, a tall, good-looking athletic fellow with an air of genial authority. It was the happiest of choices. Tib, then twenty-eight, had been a sergeant in the militia before transferring to the Air Force. He was a scrubbed pilot, destined for high accomplishments as a navigator. In Bundaberg his father was known as 'the Colonel', a decorated Boer War man.

Achilles shadowed us as far as Pago Pago; by then we were probably reckoned the responsibility of Hawaii. On October 1st, 'planes from Honolulu came out in spectacular welcome, flying low over the ship, zooming up, waggling wings. At the docks a fleet of cars driven by young women in Red Cross uniform was waiting to take us sight-seeing. They drove us up through heavily-scented forest to the high Nuna Pali, sea and city far down at our feet.

On the way back our driver confided that the people of Honolulu were living in fear of a Japanese air attack. We hardly knew how to reply to such an absurdity. Although a few journalists at home had thought Japan might strike south while Britain was occupied in Europe, we had taken the supposition lightly. For one thing, we knew the Japanese were no match for Europeans; for another, Singapore was impregnable. As for Honolulu, even if Japanese 'planes were able to reach it, the American air power we had glimpsed that morning would overwhelm them. On our return to the ship we found that several others had heard the same fears expressed. As the bright streamers parted that afternoon and ship and shore sang *The Maori Farewell*, we laughed off Hawaii's fears as 'Yank panic'.

Over dinner Johnnie assured us that our welcome in San Francisco would far outshine Honolulu's; there was no place like 'Frisco. Wing Commander Richards had us practise marching on the promenade deck, the American tourists watching admiringly. But when the day came and we parted from the *Monterey*, the only welcome we received ashore was from the ship's crew, among them a much-inebriated Johnnie. Our hearts went to them, for most citizens' faces showed stony distaste for us, harbingers as we were of an unwanted war. We were hurried to an Oakland-bound ferry with scarcely time to take in the scene of skyscrapers and bridges before we were

13

marched onto a sealed train bound for Vancouver, thirty-six hours north.

At 6 pm we pulled out, our locomotive clanging its bell, its whistle whooping, Negro conductors calling us to dinner. All this was pure Hollywood. After dark the train climbed high into the Cascade Range. In the early hours of the morning Mt. Shasta towered over us in moonlight, its snows spilling into forests of fir and spruce, ghostly under the moon, the first snow most of us had seen. As we gazed on the enchanted miles we came to a brilliantly-lighted construction site of enormous proportions. Hundreds of men worked there like ants on a disturbed mound. They did not spare a glance at the train. If we had been passing on foot, I doubted that they would have afforded us a 'G'day'. They were building the Shasta Dam.

When morning came and we sat to bacon and eggs, maples flitted by in hectic colours among fir and spruce; snow lay either side of the line. Thoughts of war were unreal.

For Australians and New Zealanders Vancouver was the receiving point in Canada's aircrew production line. There trainee pilots, observers and wireless operators split up, each group going to specialist training schools. The separate trades seldom saw each other again until they were delivered as finished products at the other end of the country.

One or two of our trainee observers had managed to find that there would be a choice of destinations offered us: sixteen men were wanted for Malton, near Toronto, the rest were to go to Edmonton. The one or two spread word among their friends, arranging to have sixteen ready to step forward when the announcement was made. The attraction for them was proximity to a large city. The announcement came on Vancouver station; the sixteen stepped forward as a man. This left twenty-six for Edmonton, most of them not at all happy about the subterfuge. As far as I was concerned, I was going where I had expected to go and the men I knew best were left with us:

Tib Barker, Col Cooper, Johnnie Gordon, Blue Freeman, Ron Wheatley and my tablemates Bryant, Burrows and Charlton. By nightfall our Canadian National train began climbing through the Fraser Canyon, the moon shining on water that tumbled between mountain walls such as we had never seen. Caught up by the unearthly beauty, we opened windows, admitting a roar of water and the labouring of our two locomotives up the gorge. But the cold that struck us was cold such as we had never imagined.

In the morning we halted at Jasper. There, under snow-capped peaks, the whole *Monterey* contingent marched, three hundred and seventy-eight aircrew all singing as they swung through resinous forests. Then we went to our separate trains; the contingent had split up forever. I doubt that a hundred of us ever saw home.

Our own train left the Rockies and emerged onto rolling prairies. Darkness had not long fallen when we saw ahead the lights of Edmonton. The railway track ran along the boundary of the municipal airport which was to be our base for the next three months. There, in cavernous hangars, bright as day under fluorescent lights, we could see men working on yellow fuselages of Ansons. Here were our aircraft; here was what it was all about!

As the train drew in at the 'Canadian National Railroad depot' we saw a crowd waiting to receive us, in the forefront the Australian courses preceding our own, behind them a throng of bemused local people, whole families of them come to witness the meeting of these strange antipodeans. The Australians pressed forward, shaking hands with those they knew, asking news of home, deluging us with information, all the time playing to the gallery of Edmontonians. We were going to like this city, its people were the most hospitable on earth. We could go out to dinner every night if we liked, but it just didn't pay, the course was hard slog; if you failed the

15

scrub tests you were likely to end up in Trenton for remustering, or be put back a course, or even be sent home. The barracks were great, except that they were over-heated and Canucks didn't like windows being opened – reckoned it would freeze the plumbing. The weather? Perfect; no snow yet, 'But the locals keep saying, 'Wait till it's thirty below, forty below...'

'The pilots here know every inch of the country, but they'll only step in if you get yourself really lost.' The greatest aids to navigation were the grain elevators. 'Each town has one, even the smallest. The town's name is painted on them in bloody great letters.' Added to this were the fences, 'They all run north-south and east-west.' It was country made for navigators.

An Adonis among the welcoming men declared the local girls 'easy'. 'But they don't have the ... ' He sought the word, wrinkling his brow, 'the *finesse* of the girls at home.' The girls at home were never to receive his attentions again.

We knew nothing of Canadians, beyond the fact that they were some sort of Empire cousins. We were surprised to hear that they sounded like Americans. They appeared highly amused by our exchanges. Two RCAF NCOs waited to direct us. One with a crown on his sleeve was referred to as 'Major'. He shouted good-humouredly, 'Fall in, eh!' The addition of 'eh' made his order sound like a friendly suggestion. When we ignored it, he roared, 'All right you goddam Osstrylians, *fall in!*'

After Somers, the Canadian barracks proved astonishingly luxurious. Built in H form, the bar of the H housed ablutions, laundry and drying room; the two sides were given to rows of double bunks. The whole place was clean and gleaming and centrally heated. To our surprise there were sheets on the beds; not only that, they were to be laundered for us. The Major made an announcement: trainees flew navigation exercises in pairs, therefore would we please determine without delay who our flying partner would be. It was the practice for partners to take the upper and lower levels of the same bunk; this avoided disturbing others after night flying.

As a matter of course, Max Bryant and I paired together, he in the upper bunk, I below – this, he felt, was something he owed my antiquity. Next day, Saturday October 11, he chanced to go to the orderly room. The Major was speaking on the telephone. Cupping the mouthpiece he said, 'Hey Aussie, I have a lady here who would like two of you guys to go to her place for supper tonight. Want to be in it?'

Max accepted and gave my name as the second man. He came to me with a slip of paper reading: 'Mrs. East. 10174-115th Street.'

Before we had attended a class or become familiar with our surroundings, Max and I caught a bus to the city. Edmonton then numbered about 80,000 people, a small lively place, its avenues running north-south, its streets east-west, its long house numbers giving, in effect, the co-ordinates of each home. The only thoroughfare given a name was Jasper Avenue. Along it ran street cars, each with a small furnace for winter heating. But winter was weeks off. Shoppers crowded the main stores – the Hudson Bay Company, T. Eaton's, Birk's. It seemed as if half the population was bent on hospitality; several times we were stopped and invited to supper. We began to realize that the conspicuous colour of our uniforms was going to have some benefits: RAF and New Zealand trainees wore the same dull grey-blue as RCAF men.

In the residential areas the houses were two-storey wooden structures with porches and dormer windows and steeply-pitched roofs. They seemed extraordinarily tall and close together; very few had front fences. We walked as strangers in a strange land, wondering what might lie ahead.

East's turned out to be a place of two apartments, an upper one which they occupied, a lower one which they let out. A diminutive, plump lady opened the door to us. When we had introduced ourselves she asked eagerly, 'Where do you boys come from?'

'From Cowra, New South Wales,' said Max.

'From Melbourne,' I said.

My reply delighted her. 'I came from Melbourne thirty years ago,' she said. 'I have never been back.'

She had married a Canadian goldminer, one of five brothers who had successfully operated their own mine in Western Australia. She had met him while she was training as a nurse in Perth. This much we learned while standing between the door and the stairs. As we talked I looked up and there, leaning over the landing rail, looking down at us, were two attractive girls. One with brown eyes and a lively expression was studying us with anticipatory glee. At once an absurd thought struck me: 'There's the girl you are going to marry!'

Nell East was a primary school teacher of twenty-two who had been raised on a lonely farm near Vermilion in Alberta's far east. Her mother had come from a comfortable, well-to-do Melbourne home to pioneer in a log cabin. Nell's father proved the most formidable man I had ever met or ever would meet. Neil East was tall and ruggedly built, his eyes piercing; he had spent eight years in Western Australia and declared it had made a rebel of him. That first evening he told us of a six-month camel journey he and his eldest brother had made from Laverton to the Warburton Range in a fruitless search for further gold. In that country Neil had been the first man to use a sextant, his artificial horizon a small bath of mercury. He was still immensely strong, his voice loud and resonant. He was very deaf, an affliction that deepened his inclination to distrust. I might have imagined marrying the beautiful girl across the table, but I could not imagine Neil East ever being my father-in-law.

It was relief to escape to a table-tennis table in the basement. All houses, we learned, had basements; that was where the furnace was installed for central heating. If Australians didn't have basements, where did they have their heating? We didn't need it, we claimed.

The evening became hilarious. Nell's friend was Billie Willson; the subject of much of their laughter was our accents. We were nonplussed. 'Just talk,' they begged – 'tahk' they pronounced it. 'Oh, they're really kinda cute, aren't they!' Useless to convince them that *they* had accents. 'And the *words* you use!' 'Words?' 'Well, you really mustn't say ...' Embarrassed laughter. 'You mustn't say 'knocked up' y'know.' We didn't know and were left unenlightened. When I played Max singles Nell said enthusiastically, 'I'll root for you.' I concentrated on the game, not daring to look at her.

As she had been teaching at outlying schools, she had bought herself a black Pontiac coupe – pronounced 'coop'. She drove us back to camp in it, she and I in the front seat, Billie and Max in a small outside rear seat called 'the rumble.'

When they had set us down I said to Max, 'I think I've met the girl I'm going to marry.'

'Nell? You couldn't do better,' he said sagely, then he added 'Mind if I'm your best man?'

'Delighted!' I laughed then added, 'Let's talk realities – we've got to survive first.'

Max answered, 'I think you will; I think ours is going to be a lucky course.'

3

Edmonton

OBSERVER: High standard of energy and stamina to cope with long work in high, cold altitudes; a combination of alertness and steadiness; analytical mentality, accuracy in detail; determination, tenacity, and courage. From the Empire Air Training Scheme *Brief Book Vol. 2: 'Interview Methods and Aircrew Types.'*

From our bunks we heard the giant locomotives of Canadian National and Canadian Pacific thundering through the night, hauling mile-long trains, whistles wailing, sometimes near, sometimes far, their note strange and forlorn. Stirring from sleep I remembered we were far indeed from home. I was dimly aware of twenty-five other men sleeping around me, each on a journey much longer than these coast-to-coast trains, each with homes and anxieties and store of Australian memories. Vancouver was over 500 miles back across the Rockies; 300 miles eastward was Saskatoon, next town with claim to being called city; 450 miles east of that again was Winnipeg; in between were numerous wheat villages. All were linked by the great railroads that drew wheat from hundreds of 'grain elevators' along the way.

Edmonton was dubbed 'Gateway to the North', a sub-Arctic north of lakes and muskeg and isolated settlements. From our airport the legendary 'bush pilots' headed out in light aircraft fitted in summer with floats, in winter with skis. Our Anson pilots had been selected from among them; they were employed by the Edmonton Flying Training School Ltd. The same company was responsible for running the barracks and mess, but our officers and classroom instructors were from the RCAF.

A sign at our entrance gates read:

ROYAL CANADIAN AIR FORCE
No. 2 AIR OBSERVER and
No. 16 ELEMENTARY FLYING
TRAINING SCHOOL
BRITISH COMMONWEALTH
AIR TRAINING PLAN

'The Plan' was what other Commonwealth countries called the 'Empire Air Training Scheme'. Canada, more independent of Britain than the rest of us, eschewed mention of Empire; besides she had her French population to placate. But if the official line was more independent of Britain, we found most English speaking Canadians as loyal to the crown as we were ourselves, perhaps even more loyal in that they lacked our infusion of Irish rebelliousness.

Six observer courses were running concurrently, ours No. 35. Our three months in Edmonton were to be followed by shorter courses on other stations: bombing and gunnery at one, astro-navigation at the other. On our first working day we were required to nominate a course 'senior'; unanimously we named Tib Barker. Though very much one of us, he was our natural leader.

A dapper young French Canadian was put in charge of us; we were his first course of Australians and it was soon evident that someone had warned him to assert his authority from the outset. Addressing us in English scarcely better than our schoolboy French, he said with great seriousness, 'My name iss Yarry,' He wrote 'Jarry' on the blackboard. 'You may yoke about anyt'ing but t'ree t'ings: one, my race,' he drew himself up. 'I am French. Two, my religion,' his voice lowered; 'I am Cat'olique. T'ree, my vife: I am yoost married. Iss dat unnerstood?'

We were too close to laughter to risk exchanging glances. *'Iss dat unnerstood?'*

21

'Yes sir.'

'Ver' well.' Raising his voice suddenly, 'On ze parade groun', fall in!'

Astonished, we clattered outside and fell in with Tib as marker. Having brought us to attention Jarry shouted, 'From ze lef' noomber!'

Never having numbered from the left, we were momentarily silent. Jarry rose to the tips of his toes. Glaring at the impassive Tib he repeated the order, his voice close to a scream. From the other end of the line Wilf Burrows uttered, 'One!' which was quickly followed through to five, by which time Jarry spluttered, 'Ass you were!' In conciliatory tones he ordered, 'From ze *righ'* noomber.'

We sensed his relief as he wheeled us about the parade ground. By the time he returned us to our desks, his demeanor had relaxed. We had no more trouble with him. The course, he assured us, was easy. 'Eet iss cheeken sheet.'

Even if I could have understood him better, I would not have found it 'chicken shit.' Speed of assimilation was going to count for much; there was no time in the training scheme for the slow to catch up, however good they might eventually have proved. Jarry was to teach us navigation, maps and charts, altimetry, everything, in fact, except wireless telegraphy and meteorology. For meteorology we were blessed with Denny Ross, a pleasant Canadian civilian who inevitably became 'Met Mick'. He seemed well accustomed to Australians. The classroom walls were plastered with photographs of cloud types and examples of weather charts; these shared space with silhouettes of Allied and enemy aircraft, all of which we were required to know for 'aircraft recognition,' along with their wing span and performance.

There were to be six hours of lectures a day; on flying days, three hours. Though reveille was at 0630 and breakfast 0730, our first compulsory appearance was at 0800 parade. We were not asked where we had been before then; we could breakfast or sleep. Those who couldn't tolerate hotcakes and bacon, with the option of maple syrup, usually slept, or made do with biscuits from the Legion canteen. But daily parade was a serious business; the flag was so revered that we had to salute each time we passed it during the day. In later days exasperated Australians at Edmonton's Manning Depot were blamed for the ultimate in disrespect: one morning when the flag was broken, a pair of female knickers fluttered with it at the masthead. On another occasion there was no flagpole; it had been chopped down during the night. Australians were blamed again – the distinctive uniform had its disadvantages.

Morning parade ended with a half-hour route march. At first we considered our marching distinctly superior to that of the Canadians. They held their arms farther from their sides than we did, they turned their toes out slightly and their bodies had a lateral sway. But the day came when ice formed on the roads. The Australian marching went to pieces; men fell into each other and sprawled on the ground, the Canadians remained rock steady, mildly amused, not full of laughter and gibes as we might have been. They were a more earnest lot than we were.

On our third day at 2 AOS an avalanche of work descended on us. Jarry faced us seriously: 'I now gif you ze dates of ze scroob tests.' I realized that this was the worst possible time to have met Nell East. Already I was seeing too much of her; we made a foursome, Max taking out Billie. The girls still mimicked our accents enchantingly; Nell drove us sightseeing in 'the coop'; whenever we appeared at 10174-115th Street, Mrs. East had a delicious meal ready.

Max could afford such outings. Beside me in class he was lightning quick. While I laboured to make sense of the sentence before last, Jarry leapt ahead with Max and the other bright young enthusiasts, his English deteriorating as he gathered speed. The youngsters comprehended his broken sentences and gestures readily; I found myself turning lamely to Max for elucidations.

Commissions were to go to men filling the first half dozen places at the end of training; the rest would become sergeants. Although differences of rank in aircrew made little sense, the fact was, we were stuck with an archaic system and this seemed as fair a way as any of determining who among us would become 'officers and gentlemen'. Although we were unaware of it, the RCAF was trying at the time to persuade the RAF to commission all aircrew:

> ... there being no justification for the commissioning of certain individuals whilst others are required to perform exactly the same duties but in NCO rank.*

Not only this; if a crew became prisoners of war, sergeants could be given menial duties, while officers were spared them. The RAF was not to be moved.

My own aim did not go beyond avoiding the humiliation of being 'sent to Trenton' for remustering. Although we scarcely knew where Trenton was, its name equated with disgrace. For most of us this was a greater dread than the far-off risk of being killed in action. I resolved to avoid serious involvement with Nell however I might feel about her.

Flying exercises began twelve days after our arrival. The 'first navigator' worked at his log and chart and directed the pilot; the 'second navigator' was his assistant and had such additional tasks as taking drifts and bearings and keeping weather observations. We were to alternate in these two roles.

The first exercise left us in a state of confusion and utter despair. Gravity plucked gut and skin, engine noise assaulted us, vibration and turbulence shook our bodies incessantly,

---

* The RCAF point of view on rank in aircrew, quoted by John Terraine, *The Right of the Line*, Hodder & Stoughton, London, 1985.

clear thought seemed scarcely possible. Below us were lakes and small towns. But *what* lakes? *what* towns? We were utterly disorientated. Our Course andSpeed Calculators* lay accusingly on our navigation tables; they belonged to the quiet of classrooms, not to this elevated hell. The aircraft stank of dope, petrol, oil. Several men were airsick. Flying with a cold, I suffered excruciating ear pains as we descended. The pilot, seeing me clasp my head, levelled out and told me to scream and to keep screaming while he descended more gradually. It seemed a fitting end to what was supposed to have been a pinpointing exercise. As one of my pinpoints I gave 'Crossing Saskatchewan river'. Beside this Jarry wrote in red ink, 'Saskatchewan river 1200 miles long.'

We began a daily wrestle with the basic problem underlying air navigation: what wind was blowing at cruising altitude? At five or ten thousand feet an Anson's speed was sometimes halved by a headwind or increased fifty percent by a tailwind, or we might head in one direction while an undiscovered beam wind pushed us further and further off our intended track, so that we moved crab-like away from our destination. Some destinations we came on long before or after they were due to appear; a few we failed to find at all.

As we returned to the classroom after these first flights, there was dismay on every face.

'What wind did you get?'

'Oh-five-oh degrees twenty knots.'

'Christ! I got one seven five degrees fifty knots!'

'Well, you might have been right – bloody Wetaskiwin never did turn up for me. How's a bloke going to be in the dark over Germany with Jerries shooting at him!'

George Loder, one of our ablest men, wrote despairingly in the camp paper:

---

* The CSC was soon afterwards replaced by the Dalton computer. Both were used for solving the triangle of velocities posed by air navigation.

... if you have six or seven pairs of hands, three or four or even a dozen legs (half on the abdomen) and the energy and determination of six men you're just about in the race.

Johnnie Gordon, our classics scholar, wrote home:

... we're so busy we haven't time to notice the beauty of the country. To us the burning question is: ' Just where the hell are we on the map?' ... The concentrated mental effort and the effect of the air at high altitudes makes us ready for a rest when we get back. But it's a great life. As everyone here says, 'I could stay here for the duration'.

My main Air Force interest was not aeroplanes, nor even navigation, come to enjoy it though I did, but these men whose lot I was sharing so closely. I never tired of observing their idiosyncrasies, their differing reactions to the pressures of the course, their turns of phrase, their attitudes to life. After several weeks of flying, when we were beginning to laugh over our initial debacles, I wrote in a cautionary article for newly-arrived Australians:

... With the ground falling rapidly away, you suddenly remember that you are to give the pilot a course. Ah yes; a course. First you must estimate your true airspeed. You mutter, 'True airspeed equals indicated airspeed plus – Where the hell's that piece of paper? It was just here. Plus 1.75 something – '

Your attention is distracted by the second navigator. He is shouting to the pilot and pointing toward the trailing aerial. You hear the words, '... gone sir. Broke off -' You don't like the expression on the pilot's face.

Ah yes, the course. You suddenly find the piece of paper on the desk in front of you. You estimate your true airspeed to be 854.5 mph, then grasp your course and speed calculator in an upside down position. It suddenly occurs to you that 854.5 mph is an improbable speed ...

So it went. Navigating over Germany was too far off to contemplate; much more real was the threat of Trenton. As the scrub tests approached several of the men shut themselves in the drying room after lights out and worked night after night until 1.0 and 2.0 a.m. Our minds were crammed with scraps of information. I drifted to sleep murmuring, *'Variation east magnetic least'; 'Stand with your back to the wind in the northern hemisphere and the low pressure system is on your left'; 'Saturated adiabatic lapse rate is -'* Is what? God, I must check it in the morning! *'Transfer position lines along track at groundspeed'; 'A great circle plotted on a mercator projection is convex to the nearer pole'; 'The obliquity of the ecliptic -'* How had Jarry explained it...? For my part I often fell asleep consoling myself with half-dreams of Nell's brown eyes, lively, gentle, endlessly understanding.

Although we jested self-depreciatingly about the outcome of the scrub tests, all of us were in a state of tension until November 25 when Jarry announced the results. Max was second on the course; I was sixth, which was much better than I had expected. None of our number was to go to Trenton, but three were put back a course and, worse, two were to be repatriated. The two were utterly dejected. One, a New South Wales schoolteacher, murmured ashamedly, 'What can I tell my kids at school?' By 1944 he could have told them that twenty of the men he had parted from went to Bomber Command; that fifteen of these were killed, that one became a prisoner of war.

In a small group of men of similar backgrounds, all feeling the pressures of a new task, all deprived of family life, all waiting two or three months for home mail, comradeships developed that lasted as long as lives lasted. Unlike most service units we were not a group of men who would go into action together; instead, we would each marry into a crew. We were more like brothers sharing an upbringing, each of us

27

later to establish a family of his own. This kinship meant that we later heard of the deaths of our course members with feelings close to family sorrow. So it was with all aircrew courses, of all trades.

Our generation had been brought up in an era of religious bigotry between Anglo-Scottish Protestants and Irish Catholics. All that was left behind. As one of the Protestant majority, it sometimes struck me that our course would have been staid but for four men with strong Irish Catholic infusions: Johnnie Gordon, Harry Wright, Tom McNeill and Blue Freeman; all lent colour to the course. They by no means shared our respect for petty discipline; but in the end each of them exhibited on operations the strong self-discipline that was the hallmark of good aircrew. Harry Wright was a long, thin, twenty-year-old Queenslander with untidy hair and a self-mocking physiognomy. Tom McNeill was the biggest man among us; he had represented Queensland in rugby union. He was big in every respect; his eyes fairly shone with good fellowship. I regarded him and Tib and Blue as natural warriors. They would have been outstanding men in any of the services.

Although each of us had private anxieties, we seldom confided in more than one of the others – usually our flying partner. Worst hit was George Loder. He had just turned twenty-three, but had a high degree of maturity as well as easy efficiency and a sense of fun. He had sought to have his embarkation date from Sydney deferred, as his wife was pregnant. At the last minute the deferment was refused. Nearly all of his pay went home, most of it to his wife, but some to his brother to help him to an education that George himself had been denied by the Depression. We never heard him complain; he was everybody's favourite.

The day after the 'scrub' results were announced the first snow fell. We were entranced by the host of gently spiralling flakes and the transformation of our surroundings. Once out of class a second childhood possessed us. The Canadians, who slept at the far end of our long barracks, watched bewilderedly as we snowballed each other.

'How'll you guys be when yuh snowed in? when it's twenny below? thirty below? when yuh shovellin' the goddam stuff?'

As the temperature fell the world changed to a white, muted place in which people wore clothing such as we had never seen – furs, beaverskin caps, heavily-lined overcoats, mittens. Although RAAF trainees had been coming to Canada for over a year, Australia still issued nothing more than normal RAAF clothing. Our CO at first banned balaclavas, but he relented when George Loder suffered a frost-bitten ear on parade. The RCAF provided us with overshoes, but it was left to the Australian Comforts Fund to distribute sheepskin vests and gloves and the disputed balaclavas. The parade ground was rolled hard to a grooved surface. The days closed in; on morning parade the last stars glinted over us.

From our Ansons we saw the great Saskatchewan curdle then freeze. Eventually Nell took me walking on its surface to a place where men with saws cut large blocks of ice for refrigeration. There was great beauty over the world, a soft-ness, a transformation from angles to curves. Conifers drooped gracefully under heavy loads; whistles of night trains sounded clearer, more forlorn as we drifted to sleep. Australia was far off indeed.

I asked Johnnie Gordon, 'Are you going skating again tomorrow?'

'You can't skate two days in a row,' he replied, ' – not the way I skate.'

We sometimes saw Johnnie sitting with his head close to a radio. If we went by we heard symphonies from Montreal or New York. 'I like the noise they make,' he remarked defensively. If we saw him reading the Greek dramas, it was because he 'liked the murders in them.'...

Having escaped Trenton my resolution faltered. I went to see Nell one night when Max was at a skating rink. Her mother was out of bread and asked us to go and buy a loaf. We went for it in 'the coop'; whether we bought any I no longer remember. I talked my way into camp at two o'clock next morning, knowing that if life were normal we would marry.

Neil East soon sensed our feelings and told Nell to cease seeing me. The situation was ironical: I was bound for a war in England; I had fallen in love with the daughter of a ferocious pacifist. He had been so outspoken a critic of the First World War that he had been threatened with imprisonment. He was outspoken to Max and me. 'There are industrialists in Britain who viewed Hitler as their protector against Russia.' We put it to him that our generation was left with consequences, that it was too late for us to look back on causes. He agreed that we were reaping what had been sown earlier, but so it would be in the future; war led only to further wars.

Max was dismayed that the father of such a girl could speak so heatedly against the course we had taken. Privately Neil warned Nell that if I came back, which he thought improbable, I would be a man calloused by war. It was double irony that his wife, a gentle, sweet-tempered, loveable soul, was Jewish. She came from a Melbourne family of Ellises and Phillipses distinguished in arts, law and medicine. Her quiet courage in enduring pioneering days on the prairies was something I came to admire deeply.

Unlike the brothers with whom he had gone to Australia, Neil had long since rejected religious beliefs. A sanctimonious Methodist father and the church's support of the First World War had finished him. But he retained methodist zeal which found outlet in prodigious physical endeavour. If it involved hazardous travel to remote parts of the world in search of gold, so much the better. It was this zeal that led him to drop his guard over Nell. Not that he went far away. He decided to work in the Vancouver shipyards, mainly because he wanted to study at close quarters what profits were being reaped from war contracts. He saw big business and banks as conspirators, but he was no mere crank; in 1923 he had been a member of the Banking and Commerce Committee set up in Ottawa by the Dominion Government.

Nell and I began seeing each other almost daily, she love-lier than ever in muskrat coat and hat and fur-trimmed overshoes. My life was being lived on two levels, one normal and joyous, the other, the Air Force life to which I had committed myself and which began to seem more than ever insane. My work began to slide. Since I equated survival with efficiency, this troubled me deeply and troubled Nell, but with separation impending, our folly continued.

Our course was now flying every couple of days and classwork flowed in unremitting volume. As I found in the end, navigation at the level required of us was not difficult; for all that, I could scarcely master it when so much of my time was spent away from it. Realizing this, Nell drove me to work when I visited her – but inevitably she was a bewitching distraction.

On December 7 news that we could scarcely believe was broadcast: Pearl Harbour had been disastrously bombed. After our initial shock we began assuring each other that America wasn't Britain; America had always over-estimated herself; protecting Australia were the British, undeterred at Singapore.

Three days later came news that *Prince of Wales* and *Repulse* had been sunk. Surely this was impossible! – British battleships sunk by little yellow men whose eyesight, we had been assured, was too poor to allow them to become good pilots! We began to talk of the need to go home as soon as our training was over.

These days were close to Christmas. Nell and her mother were going to join Neil in Vancouver at the home of Nell's doctor brother. Before they left they prepared us an early Christmas dinner – 'a turkey as big as a sheep', as Max put it – and had presents for us under the first Christmas tree we had ever seen. Then they were gone. Instead of spending hours seeing Nell, I spent hours writing to her.

Bright lights from Christmas trees spilled from house windows onto curving snow; hoar frost bearded every twig of every bush; our words rose in vapour on the chill air. Carols were sung all through the brightened city, yet on Christmas Eve I wrote darkly to Nell:

Here we are, cramming specialized knowledge into our heads, worrying, often feeling lonely, and soon we will be put into 'planes from which we will have to bomb people we don't know...

On Christmas Day I went with Max and Col Cooper to church. We were taken in hand by a family who whisked us home. Even as we toasted each other, there was one more shattering news broadcast: Hong Kong had fallen; the garrison included 2000 men of the Canadian army.

There was small time to fret over Japanese victories, to ask why she had been so grossly under-estimated, to wonder what was going to become of our people, for work in class continued at high pressure and our navigation exercises were becoming more complex. On Boxing Day we flew an interception. I wrote that evening to Nell:

We started from Holden and the 'rabbit' (the pursued 'plane) from Strome. I caught him near Chaton. You have to tell the pilot at what time you will intercept. Then you hope and pray. Sure enough, just as I was despairing, a tiny 'plane shot over the horizon. We caught up to it so as Harry Wright (who was navigating it), could get our number, then we turned away.

When I returned from posting this letter I found an Australian civilian waiting to meet me. He introduced himself as Len Dobbin, a large, amiable fellow who knew relations of mine in Melbourne. He was a senior ground engineer responsible for maintenance of our 'planes. We yarned for a time of home and the threat of Japan, then, in a matter-of-fact way, Len said, 'I had a letter the other day from one of the chaps who went through here a year ago on the first Australian course.' He added in an inconsequential way, 'He tells me only two of them are left.'

For a moment I was unable to reply. Two men left out of twenty or twenty-five – was this possible in so short a time? I walked away resolving not to discuss it with the others and certainly not with Nell. Her father was right in one respect – my prospects of returning were remote. I tried to put it out of mind.

By the time night exercises began, our confidence in our navigation had mounted. We flew between jewel-like clusters of villages and towns. From seventy or eighty miles, the large, reassuring glow of Edmonton drew us unfailingly home. Home it had certainly become; we felt ourselves locals. Not one of us remained unadopted by an Edmonton family.

On December 13 we lost one more of our number, this time through an incipient ulcer. Max wrote:

Owen Lloyd grounded. Flight down to 21 – brr! Wonder how many of us will see Berlin from the air?

On Bomber Command squadrons in England the observer had a dual role: he navigated the 'plane to the target, then, lying in the nose, aimed the bombs. In a matter of six months this was to be changed; separate categories of navigator and bombaimer were to be introduced; the First World War mustering 'observer' would become archaic. In Canada we knew nothing of these changes. As far as our training was concerned, a ten-week course in bombing and gunnery was still included. We were given an introduction to bombing theory and practice during our final weeks in Edmonton, first of all being introduced to a mythical projectile termed 'the ideal bomb'. Unlike the 'real bomb', it was unaffected by the speed of the aircraft from which it was released, or by any of the other forces that made the 'real bomb' such a difficult weapon with which to achieve accuracy. As someone put it, 'The ideal bomb is ideal in that, by not existing, it can harm no real person'.

By turning a knob on the bombsight the bombaimer aligned a parallel pair of drift wires with the direction in which the aircraft was tracking over the ground. Lying in the nose of the Anson he could then watch frozen ponds, snow-roofed homesteads and large red barns move in more or less orderly procession down the drift wires. Once over the bombing range he released the eleven and a half pound practice bomb onto the target. Being far from ideal, it followed in curving flight under the 'plane, down, down through the translucent prairie air gathering momentum, until it struck with a puff of smoke. But sometimes the Anson would pitch or yaw at the moment of release and the puff of smoke would be like a bowler's 'wide.' Some bombs fell outside the range altogether, for even on bright days without any enemy to fire on us, bombaimers often suffered over-anxiety. Down below, the range crew measured errors. Like the God of Israel, they made scant allowance for human frailty.

The bombing record at 2 AOS stood at forty-two yards from 10,000 feet. For five of six bombs on our final exercise my error was thirty-one yards; the sixth missed by 200 yards, giving me an average of sixty yards. Even so, this was our best for a few days, then Johnnie Gordon broke the school record by a yard and was awarded a case of beer. Dear Johnnie; I well

34

remember his anguish a year later over Bomber Command's lack of accuracy and the policy of area bombing.

On New Year's Eve most of us escaped for five days to Banff, taking our study material with us. Every encircling mountain there, every roof, every tree and post bore its load of snow. Max and I climbed the minor peak of Tunnel Mountain with George Loder and his flying partner Harry Waddell; these two had been bushwalkers together in Sydney. Though Harry was plump and enjoyed good living, he was a vigorous walker and the most cheerful of companions; everything he undertook, he tackled with zest and joy. Johnnie Gordon had brought his case of beer with him. As its contents diminished he telegraphed Denny Ross, who was setting our final meteorology paper back in Edmonton: SATURATION POINT REACHED. PLEASE FORWARD WET ADIABATIC LAPSE RATE. Denny's reply came promptly: WET ADIABATIC LAPSE RATE SHOWS INSTABILITY AND TURBULENCE REGION.

Max and I had a party. He wrote cheerfully:

All the boys rolled up – we had about 15 in the room. They brought along varying supplies of tinned stuff from home, and we had a mixed supper of cheese sandwiches, Christmas pudding and cake, and sliced peaches, not to mention beer and soft drinks …

I could not have guessed that night how deeply concerned George Loder was over his wife's impending confinement. Back in his room, he wrote to his parents:

Every day I find myself wondering how Betty is getting along, wondering if this is the day and hoping and praying. I know you'll be good to her and look after her. It's rotten being so far away just now.

Perhaps when we've finished training they might send us back because of the Japs – though I doubt it very much. What a break if they did – even if I could just be in Sydney long enough to see you all and Betty and the baby.

Nell met me on our return to Edmonton; she was just back from Vancouver. Time was closing in; final examinations were three days off. In the mail waiting for me was a letter from Jim Riddoch. He had been posted to Coastal Command Whitleys in Cornwall; if we both tried when I reached England we might still be able to crew together, or at least be on the same squadron. I wrote assuring him that, if we were sent over, I would make the attempt. But now I wanted a posting home.

The oldest men on our course were Johnnie Gordon and Keith Webber, both of them aged twenty-nine. Both were fine sportsmen, Johnnie playing Country Week cricket, Keith Pennant tennis. But it surprised me that Keith had been accepted for aircrew, as it was evident that he suffered digestive problems that made many of his days a misery; in the two years I was to be with him he existed on a bare minimum of food. He was gentle and courteous and warmly companionable. He wrote in his diary on January 10:

The 'finals' are over after a week of strain and sheer hard work. Writing all day, studying every spare minute, up to 2 o'clock the following morning. All on three pieces of toast a day. They are my meals. I just can't eat the meals in the mess.

He wrote of the fear of being 'scrubbed' that hung over us until our final results were announced. As it turned out, our class average was 76.7%, the highest of any course to that time. With a 70% average I not only pulled this average down, but was deservedly last. At our end-of-course dinner Harry Wright, fired with beer and relief, proposed a toast: 'To Don, who filled last position – something that can perhaps be attributed to a black coupe that used to park outside the main gate.'

Max had come second. Jarry viewed him as officer material, but not suitable as an instructor. 'Which couldn't be better from my point of view,' he wrote, 'thank the Lord I am not suited for an instructor.' On the morning of January 13 I woke him to congratulate him; he was twenty-one. That evening Nell and her mother held a party for him, with cake and candles. Nell and I gave him a volume of Rupert Brooke. There was an unspoken plea in my heart as we handed it to him: 'Don't emulate him; don't thank God who has "matched us with his hour"; see this business in its true colours.'

But it was a futile wish. Four days later we were to be posted to the bombing and gunnery school at Lethbridge, 430 miles south of Edmonton, not far from the United States border. I had no idea whether I would be able to return on leave, or even whether leave would be granted at all. Our third and final school was to be much further off. Thus, as far as Nell and I were concerned, our Edmonton farewell had an air of finality to it. I wrote that night:

Scores of people were at the station to see us off. I'm afraid I existed for one sad-eyed lass and she for me. The goodbye came suddenly. Nell rode a few moments on the step of the moving train. We kissed and she stepped down. I watched the space between us grow, then saw her suddenly turn away with her head bent and her arm in Billie's ...

4

Officer and Sergeants

For all the massive technology embodied in the bomber aircraft, its load once released was an astonishingly crude and imprecise weapon. (Max Hastings, *Bomber Command*, Michael Joseph, 1979.)

The people who had seen us off diminished and diminished against shrinking Edmonton. We rumbled over the High Level Bridge, glancing down on the broad frozen Saskatchewan. My real world, I knew, was this forever-shifting group of brothers. Nell and I had made no commitments; we clung only to slim, far-off hopes.

I stretched with others on the seats and slept. We had no escort; Tib Barker had been entrusted with delivering us. Near midnight we reached the small city of Lethbridge; No. 8 Bombing and Gunnery School lay six miles out. An open truck with high sides met us and we rode through the night standing up, bleating like sheep.

No. 8 Bombing and Gunnery School, Lethbridge

The air was milder than Edmonton; no snow had fallen, but No. 8 B & G proved dry, dusty and dispiriting. Perhaps no place could have pleased us just then, so soon after our Edmonton connections had been severed. By day we could see the Rockies, glinting ninety miles off in the clear air; a gap in them funnelled westerlies onto 'windy Lethbridge', swirling dust between large hangars.

For me there was one consolation: Trans-Canada Airlines ran an evening Lockheed 12 service from our aerodrome to Edmonton; mail was delivered next day. I began writing Nell daily numbered letters and received daily numbered replies.

At my end, there was ample time to write. For the time being our studies were over; our six weeks in Lethbridge were to be spent perfecting the gentle arts of bombing and gunnery. This we were to do two at a time, not necessarily pairing with our Edmonton partners. There were twenty short flights to be done in Fairey Battles; most of our duty hours were to be spent awaiting turns to fly. We lounged on benches and floors, read books, talked, wrote, quizzed each other on aviation knowledge. Occasionally we had intensive bursts of the wretched morse code; men had to be prodded awake from *dah-ditting* dreams.

Although the Battles looked handsome, they were ancient and prone to all manner of failures; worse, they were flown by 'browned off' pilots who resented that we, not they, were going to joust with the enemy. It was as if their manhood had been doubted and demonstrations of daring were called for. They put the aged planes through manoeuvres they had not been designed to perform. While one of our number went to work over the bombing range, the second clipped himself into the large, open cockpit by a G-string. If the pilot decided to fling the aircraft about the sky, centrifugal force might pluck the man to the string's full length. His bulging eyes beheld the Rockies above him and a dome of sky below. Gradually we became blasé and even began to enjoy ourselves.

The dusty conditions ended overnight when a blizzard howled in from the Arctic and released so many millions of tons of snow that a way had to be dug out of the barracks and into the mess. We were beginning to regard winter as dourly as the Canadians. Snowploughs spewed white streams to either side of our roads so that they soon lay in chasms eight feet deep. But flying was not long held up. As we were no longer flying with a regular partner, we came to know each other more closely. I found myself hoping that Max was right, that ours would be a lucky course in the way ahead.

We had forty-three bombs to drop by day, twenty-eight by night. By night was what most counted. My average error was 231 yards. It seemed to me that our prospects of accuracy equated with hurling a bottle from an express train at a farmer in a field. How accuracy could be achieved under fire was beyond imagining.

Next was gunnery, our weapon a Vickers gas-operated .303. Before the air-to-ground exercises the gunnery leader paraded us. 'Now see here you guys: do *not* – repeat *not* – fire at the Indians' cattle; they don't like it, we don't like it. If you kill one, you'll pay for the animal and pay the fine.'

Some one at some time must have been guilty. We could only admire his accuracy; we could seldom hit the official target. Firing air-to-air was worse. We aimed at a drogue towed like a giant stocking behind a plodding Lysander, firing bullets dipped into paints of differing colours so that each man's strikes could be identified. Our results were ludicrous: of 300 beam rounds I scored 7.33% strikes. We consoled ourselves that only in the direst emergency would we man a gun.

We seldom bothered to go to Lethbridge. When Ron Wheatley, one of the four Somers volunteers, went in with some of his friends to celebrate his twenty-first birthday, he was taken by the police to the lock-up: he had unwittingly broken the Albertan liquor laws by opening a bottle of champagne in a public restaurant. The course members who had given it to him had to bail him out.

News from the Pacific worsened daily; even impregnable Singapore of our schooldays began to look vulnerable. Keith Webber wrote sombrely on January 30:

Churchill seems to have gambled with Singapore and lost. He may have to pay the price. It's characteristic of him. Hope I return to Australia when I finish my course. So do most of the chaps.

Sixteen days later I walked into our barracks from a gunnery flight and saw the men gathered at a radio. Something about them prepared me for the worst. Churchill was announcing the fall of Singapore. Only four days later I wrote:

February 19: ...Darwin has been bombed – we do not yet know how badly. God help our people ...

The day we heard this news of Darwin George Loder received word of the birth of his daughter.

What more could I ask for! Needless to say I feel thrilled and relieved in the one moment. ...There is still the future to consider however and that also makes me wish I were there ...

The desire to go home was running so high that RAAF Ottawa sent officers out to address Australian courses. There was scant hope in what they had to say; our postings would almost certainly be to Britain.

Our wings parade was scheduled for February 27 and was to be preceded by a twenty-four hour leave. I wanted to see Nell once more before we moved east, but to get to Edmonton and back in so short a time was impossible. I decided to seek the co-operation of three of the men I knew best and go absent without leave the day preceding leave. Detection seemed unlikely as our names were very casually checked. Harry Wright undertook to fly my last air firing exercise, George Loder to fire my ground exercise with the Browning machinegun; Max would mail my twenty-four hour leave pass to Edmonton and answer awkward questions.

The Lockheed 12 was due to leave for Edmonton early in the evening. That afternoon I flew a gunnery exercise with a particularly browned-off pilot.

[He] executed a couple of barrel-rolls...on the way out to the range. Just as we were drawing up to the drogue, our engine began spluttering and finally cut... In deep snow, on the bombing

41

*range, he landed splendidly. Great chunks of snow flew up behind
us and within a hundred yards of the quadrant the plane stopped
dead. ... Now I was in a fix – it was almost time to cancel my flight
booking if I were unable to go. Fortunately we soon covered the
11 miles back to camp in a truck.*

* * *

While I ate a meal on the Edmonton-bound flight, Harry
Wright flew for me and recorded a better score than he had
done for himself; in the flight office Max parried questions
about the forced landing and my whereabouts; next day
George Loder presented himself without difficulty when my
name was called on the machinegun range.

On that blissful leave Nell stitched sergeant's stripes and
observer's brevy on my tunic for a photograph, then demoted
me for the return flight. Only a handful of people witnessed
our wings parade. When the commanding officer had pinned
on our wings, we marched past him as sergeant observers, led
over dazzling snow by the station band. Of more importance,
our pay went up to $3.60 a day – more than most of us had
earned in our lives; moreover, we were entitled now to sleep-
ers on the long train journey to Rivers, in a remote part of
Manitoba.

No. 1 Advanced Navigation School, Rivers

The School was in a daunting, white world which seemed on
the edge of the Arctic; Rivers was only a scattered village;
Brandon, the nearest town, was twenty-five miles away.
Mainly we were there to learn to use the Mark IX bubble
sextant, first by day on the ground, finally by night in the air.
We were to take 250 shots, 70 of them sun sights, the rest, stars
and planets. Added to this there were long classroom navigation exercises to be done, involving use of the Marc St. Hilair
method of plotting astro sights.

On sub-zero nights, as we stood in fleece-lined boots in the
snow, taking shots of stars and planets, curtains of the aurora

borealis undulated fold on fold over the northern horizon; behind them were shifting beams of light, like celestial searchlights. On one of those nights, George Loder wrote home:

...the beams gradually contracted and moved together and became full of the most glorious colour. After a little while the colour faded and the lights began to break up. ...it was a thrilling sight and left me with a superstitious feeling, like one who has seen an omen.

The Pacific news was wholly bad. Broome, Wyndham and Port Moresby bombed, 60,000 Japanese troops in Java. I knew by now that Ian, one of my younger brothers, had gone into action in New Guinea with the 39th Battalion of militia; he had not long turned twenty. And we knew that thousands of Americans had arrived in Australia under MacArthur. It was beyond our comprehension that the RAAF was sending us in the opposite direction.

As well that work in class kept us fully occupied. Our long navigational plots simulated flights to German targets. On Mercator charts we drew the track we must try to follow from 'base' in Lincolnshire to 'point A' on the enemy coast, then made a change of direction by a short leg to 'point B', then dashed to the 'target' – Cologne, Hamburg, Berlin – and made a roundabout return home. So great was our concentration that we did not pause to consider what sort of reception might await us in reality; our overriding concern was to get there. The instructors saw to it that perverse winds raged. We changed altitude; we iced up, were attacked by fighters. All the way we were given clues to our whereabouts. At 0132 hours the altitude and azimuth of Spica were such and such; eight minutes later Vega read so and so. By transferring the first astro reading to the second we obtained a fix which revealed an alarming change of wind. But by no means everyone obtained the same wind, consequently not everyone altered course by the same amount. We started these plots sitting at our tables; half an hour later two or three men could sit no longer, they rose and worked with bent backs. After two hours half the class was standing. Now, said the test paper, your wireless operator has obtained bearings. When we plotted these, the fix obtained did not by any means tally with our positions. 'Oh shit!' A burst of laughter, then silence again.

I could never shut from my awareness the reactions of my fellows; it was a fascination that cost me dear. On March 4 I wrote despairingly:

Tonight we did a D.R. plotting paper and I did not properly complete it for 5 ½ hours. Certainly I did not hurry and I did several parts two or three times, but 5 ½ hours!

We all seemed to do better in the air, nevertheless Max and I found ourselves one night deep in the United States and scrambled home full of gloom, not sure how we had got there. The north magnetic pole was close by in Baffin Land, consequently magnetic variation changed every few miles. But even this, we decided, was not the cause of our debacle.

Late in March the worst blizzard in twenty-five years swept Manitoba; the Arctic engulfed us. Drifts built up outside our classroom windows, mounting against the glass until they met Damoclean icicles hanging from the eaves. We became sealed behind a white wall. Guide-ropes were positioned to link classrooms to mess and barracks. We bent double over them, scarves over mouths and noses, mittened hands grasping them. We did not dare stray from them, as we could see no more than a few feet in the deathly whirl of snow.

Flying halted; our departure date on pre-embarkation leave had to be revised. It struck me that our leave would coincide now with Nell's Easter holidays. I wired her: would she join me at Rivers and travel as far east as Quebec with me?

She accepted. As expected in those far-off years, I wrote also to her mother, thankful that her father was still away in Vancouver. The blizzard abated and we got on with our flying.

On April 2 all our training in Canada ended. We had each totalled about 120 hours of day flying, about 40 by night, all without loss of a life. With this meagre experience the six top men on the course were automatic choices to go to Ferry Command in Montreal, there to team with seasoned pilots to navigate across the Atlantic to Britain. Each of the six was commissioned: Tib Barker, Max Bryant, Tom Cunliffe, Ted Freeman, Tom McNeill, Ron Wheatley. As it was to eventuate, each could have remained with Ferry Command in relative safety, but only Tom Cunliffe, a married man, chose to do so. Many of us regretted that George Loder had not had the same option; as a man suitable for commissioning, I saw him as second only to Tib Barker.

Next afternoon Max and I met the eastbound train at Rivers siding. Nell was safe on board. She and I looked at each other incredulously; the seemingly impossible had happened; we began to dare to think it might always happen, that somehow we might come together in that far-off tantalising time 'after the war.' Max looked on us with indulgent affection and repeated his claim to be my best man. He travelled with us as far as Montreal, then left to join the rest of the course in New York.

Even now I associate Quebec with contrast, with the joy of being with Nell in so charming a place and the impending wrench of departure. On April 10, in Montreal, we went our ways, she homeward-bound, I to join our course in New York. We had still imposed no bonds; we recognized that we might never meet again, that almost inevitably others would come into our lives, but we clung still to a far-off hope.

45

Halifax was so overcrowded with aircrew that our course was sent to Moncton, New Brunswick. Keith Webber was hoping still that we might be sent home:

How long we will remain here, is of course a mystery to us. Where we are going is also a mystery. Home or England? – The rumour says home – good sense says England. The New Yorkers and Canadians are quite convinced we will go back. Somehow I think the chances are 50-50.

Until the Fall of Singapore, Keith had been as loyal a 'son of Empire' as any of us. In New York his disappointment in Britain had been swept away by the warmth and vitality of Americans.

It seems evident to me that after this war Australia will lean more to the States than Britain. I have always plumped 100% British but after the 'disclosures' of this war – the mishandling of every campaign – the absolute effeteness and public 'school tie' of everything Britain touches has made me against my will look to America. ... The handling of Singapore from a military point of view was pitiful in its unpreparedness. 'We never thought they'd come from the land.' How characteristic in its complacency, its puerility, in its inefficiency ...

At Moncton the six men commissioned off course decided not to be separated from the rest of us; together we took over an upstairs barracks. But this lasted just one night, then they were posted to Montreal for their Atlantic ferry duties. Our course was never again to be together. The rest of us remained only three days more, then went on to Halifax, to the end of the great training scheme production line. Until this point each trade had attended separate schools across Canada; here was the coming together.

The place was packed with men awaiting convoys, Englishmen, Canadians, Poles, New Zealanders, Norwegians,

Czechs. Fifteen hundred trained aircrew were passing through every four weeks.

Our destination was formally announced to our group: England. A silence fell over the men. Keith wrote despondently:

> I think every one of us is disappointed. With our own country in such peril it seemed reasonable to us that we would be posted back. The Yanks are going to our country – why must we be going in the opposite direction?

Next day we were marched to hear an address by Sir William Glasgow, Australian High Commissioner. Keith's indignation overflowed:

> He told us that perhaps – I repeat perhaps – when we have had extensive operational experience, we may get a chance to return. The boys, including Australian sailors, told him later in no uncertain terms, what their ideas were.

The posting hit George Loder hard; he was conscious of the responsibility now falling on his mother for keeping an eye on his wife and their baby daughter.

> Poor darling old Mum! I know how you must feel at the present time… I'll take every possible care and we can only trust in God for the rest… I'm glad in a way Dad is not well enough to enlist. I think you need him with you.

On May 1, carrying full packs, complete with gasmasks and tin hats, we boarded the 12,000 ton Polish *Batory*. Most of us were carrying as well a load of foodstuffs for British families yet unknown to us.

By troop-ship standards *Batory* accommodation looked good: six of us were to share a cabin twelve feet by ten, two taking turn to sleep on the floor. Three others besides myself were from our training flight: Col Cooper, Johnnie Gordon and the youthful Ian Heatley; the other two were former *Monterey* observers who had trained in Ontario.

May 3: ...I went to breakfast and presently saw that we were moving slightly. I came to our cabin and now am writing beside our open porthole. ... A second tug has just raced past. A man on board shouted, 'Good luck boys!' and a Canadian replied, 'Look after the girls!'... We are gaining speed. Soon Canada will be a shadow just as Australia was. In faraway Alberta it will be early morning. I wonder if Nell is stirring in her sleep as my thoughts go back over those miles?

5
To 'The Homeland'

For Britain in 1942, the only area where unilateral action was in any degree possible was the continuation or non-continuation of the night offensive of the bomber force against Germany, because no allied (American) forces were engaged in it and no German initiatives were involved ... (John Terraine, *The Right of the Line*, Hodder & Stoughton, London, 1985.)

Wraith-like we slipped into the Atlantic and began taking up convoy stations. The U-boat war was entering its darkest period; that month 125 ships would be lost. The main units of our defence clustered around the immensely dignified *Aquitania* at the centre of the convoy; she was said to be carrying 6000 troops. Between her and the *Batory* rode U.S.S. *Texas*, comfortingly abristle with guns. Destroyers raced about us like sheep dogs, chivvying us into position. By the time we were ready to sail it was evening, the Canadian coast still in sight. Keith Webber went on deck for a last look at Halifax:

> *Lights twinkling around the harbour. ... Take a look at those lights, pal. It will be a long time before you see them again, twinkling as they are now.*

Emphatic orders came over the public address system: *always* carry lifejackets; *always* carry a full waterbottle; *always* lock portholes when the blackout signal sounds; *no* smoking on deck at night; *never* shut cabin doors in case they jam in an explosion.

It was said that U-boats lingered outside ports of departure. Sure enough depth charging began next day from racing destroyers, the *Batory's* hull shuddering like a tin can. We joked uneasily about the possibility of all our training being wasted. That afternoon aircrew attended a church service in the lounge. As we sang 'For those in peril on the sea' the ship continued to rock to detonations.

We never heard the *Batory*'s full complement; we only knew that aircrew numbered 600. Somewhere below us were RCAF ground staff; Canadian army men were below them again, hammock to hammock below the waterline. I felt embarrassed that these men were required to wait on our tables:

Tonight one said to me, 'I'll be able to tell my children how I worked my way overseas to fight for my country.' I suppose most of them will get back and some day have families, whereas our boys have a much slimmer chance –

Less than thirty-six hours out, fog closed over us limiting visibility to a couple of hundred yards.

It is damp and eerie on deck. The mast tops disappear in the greyness above us and from the stern we cannot see the fo'c'sle. Sailors are wearing rubber kneeboots and oilskins. The rest of the convoy is completely hidden from us, but occasionally the ships exchange mournful blasts on their sirens ... Eddies of air bring little clouds of fog across the deck. They cling awhile to the superstructure then vanish away. ... Our ship is number 22. In the fog it wails that number on its siren, then, from out of the mist, comes a hoarse wail from 23.

Our cabin reeked of cigarette smoke and inadequately-washed bodies – we were limited to seawater baths. We read and wrote and argued. Chiefly we argued about the Empire. Since the fall of Singapore a great deal of disillusionment was being expressed. Col Cooper remained staunchly pro-British; I was less so than I had been. The other four had a good deal of Irish in their ancestry. From three of them we heard much of Henry VIII, Cromwell, the Potato Famine, the Black and

Tans. The fourth was Johnnie Gordon who was trying to read *Romeo and Juliet* on a top bunk. He complained presently that he was suffering enough noise from depth charges and sirens without having loud, inaccurate history assailing him. He had taught history; that day he proceeded to teach it in our foetid cabin. He addressed us on the Norman Conquest, perhaps seeing it as the beginning of Britain's stratified society. At all events, he spoke so lucidly and interestingly that scarcely a word interrupted him. It was an artless exhibition from a born teacher.

May 5: We are still enveloped in fog. On deck we stand peering into it, impelled to listen and to watch. The sea is calm, almost lifeless. We know that the rest of the convoy still surrounds us, but it is hidden completely from our sight. As we stared out into the grey wall today, we saw a ship's bows close against our stern and saw the great superstructure above it. It looked a ghost ship, but white foam was falling back from its prow and it was coming on steadily. Presently it tilted and turned, coming onto our starboard side. ...

May 6: The fog has cleared and our 'great cloud of witnesses' is visible. ... According to the Batory Blackout, *... our captain has been almost continually on the bridge during the past three foggy days.*

May 8: The AA guns have been practising, as we can expect air attack within the next few days from Focke-Wulf Condors...

No attack came. On May 11 I went up into a wet dawn. Land lay off to starboard – Donegal, someone said. Then a full-throated roar sounded over the mastheads. A Polish sailor, flinging grateful arms above his head, shouted, 'Spitfeur! Spitfeur!' Soon we had the wild heights of Ailsa Craig off to port, then, to starboard, Arran. My mind went to the departure this way in 1849 of a five-year-old boy, a Gaelic-speaking

51

Cameron of Glen Nevis, who became my grandfather. After ninety-three years I was the first of his descendants to return. If I can, I thought, I will go to Lochaber.

George Loder wrote home that evening as we rode at anchor in the Clyde:

The colours of the landscape are beautifully soft and moist, the green of the fields and the trees the gentlest I ever remember. ... Well, at any rate our journey is safely over ... tho' early this morning the crash of depth charges was so close and loud that they woke me up. ... altho' things haven't turned out perhaps as one could have wished, I am looking forward to the future, which should hold lots of interest, if one is prepared to make the best of it.

'Making the best of it' did not come as easily to Keith Webber:

And so here we are in Britain. For how long and whither bound, we know not. We hope not for too long. Somehow I think we will have to do a fair bit of 'ops' before being returned home. If one can last that long. That is the question burning everyone. The N. Zealanders also would much like to return home ...

That night we remained on board ship, conscious of stillness, wondering about the way ahead. With double daylight saving, evening seemed endless. I had not expected the banks of the Clyde to be beautiful.

It is like a garden. The hills that fall down to the harbour are vivid green and patterned with hedges. Among clumps of trees are church towers and steeples and along the waterfront stand rows of straight-fronted houses – very Presbyterian-looking ... we go by train tomorrow to Bournemouth – an 18 or 19 hour journey ... Barrage balloons went up over various points tonight – silver sausages ... Col Cooper went to hospital today with something like tonsillitis.

52

This setback to Col's health put him seventeen days behind us. Although it separated him permanently from the old course, it probably saved his life; he was eventually posted to Coastal Command in Northern Ireland.

When darkness at last fell, searchlights sported lethargically over Glasgow, their beams innocent of the menace in store for us.

In the morning, May 12 1942, 1500 aircrew were ferried ashore from various ships to a miniature train. After the Canadian locomotives the engine seemed a bantam of self-importance, its whistle high, thin and peremptory. It puffed off with us into the south, the men staring bemused onto unfolding fields and woods and dry stone walls and grazing sheep and white cottages. All this, too, was in miniature, groomed, measured, willed, sold, squabbled over generation upon generation; all strange yet not foreign.

The greater number of men in the convoy were Canadians. Like ourselves, they had arrived in a land which was subtly familiar, not only familiar from schoolboy history and literature and geography, but from an inherited consciousness of which they had scarcely been aware.

We bustled out of Scotland and into England, whistle shrieking. Again, day seemed to have no end. Scene on scene flowed by, hedged and beautiful, distances limited by diffused light, Constable skies overhead. But at dusk we neared Manchester and were assailed by packed, grimy chimneypots, darkened walls, wet slate roofs, people moving in chasms of melancholy. How was it possible to exist in such places?

An order came to draw blackout blinds. In the carriage ceiling dim blue lights came on and remained on all night, too weak to read by, too strong to allow easy sleep. We curled on floors and seats, in luggage racks, journeying through darkened miles of this unknown, well-known country.

Johnnie Gordon wrote in the morning:

The country, every inch of it, is something more beautiful than ever I could imagine. It was a real tonic to see the rich colours of the fields after Canada ... I can understand after seeing it, why the English are so keen to hold it.

We came to the edge of Bath and saw gaping bomb damage from a raid of three weeks back when 600 had been killed. It was our first intimation of war. Church towers then and thatched villages, grazing sheep, thick woods and always multi-shaped, hedged fields, as if boundaries had been ordained by the creator. It occurred to me how much of Australia and Canada were beyond man's detailed ordering. Though spellbound, I began to cherish an inheritance of boundlessness.

The farther south we moved, the more lush and beautiful the scenes became until, at Bournemouth, we felt we had reached another Eden. 'This town,' Johnnie wrote, 'is the most beautiful I have ever seen. The trees and gardens almost smother the buildings.' It was thronged by men and women in uniform. We marched up a hilly street to 'Bath Hill Court', a block of flats previously the abode of affluent holiday makers, now stripped of furnishings and, like several other such buildings, used as barracks.

In the morning, as I leaned at a window absorbing the beauty of the place, I heard an Australian from an earlier contingent say, 'Listen to this – you blokes are being given a welcome from Germany!'

Over his radio a supercilious voice declared, 'We know you Australians and Canadians have just arrived in Bournemouth. We'll pay you a visit before long. In any event, most of you will kill yourselves in training.'

'Lord Haw Haw,' said our informant 'He says the town hall clock is two minutes slow – it is you know!'

This then was the voice of the enemy; his coast was scarcely seventy miles off. We were on an island struggling to survive at the edge of a darkened continent. Only the RAF and the

Luftwaffe passed between the two lands.

Mail was waiting for us, forwarded from RAAF Base Post Office, Kodak House, Kingsway, London, our official address. A letter from Jim Riddoch gave me the number of their sergeants' mess at 502 Squadron, St. Eval, Cornwall. I phoned that evening and spoke to him for the first time since his departure from Nareen, feeling for a moment as if the intervening months had melted away and we might speak of next weekend's tennis. But our subject was how best I could try to join his squadron. I put in application that night.

When I look back now, our stay at Bournemouth seems a long delightful interlude before the blood-letting ahead; in fact we were there only eighteen days. The pleasures open to us were endless: concerts by the Bournemouth Municipal Orchestra; long walks in the New Forest – shared for my part with Harry Waddell and George Loder; slow perambulations about Christchurch Priory with Johnnie Gordon. These last I cherished most. I see Johnnie yet, cap in hand, tunic unbuttoned, pausing to construe Latin inscriptions for me from graves against walls and under our feet, sometimes puzzling over a stonemason's incised abbreviations, his mind seeming as much with those of whom he read as with me.

'The jokers who built these places were in no hurry. They were building to the glory of God.'

He wrote home: 'We like this place so well that we don't mind how long we stay here.'

And George Loder:

It is really hard sometimes to believe that war is near. The sun doesn't sink until about eleven o'clock. I go to bed when it is light and wake up – 6.30 – and it is light again. Twilight is the most beautiful of times when the day begins to cool off, the sky is still light and the hedged lanes are all a-twitter with birds and you can hear the cuckoo calling.

Keith Webber explored further afield than most of us, going alone to Salisbury. A complete change had come in his tone:

I was buying cards at a little shop near the market square – the sort of shop you step down to and a bell tinkles as you close the door – the alert sounded and the woman told me it was the second for the day. ... Whilst still in the little shop some sheep being shepherded by a farmer in gaiters ambled from the square into the street ...

Although we were aware that people were in no position to offer us hospitality on the Canadian scale, we each hankered for home life. Many of the men found it through the Lady Francis Ryder scheme which matched servicemen with people willing to accept them into their homes. Thus was the food distributed that we had brought from Canada. My own wish was to locate two middle-aged sisters, girlhood friends of my mother's, whom I had known in my 'teens. I knew that they ran a small guesthouse at Burnham-on-Sea, in Somerset, but I lacked their address. When I saw that Burnham was scarcely sixty-five miles from Bournemouth I decided to go there, supposing it to be small enough to make locating Nora and Stella's place easy.

The train jogged through the drowsy afternoon and, at Evercreech Junction, stopped for an hour to wait for a connection. By the time I reached Burnham the shops were shut. It was larger than I had expected; my search took hours. In the end I was greeted with such surprise and joy and affection that I came near tears. I produced Nell's photograph for approval, as if I had arrived home.

In Bournemouth we were given a weeks leave with free return tickets to any railway station in Britain. Feeling that time might be running out, I planned to walk across Scotland, from

Inverness to Fort William along the Caledonian Canal, finishing in my Cameron grandfather's country. It did not occur to me that any of our course might like to join me, so I was delighted when George Loder and Harry Waddell asked if they could come.

These two had first met in Sydney as Junior Trust Officers in the Public Trust and had joined the same bush walking club. They were to prove such lively, equable company that I hoped our service lives would continue together.

Although Harry liked good food and comfortable lodgings, he was physically tough and our pace-setter. He walked with great vigor, swinging his arms, leaning aggressively forward, at the same time conducting preposterous arguments on war strategy that brought amused smiles to George's lips. We knew there was scarcely a grain of aggression in him. I was unaware that he, too, was troubled by the prospect of bombing civilians and was hoping for this reason to go to Coastal Command. On our walk we seldom discussed the future, so I was startled when he announced one day that he did not expect to come through. George, with a wife and child waiting for him, allowed himself no expression of premonitions. He was extraordinarily poised and self-disciplined. I thought him the most whole man among us.

I had imagined we would be tramping across heather like latter-day Alan Breck Stewarts. The reality was disillusioning; the eastern end of the Great Glen was scarcely less manicured than England. We walked thirty miles on bitumen above Loch Ness. But at Fort Augustus all this changed. The skipper of a small oil tanker, *Ben Henshaw*, bound for the Western Isles, offered us a ride to Banavie. His crew welcomed us like brothers. We entered Loch Oich with them, gliding past islets and wooded capes and white cottages, the ship sending a gentle wash against the banks. In Laggan Lochs we were called below to share a curry. As we ate and talked, the lovely

57

avenue to Loch Lochy slipped past the portholes. Gradually the colours outside changed. On either side of the narrow loch, steep mountains rose; the water was dark and the scene ahead indistinct. The great bulk of Ben Nevis was half hidden in cloud, but here and there I caught a gleam of snow.

In Fort William we booked into a cheap hotel fronting Loch Linnhe and in the morning set out in wild weather to Ben Nevis. George wrote later:

As we climbed the first thousand feet, the rain and wind beat in our faces with discouraging persistence. About half way up ... snow began to fall, large soft flakes, but we kept on and this soon ceased; the clouds began to break and occasionally we got a fleeting glimpse of sunlight. On all sides lay the most beautiful scenery – rugged mountains, jagged cliffs, sharp peaks and grey lochs ... As we climbed we came amongst snow-drifts and on the summit snow lay all round ...

We were looking over the dark precipice that falls a couple of thousand feet from the summit, when mists closed over us. We stood there, listening and watching.

... presently the silent company departed and marched away over the chasm, leaving us again in sunshine. ... Our way down turned. Every stone in the path before us was wet and glistening. ... Harry was in the lead, taking barbarous shortcuts, muttering to himself 'Time for tea.' ... We were soon in grassland again, fit country for mortals to live in. Ewes and lambs lifted black faces from the grass and regarded us blankly. George lit his pipe and a wisp of smoke passed my nostrils. ... We would, we agreed, miss tea anyway ...

These were moments to cherish for the rest of my life. In the morning we started back to Bournemouth. The Japanese, we read, had reached the borders of India. That night a thousand bombers attacked Cologne, a force augmented by crews finishing operational training. The defences, the reports declared, were overwhelmed; the British press was exultant; people we met rejoiced at the blow, a few even thanked us as if we had taken part. I was unaware then of the extent of Britain's own losses, of 40,000 civilians already killed in bombings. Better knowledge might have tempered my diary entry:

The destruction and suffering must be worse than anything England went through, but Germany chose the weapons. It is a terrible thought that inoffensive fellows are killing women and children, but I can see nothing else for it now.

Next day our postings came through, my own with the rest. It was to Bobbington, in Shropshire. Half the course were going there, the other half to North Wales. Whether the Bobbington move would decrease my prospects of joining Jim Riddoch, I could not tell. I had a last walk with Johnnie Gordon in the New Forest and, afterwards, we ate supper in Westover Street.

We lingered talking. I value his company above all others. ... Tomorrow we leave here – and lose Johnnie, Bill Charlton, Wilf Burrows and Ian Heatley. I am very sorry indeed to lose any of them. We are a family ...

Blue Freeman, first of the Atlantic Ferry men to reach Bournemouth, arrived as we were leaving. He alone of our course was there for Lord Haw Haw's promised raid. The German planes came low over the sea the next Sunday morning, attacking indiscriminately, taking many lives.

6

Bobbington

The danger of jumping to the wrong conclusion is most real when the Navigator imagines he has lost his way and cannot quickly recognize expected landmarks; or when a landmark fails to show up at the appointed time and something similar presents itself. These moments call for self-restraint and quiet reasoning which do not always come naturally to the beginner. (Air Navigation; HMSO publication A.P.1234)

No. 3 Advanced Flying Unit, Bobbington,* was not a large station; it lay in gentle countryside between the Severn Valley and Birmingham. As all its barracks were occupied, we were quartered in bell tents, I sharing with Harry Waddell, George Loder and Keith Webber. A more companionable quartet I could not have imagined. Languorous summer was in the air and scents of hayfields and blossom; the grass around our camp was soft underfoot. The scene and the good company reminded me of boyhood camps. Sometimes I heard Keith Webber savouring aloud English woodland terms: 'spinney', 'water meadow', 'coppice'.

The purpose of Advanced Flying Units was to introduce us to the complications of navigating over England after having learnt the craft in countries of vast spaces, free of war and with maximum visibility. For this we would have three weeks. We were a mixed intake of Australians and Canadians, again flying in Ansons, one day as navigator, next as bombaimer-second navigator. At the end of the course there was to be a limited degree of choice: each man could say whether he

---

*   This name so resembled RAF *Bovington* that, soon after our time, Bobbington was re-named *Halfpenny Green*.

wished to become a navigator or a bombaimer. This was an interim arrangement while the RAF waited for the new specialist bombaimer category to yield adequate numbers. Our Anson pilots were a fairly scruffy-looking lot of sergeants and pilot officers.

We were issued with a set of topographical maps of Britain, scale 1:500,000. After the maps of Canada with their vast, open prairies, large lakes, mountain barriers and widely-separated villages, the detail of these was overwhelming. It was as if the whole of Canada had been compressed to a fiftieth part of its size, its cities, towns and villages drawn tightly together.

In class a pleasant RAF Flying Officer referred us to Sheet 5. This, we saw, stretched from the coast of Ireland in the west to a glimpse of the Humber estuary in the northeast. Its congestion reminded me of an aged body with knotted veins, thickened arteries, enlarged organs, with here and there hideous conglomerations, like cancerous growths. These last, all closely shaded brown, were marked LONDON, MANCHESTER, BIRMINGHAM. Black railways, red roads, blue canals wove in and out like intestines through the prevailing brown of these growths. But there were also places that promised beauty: deep estuaries, splendid capes and straits, purple high country with precipices and lofty lakes. Man had measured these areas and heights and depths and angles and curves and distances for centuries; in Australia and Canada he had scarcely come to grips with his geography.

Our first essential was to mark the whereabouts of Bobbington, since it did not rate mention. Its nearest town was Stourbridge; a prominent high ridge about sixteen miles off to the northeast was the Wrekin – a good guide, the Flying Officer told us, to the aerodrome. He then uttered warnings. As we could see, the country was much more congested than Canada or Australia; its vast number of landmarks would at first make pinpointing our whereabouts confusing.

'Don't risk following railway lines or roads that look familiar from an earlier flight, because they are likely to be some other railway or road, you could end up coming in at Waterloo Station. If flying cross-country exercises in poor weather, *always* fly a thousand feet higher than the highest terrain to either side of track – the mountains of North Wales are an Air Force graveyard. *Always* remember that the skies over Britain are congested. Look at the number of aerodromes on your maps; Bomber Command alone has over ninety along the east coast.

'Avoid built-up areas because anti-aircraft gunners around places like Liverpool are trigger happy after frequent blitzing. Not only that, the cities are protected by balloon barrages; their cables can bring a plane down. If you need to call for a radio bearing to guide you back to base, remember that if the answer is prefixed by QBY instead of the usual QDM, it means that balloons lie between you and home. The balloons are equipped with squeakers which can be heard on the aircraft's radio; the closer you fly to them, the louder they sound.'

Then there was the matter of airfield control. Take-off instructions were not given from the watch-office by R/T; Bobbington would prepare us for operational stations, to which the enemy was always listening. A green take-off light would come from the control van by the upwind end of the runway.

This talk, both helpful and disturbing, was followed by one from an obnoxious Wing Commander. Keith Webber was incensed:

The attitude of the RAF towards us is obviously one of repugnance. He told a bunch of us, Canadians and Australians, that we were not in Canada or Australia any more but in an Air Force ...He impressed on us that because Britain was trying to build up her aircraft production, loss of a plane mattered more than loss of a crew.

As a consequence of our mixed intake, I was listed to fly with a Canadian named Gemmel. He could not have been more than twenty-one, a quiet, intent, efficient youngster. Our first flight together was my first since Rivers, two months earlier. For three and a quarter hours a RAF sergeant with enthusiasm for history and literature flew us at his own sweet will on a map-reading exercise. It was purely a familiarization flight.

The day was beautiful – really hot on the ground – and we flew without flying kit. The horrible smoke pall over Birmingham and Wolverhampton lay over half the horizon. We circled over Clive's birthplace and over Stratford-on-Avon. Map-reading in this congested countryside is very different from Canada, though not as bad as I had anticipated.

On our first true cross-country exercise, on a 'clear, breezy day with a few alto-cumulus clouds', Gemmel was navigator. We flew low over Wales, and then across a silver sea, grandly mottled here and there by clouds shadows. We circled over Douglas on the Isle of Man and came back to Rhyl.

With the coasts of North Wales and the Isle of Man as clear as a map, I never had doubt of our whereabouts and passed Gemmel regular pinpoints. For his part, he navigated without setback and the Wrekin welcomed us home. But next day, in poor weather, I flew as first navigator in the opposite direction. Instead of Rhyl, clear on the coast, I was to make a first change of course at a church somewhere in the Cotswolds. Gemmel reported church towers every few minutes; they appeared in impossible numbers.

Never have I had such a trip. On my ETA at our first turning point, we were somewhere west of our objective, but the pilot – a pleasant young NZ sergeant – said he knew a railway line close by that we could follow to the spot. He got onto the wrong railway line and we became hopelessly mixed up…. We climbed to 8000 feet, for no apparent reason, but our view was obscured by clouds. Eventually the pilot came spiralling down, intending to make for the coast. The coast was out of sight and we landed at the experimental drome of Farnborough. We set off again, but there was a strong smell of burning, so we returned to Farnborough and were there forty minutes while some minor repairs were made. After this we decided to go straight home. ... By now we had bumped so much that I was feeling thoroughly sick and did not care what would be said at Bobbington.

Nothing much *was* said, but I was mortified from having fallen in with the pilot's decision to follow a railway line and having landed at such a high security aerodrome as Farnborough. I threw off depression by immersing myself in an account I was writing of our journey across Scotland. I wrote alone in our tent, aware of the bleating of ewes and lambs and the dreamlike call of cuckoos. When the others came in and dropped despondently on their stretchers, and started their catalogue of disasters, I was reminded of our first days in Edmonton, and said so. Before long we began laughing at ourselves.

Then we were further cheered by an unexpected letter I received from Johnnie Gordon.

Hanged if I know why I'm writing this, but at least it'll kill time. Maybe kill you too. Or even me – 'a consummation devoutly to be wished.' Anyway it's just possible that you guys still remember us and may be interested to compare misfortunes. Have at thee then!

They were billetted 'among the reluctant Welsh people at Llanbedrog', but were flying from Penrhos, 'a suicide 'drome with no runways at all and a hollow in the middle of it. Pilots who land every second time without crashing are held to be very skillful.'

The people speak Welsh among themselves and many cannot speak English. … At first you think they're sullen and unfriendly but they're only waiting for you to say 'Good day' first. Then everything is OK. But if you pass a group of them without, as it were, giving the password and the colour of the day, the letter of the day etc., they stare after you with that same dumb look with which a cow stops eating and watches you pass.

Although the remainder of our Bobbington exercises brought us no further humiliations, Gemmel and I had feelings of repugnance each time we sighted the industrial Midlands. As we groped around them, smoke and low cloud sealed off landmarks. Then we would glimpse wet slate roofs of terrace houses, see awful segments of them twisting in rows, up hill, down dale, like elongated slugs, vanishing at length into disconsolate smog. I could hardly imagine people living in such places. In our ears we often heard the caterwauling of their protective balloons.

After ten days in tents we moved into barracks and I began to share a two-bunk room with Harry Wright. He and I were to continue rooming together on three different stations over the ensuing four months. His nature and outlook were a lift to my spirits. Like Johnnie Gordon, Tom McNeill and Blue Freeman, his Irishness brought a breath of levity to war's insanity. Although all four of these men were meticulous in their navigation and deeply loyal to friends, they cocked a snoot at things 'not done.' They were an irritation to some of the RAF administrative officers, even more to disciplinary NCOs, but to RAF aircrew they proved brothers. Johnnie wrote home:

We get on quite well with the civilian population. It's the professional soldier type, the military careerists who were born standing to attention and have worn a uniform ever since, its that kind of generally dull-witted creature who dislikes us. And

simply because we do not conform to a conventional pattern that
they *have always accepted without question.*

Bobbington afforded us only one night flight; it was intended as an introduction to blacked-out England. For two and a half hours we flew over darkened country and towns, seldom sure of our whereabouts unless the pilot revealed it. Though the black-out was effective, the glow of foundries and factories was often beyond concealing. We sensed a pulsating heart, going night and day, everyone striving for far-off victory. Aeronautical beacons, some white, most red, flashed identification letters in morse code.

'The red beacons mark aerodromes; they're called 'pundits'' said the pilot. 'The white are navigational beacons called 'occults.' Codes are changed each day. You'll get an identification sheet on rice paper when you fly cross-country exercises.' We had already heard about these flimsy sheets: if we were brought down on operations we were supposed to eat them.

Aerodromes where night flying was in progress were outlined by perimeter lights; a 'funnel' of lights led to the runway in use; taxiway lights were in blue. Over Birmingham searchlights lolled about the skies. Gemmel and I were silent, perhaps he was thinking as I was, 'So this shadowy land is 'home', the land to which navigators must guide their crews. How are we going to be at the daunting task ahead? Whether I would be guiding a crew to Coastal Command's St. Eval, or to a bomber base, I still didn't know.

My flying time at Bobbington was 34 hours 50 minutes. I wondered what it would be like when we went to a crew and each crew member was as inexperienced as we were ourselves, their errors compounding our errors – or perhaps miraculously cancelling them out.

A few days before we left Bobbington the way cleared for me to join Jim Riddoch. The best of it was, he happened to visit me the day the news came through, so we went off to have a celebratory dinner at the 'Wagon and Horses' in Wombourne. It was two years since we had applied to join aircrew; fourteen months since we had last met. But next day our hopes were dashed. One of our men was spirited away from Bobbington as a VD suspect and I was listed to take his place at No. 27 Operational Training Unit, Lichfield, an OTU that fed Bomber Command.

'It's just a matter of making up numbers, sergeant,' declared the postings officer. 'I should pursue your application for 502 Squadron when you reach Lichfield.'

Jim and I decided on an appeal to Tommy White. Next day our course left for Lichfield; all had decided to be navigators in preference to bombaimers.

7

Lichfield

Fear of flying was a factor to be reckoned with. Fear of operational flying was something that very few escaped. Bomber Command's 8000 aircrew killed in training or accidents supply a sufficient reason. (John Terraine, *The Right of the Line.* p. 521)

Although Lichfield lies little more than thirty miles northeast of Bobbington, slow trains and long stops left me the lasting impression that the two places are far apart. In Walsall we waited four hours for a connection. I drifted with some of the others to the YMCA and dozed there in armchairs, tumbling soon into dreams of being on a conveyor belt to Bomber Command. I got up and went out into the street and began aimlessly walking. Coming across a bookshop I browsed a long time, finally buying Penguin biographies of Shakespeare, Keats and Newman, with notions of escaping our world for theirs.

From Lichfield City station a transport took us four miles up the Burton-upon-Trent road, the way lying mostly through fields. This way hundreds of aircrew, half of them Australian, had preceded us to No. 27 Operational Training Unit; many more hundreds were to come. Every ten weeks that summer, eighteen crews arrived of five men each. We were adding our quota to the road's long history: this was the Roman Rykneld Way; here the Legions had marched, men also missing the sun of home. Centuries later men of Cromwell's Model Army had come this way, bent on sacking the city. The very name 'Lichfield' was said to mean 'field of the dead', deriving from some far-off slaughter.

Fradley

Lichfield's main aerodrome was close by a small village called Fradley of which there was little but cottages and a church. Today, in Fradley churchyard, there are thirty-one graves of men killed in training accidents at 27 OTU, twenty-four of them Australians.

The aircraft in service were Wellingtons, affectionately dubbed 'Wimpies', or 'Wimps'. As a type their reputation was good; they could take a great deal of punishment and still get home. But in a crash their geodetic construction of magnesium alloy imprisoned the crew in a cage which could become an inferno. They had Mk. Ic Wimpys at Lichfield, with Pegasus engines and wooden airscrews; they had long since been superannuated from operational squadrons, nevertheless they were still flown, usually once a month, on 'thousand bomber' raids over Germany, flown by pupil crews. This marked the end, one way or the other, of a crew's training.

In this summer of 1942 most of the senior officers at Lichfield were RAF men; the pupil population consisted of 180 RAAF, 132 RAF, 26 RNZAF, 24 RCAF. Mainly the RAF pupils were the youths who would become our rear gunners. Most of them were short, cheerful, waggish characters who flew in the most vulnerable part of the aircraft; crews would be dependent upon their vigilance and speed of reaction. The great majority of them were volunteers from the 'lower orders' of Britain and were seldom regarded by the RAF as having the qualities desired in an officer and a gentleman. As I learned something of their civilian lives, it seemed to me they had less to fight for than any other aircrew. But they had grown up within the system and most of them were happy enough to have been elevated to the rank of sergeant.

As for Australian aircrew, this was the first time I had been with men from every state. I was struck by their homogeneity of outlook and attitudes and speech. The RAF men, by contrast, spoke in a wide range of accents, even though all of them had for years listened to BBC English. Officers' spoken English was distinctly superior to that of 'erks', as the lowliest of ground crew were termed; indeed, outlook and attitude among the RAF men seemed to depend upon where in the class system they belonged. For those of us from the Dominions, all this was distinctly puzzling.

The windows of the sergeants' mess looked across gently-descending fields and woods to the triple spires of Lichfield cathedral – 'the Ladies of the Vale.' Possession of a cathedral gave the small and lovely town its designation of city.

In the mess were several RAF flight sergeants and warrant officers who seemed possessed by a joyful insanity. They were referred to as 'screens' – screen pilots, screen navigators, screen wireless operators and gunners. We found they were instructors, but the word 'screen' was new to us. Their task was to screen (i.e. safeguard) new pupils from gross errors during their first flights. There was an extended use of the word: if a man completed his raids over Germany, he was 'screened', that is, made a screen and sent to instructional duties.

These screens were given to exotic, colourful exclamations: 'Cracking good show!' 'Shaky do!' 'Wizard prang!' 'What a black!' Their raids over Germany were 'a tour of ops', as if operational sorties were a kind of jolly outing. Their mess pranks and their eagerness to get back to squadrons and 'dice with death', suggested they were still high on their own adrenalin. The flat hats of commissioned screens sagged like cakes taken too soon from the oven. Battered and soiled, they were regarded as badges of long operational experience. The spirit of these men was so infectious that our Australian chauvinism began to melt away. One or two in our mess were pianists; occasionally we heard groups of them at the piano

singing songs popular on squadrons, some wistful, most
ribald, all with melodies and rhythms that would carry me
back for the rest of my life.

There was a small magazine these men always pounced on.
It was called 'TM', or 'Training Manual', and was distributed
both on training units and operational squadrons. It fostered
efficiency through humour, the most delicious humour, which
was illustrated by the comic genius of 'W. Hooper, RAF'. It
highlighted the gross errors of one Pilot Officer Prune – a
vacuous-looking fellow if ever there was one. He was patron
of the Most Highly Derogatory Order of the Irremovable
Finger, a decoration anonymously gazetted in each issue of
the magazine, often to senior officers guilty of stupidity. Its
spirit of fun even extended to the publication's serious articles.
TM was not only a most effective training publication; it
captured the spirit of the wartime RAF as we were beginning
to see it around us.

On our first evening Harry Wright and I made a corner of
the barracks comfortable for ourselves, Harry scrounging
essentials with astonishing rapidity, then seeking other pieces
with such disarming importunings that men seemed willing
to give him anything he sought. Next evening, we heard, there
was to be a 'flap' to Hamburg. 'Flap' was an apt term; the
whole administration was 'flapping' to such a degree that no
one seemed to notice we had arrived. We viewed the men
involved with incredulity: in a few hours, for better for worse,
they would know the real thing, the end of all their training.

I went that day to Sqn Ldr Slade, the Chief Ground Instructor, to submit my 502 Squadron application. I liked the man
immediately; he too was a screen, with his own touch of joyful
insanity.

'I'll get cracking on it, sergeant, as soon as we get back from
the flap.'

Somewhat astonished I said, 'You're going sir?'

'Oh well,' he said lightly, 'might's well go as go to the flicks.'

In the early hours of the morning, before the flap men's return, there was a raid near Birmingham. As camp sirens and far-off explosions wakened us, a lunatic thought passed through my mind: surely it would be easier if *we* bombed Britain and left the Luftwaffe to bomb Germany; it would save so much travel and one would not be greeted with such hostility. But morning brought reality: one of the pupil crews had not returned. The rest were so elated to have survived an operation on Wimpy Ics that their spirits soared above the loss.

The administrative flap had still not subsided; we were given the afternoon off and took the camp bus to Lichfield. Along the old Rykneld Way it stopped at the barracks of 27 OTU's Women's Auxiliary Air Force unit to pick up several off-duty girls. We were only then beginning to have a glimmer of the scope of their work. The WAAF girls drove transports, packed parachutes, calibrated instruments, were the voices that spoke from watch-offices, as the control towers were called; they cooked, worked in intelligence, in the map section, the post office, on the switchboard. Their uniforms appeared to have been designed by someone intent upon concealing their femininity. They were referred to by their acronym: Waaf; their quarters, known as 'the Waafery', were ruled by an older creature dubbed 'the Queen Bee'. Whatever official discouragement there might have been, we soon found that liaisons between Waafs and airmen flourished; couples even overcame the bitter Australian complaint, 'A man can't make much progress with a girl in this bloody country – in summer it never gets dark and in winter it's too damned cold.' On operational stations girls not long out of school heard confessions of fear and loneliness, and had sexual longings pressed on them that most lacked sophistication to cope with. It was by no means easy for a girl when tomorrow the man who held her might be dead; if not tomorrow then almost certainly by next month.

Lichfield proved a delight, its peace and beauty a contrast with the flap of the past night. The cathedral reflection in the Minster Pool was rippled by swans; people sat in parks and gardens reading in the sun; at a pub called 'The Goat's Head' Mr and Mrs Walker presided benevolently over a small Australia House. Late in the afternoon 'Tales from Vienna Woods' was played in a park by the pool. I was with George Loder when children began carelessly dancing to it. He wrote afterwards:

... It's in little scenes like this that a country reveals herself ... – she wins the love of common people in her quiet corners with scenes of restfulness and peace ...

But in the same letter he came as close as he ever came to expressing his longings:

How pleasant it would be to come steaming into Sydney Harbour early on a fine spring morning in October, with the newly risen sun just lighting the water and the smoke haze not yet settled round the city.

We were back in the classroom, taught now by screens who 'knew the score.' We hung on their words. Perhaps because my Canadian distraction was now a girl confined to letters, I found myself absorbing work readily. Even though I still did not know my operational future, I learned urgently – just in case.

The greatest menace, the screens told us, came from nightfighters. They sought the unwary, often attacking from below. To counter them most pilots 'corkscrewed' along their track, changing course and altitude sufficiently to give the gunners a chance to look underneath; this also presented fighters with a more difficult target. Pilots had to average the courses navigators gave them to steer. Corkscrewing was also called 'weaving' and 'jinking.' Over the target the greatest trap was to be 'coned.' Bluish, 'radar-predicted' master searchlights sought bombers; once they found one, other searchlights snapped on with them, so that the bomber was caught at the apex of a cone of searchlights into which gunfire was poured. The usual counter was a diving turn, which sent the navigator's books and instruments up to the roof then plunged them to the floor.

A first tour of operations was thirty; after that one instructed, usually for six months, before returning for a second tour of twenty. On the matter of how many survived, they would not be drawn, but bit by bit we learned that the average loss rate per raid was between four and five percent. Even I could determine the answer.

Nearly all the observers of our Canadian training course were eventually to come together at Lichfield: the commissioned men, Max Bryant, Tib Barker, Blue Freeman, Tom McNeill, Ron Wheatley, were to arrive one by one from their Atlantic crossings; Wilf Burrows, Ian Heatley, Bill Charlton and Johnnie Gordon, were due after leave from Penrhos. Johnnie wrote from Scotland:

> ... *they don't want us at Lichfield until 21st July and as there's a price on our heads at Penrhos, we were bribed by a free ticket to Buggery and Beyond to clear out ... So here we are among the heather and the fog ... I advise you to go to North Wales next time you get leave. It's my favourite spot and I'll go back there after the war and live – maybe. (Maybe I won't be doing any living after the war though – which in a way would be my simplest solution).*

Until this stage of our training we had only mixed with men of our own trade, now we were to form crews. Running parallel with our ex-Bobbington navigators was a group of pilot trainees. Two were New Zealanders, Sullivan and Withell; one a Canadian named Rublee, the rest Australians. Seven of the Australian pilots came from Western Australia: Bayliss, Cook, Fletcher, Jensen, Laing, Maddern, Morphett. Six of our course of navigators were to crew with this group.

I was in a dilemma. I had not heard from Tommy White and was unaware what my prospects were for gaining transfer to Coastal Command, yet here we were, soon to crew up. I could not reasonably join a crew then withdraw. Although no crewing-up orders had been given, we knew that it was RAF policy not to intrude in the matter; for better for worse, the choice was left to the men. Some of our observers were quick to initiate approaches to pilots. One of the first was Col Miller, former schoolteacher, middle-distance runner, Presbyterian lay preacher. He was one of the most responsible men among us and he approached a similarly responsible trainee pilot, Doug Morphett, a married man who had about him an air of quiet assurance. Keith Webber approached Ted Laing, a pilot from Denmark, Western Australia, a friendly fellow whose demeanor suggested great reliability. These moves heightened my concern. But, more important than this, I had come to the conclusion that trying to judge who would prove a 'good' pilot was beyond rational judgement.

As it happened there was a pilot of similar views; he was reluctant to chance his hand choosing a navigator. Inevitably he and I fell together. His name was Geoff Maddern. I had, of course, to explain my dilemma to him, but being of the opinion that the Air Force seldom granted anything we sought, he made the fairly safe gamble that I was bound for Bomber Command. Before 1943 was over, Geoff was the only one of the seven pilots from Western Australia still flying: of the others, one was a prisoner of war, and five were dead.

In crewing up there was natural inclination for like to be attracted to like. On that basis Geoff and I would not have come together. He was pugnacious and always ready to fight for his rights; I could too easily be steam-rollered. I was retiring, bookish, accustomed to living a fairly isolated life; I knew that in Britain my escape was going to be to the country-side, whereas Geoff was likely to want to be 'with the boys' in London – which was much more the norm. If Geoff was tough and had a low flashpoint, he also had great capacity to laugh at himself. Privately he was thoughtful and responsible and no more relished war than the rest of us. Like so many of the Australians, he diligently kept a diary. Early in those Lichfield days he wrote a revealing passage:

An almost clear blue sky with white fleecy clouds … everything breathed an atmosphere of peace and contentment. If only that could be true! … On a day such as this I think to myself how purposeless my life is these days. I crave for the comfort and security of my own home, my own wife and my own children.

The pilot-navigator relationship was the keystone of the five-man crew. Once crewed, the two usually set about approaching a wireless operator, a rear gunner and a bombaimer. These five men were entering the most interdependent relationship of their lives, brief though it usually turned out to be. Even if they survived, they would be disbanded in their moment of triumph, probably never again to fly together, some never again to see each other. But these things were not yet known to us. What we *did* know was that each crew was an independent entity, which would find its own way to the target. At night there could be no such thing as formation flying.

Geoff was intent on seeking an all-NCO crew. If we were entering upon so close a relationship, he believed it ought not be broken by daily segregation. He recruited Arthur Browett, a short, brown-eyed rear gunner, cigarette on lower lip, cap jaunty. He was aged twenty-two and had served in France

76

with the RAF ground staff; after Dunkirk he had volunteered
for aircrew. When we first met him he had something of a
deferential air, a vestige of his ground-staff days. Geoff let him
know that this was un-Australian, after which he was never
quite able to suppress him. He was married and lived in
Nottingham, only forty-five miles away. We soon found he
would readily disappear there to his Hilda. He told me she
objected strongly to Geoff having dubbed him 'Shag', but
Shag he remained. He was to prove a superb gunner and his
vigilance never faltered. He and Hilda became our friends for
life.

Which of us recruited Max Burcher, a fractious young
Australian wireless operator, I don't remember. I hardly had
time to get to know him before navigators and bombaimers
were sent to the satellite aerodrome of Tatenhill, seven miles
north of Fradley, to gain further navigational experience over
Britain. The wireless operators and rear gunners remained
behind and flew with the pilots. So far our crew lacked a
bombaimer.

Tatenill
The unit at Tatenhill was widely-dispersed in woodlands.
Harry Wright and I furnished a corner of another barracks, but
our enjoyment of the place diminished when we found we
had nearly a mile to walk to the flight office. The answer was
to buy bicycles in Burton.

Burton had a chilling etymological link with RAF aircrew:
men missing on operations were euphemistically said to have
'gone for a Burton', gone, presumably, for a pint of Burton
beer. But on the day of our bicycle purchase I did not speculate
on such matters; I remember riding home with a group of
Australians, singing Air Force songs under a bright moon. On
my carrier I had a parcel, a new pair of pyjamas which had
been a more difficult purchase than the bike. Non-issue cloth-

ing needed government coupons; the RAF did not issue NCOs coupons for such luxuries as pyjamas; many of the NCOs slept in their underwear, some even in their shirts. I owed my clothing coupons to Blue Freeman – an Australian before he was an officer.

Blue, the first of the Atlantic navigators to have caught up with us, was too late to team with one of the W.A. pilots. He chose instead to offer himself as Harry's bombaimer. Their pilot was the tall, fair twenty-year-old, Syd Cook – boyish, likeable, ambitious.

As Tatenhill possessed only two serviceable Ansons, life was relatively relaxed. On July 12 one of the two was wiped off. I noted:

Keith Webber was in it. The throttle jammed when they landed and the undercarriage was torn off. No one was hurt.

At Fradley, on the course ahead of ours, accidents among Wellington crews were much more lethal. As Keith wrote:

One disappeared in the Irish Sea, one crashed into a mountain near Sheffield (they weren't killed). One came down in a street at Fishguard ... The fifth is supposed to have been shot down by either flak or fighters at Canterbury. ... Four crews and 5 machines in about 3 days is some average ...

Geoff Maddern wrote at Fradley the same week:

Only today it came to me how callous we are all becoming. We hear of these things, comment on how unlucky the individual is and then promptly forget the instance. Perhaps it is better this way. If we were to brood at all, it would in all probability reflect in our flying.

At Tatenhill I met our future bombaimer, Ted Batten, a tall, blond square-jawed Londoner who would not have looked out of place in Luftwaffe uniform. He was an old man of thirty, who had done the full observer's course. In civil life he had been an optician. He was one of the least flappable men I was ever to know. He had a paternal air and a great liking for whisky; this he could consume in vast quantities without any apparent effect. He told me he was getting married as soon as our training was over.

Each paired navigator – bombaimer were to be given a preliminary three and a half hour Anson flight with a Tatenhill screen to check their capabilities at night. Our flight was to Rhyl – St. Bees Head – Isle of Man and return. The check was cursory. I had the impression that our screen thought it safer over Germany than with us and I didn't altogether blame him. We and the other pairs were hurriedly accepted as being capable of navigating over Britain by night. Our total night flying time since coming to the country was only about six hours; our skill in finding our way matched our experience. We were relieved that our staff pilots seemed familiar with our routes, and for my part I was consoled by the fact that my bombaimer could readily identify beacons and landmarks.

On our second Tatenhill flight we ran into a storm over the Irish Sea and I was soon humiliatingly airsick. The situation was saved by Ted Batten's map-reading. A few days later I had so sharp a recurrence of airsickness that I was not able to eat and asked the medical officer for something to settle my stomach. After examining me, he sent me instead to Fradley sick quarters. This was totally unexpected; more startling was an ounce of castor oil the Fradley MO gave me. Already weak from lack of food, I came close to fainting and began to wonder if the treatment were reckoned discouragement to report sick.

Fradley again

I was held at Fradley sick quarters for an unexpected four days; I remember these days very clearly. On the first Sqn Ldr Slade came in with word that my transfer to Jim's squadron had been refused. Although I had practically given up hope of it and would have been too embarrassed to have left Geoff, the news was still a disappointment. When he had gone I lay thinking about the future, particularly about my chances of linking up some day with Nell. Knowing now the high casualty rate of Bomber Command I realized that the prospect of seeing her again had diminished greatly. But gradually a conviction settled on me, not of my survival, but of my, of everybody's, ultimate security; that when all was known, all would be well. I could put no other words to it. I was strongly aware in those moments of Lichfield Cathedral, which I had already come to love. With an inner eye I saw us like insects on its floor, oblivious to the grand designs around us. From that brief insight came a belief that there was a viewpoint from which even the chaos of war could be seen as a minor aberration in the fundamental pattern of our being. Though I was far from attaining this viewpoint, my mounting conviction of its existence became a strong reassurance. Afterwards the conviction often dimmed and I was afraid, nevertheless, I never entirely lost it.

Someone in a bed near me gave me a copy of the popular magazine *Lilliput*. In it was a photograph of a small tent, pitched by a stream with mountains beyond. Outside the tent a girl in shorts and walking boots was brushing her hair. She reminded me strongly of Nell. Beside her was a pair of men's boots. The title of the photograph was, 'The First Summer after the War.' I cut it out and across the bottom of it wrote lines from Stevenson's *Travels with a Donkey*:

> ... *to live out of doors with the woman a man loves is of all lives the most complete and free.*

I sent it to Nell with my next letter.

Another occasion from these few day remains vividly with me: a visit from six of our training course: Harry Wright,

George Loder, Harry Waddell, Johnnie Gordon, Bill Charlton, Wilf Burrows. There was elation in our spirits, a gladness to be together. I suppose we were all conscious that this could not last much longer. With the exception of Blue Freeman, the commissioned men who had flown the Atlantic had still not linked up with us. Johnnie Gordon remained on at sick quarters hours after the others had left. He had been book buying, purchasing old favourites. He passed three on to me: *A Ballad of Reading Gaol*, *A Shropshire Lad* and a collection of Ambrose Bierce's short stories of the American Civil War. The powerful pessimism of them turned me back to Borrow's *Wild Wales*, a book I had bought after our first flight over Snowdonia.

While I was in sick quarters accidents at Fradley continued, some fatal, some with extraordinary escapes. The day I was discharged I saw a Wellington Ic run into a flock of birds on take-off. One of its wooden air-screws immediately shattered. The young pilot managed half a circuit then crashed in the northwest corner of the aerodrome. Everyone escaped. In that direction, between the aerodrome and Fradley village, ran the Coventry canal. One aircraft around this time overshot and ran into it. Everyone waded out.

Geoff Maddern had finished his Wellington conversion and we were ready to start flying from Tatenhill as a crew. He had now logged 260 flying hours, which was about average for the course. At Fradley he had acquired a secondhand racing bike, repainted a pale greyish colour. He dubbed it the 'Grey Ghost' and at 10.30 one night decided to ride the eight miles to Tatenhill to join the rest of us. His account of his ride leaves its own picture of him:

Fate was against me, the heavens burst asunder with a torrential downpour – wet to the skin. After travelling for an hour and a half, discovered to my horror that I was lost. Cycled on until I struck a house. The lady said she wasn't in the habit of opening the door to men at night, and furthermore wouldn't tell me where I was. ... The next person I pulled out of bed was just the opposite, she gave me so many directions that I became hopelessly lost. ... After waking no less than a dozen more people, I eventually got home at 3 a.m., exactly four and a half hours after leaving Fradley.

He had had less than four hours sleep when we gathered next day as a crew. Like the other new crews, we were to be shown over a Wellington by our skipper. For some reason Geoff preceded us on the Grey Ghost; the rest of us went in a van driven by a Waaf. The planes were widely dispersed in case of air attack and each 'dispersal point' had its own huts and ground crew. I fancied that these 'erks' regarded us as birds of passage, themselves as the hardworking permanent residents – which was true. The Waaf told us she would wait and drive us back. Close by on the concrete lay the Grey Ghost.

Geoff was walking around the Wimpy, looking at it as a prospective buyer might look at a broken-winded hack, nevertheless he managed to infect us with enthusiasm for it. We filed up its nose ladder into the interior, assailed by smells of oil and petrol and the accumulated sweat of scores of frightened men. The navigator's area proved small and dim; there was no outlook from it; I realized I would be entirely dependent on Ted for pinpointing our position. From an Anson I had at least been able to double-check for myself.

The inspection over, we left Geoff and climbed back into the van. The Waaf reversed out of the dispersal. Suddenly a crunching of metal and bellows of rage halted her. She had backed over the Grey Ghost! When we saw Geoff hopping and cursing about the crushed bike, we hardly knew whether to laugh or to comfort the girl – she was close to tears. Geoff was incoherent. Finally he flung the bike – wheels twisted beyond repair – into the back of the van and climbed in with us, shaking his head, waving his arms, muttering imprecations that had us on the edge of laughter. Just then we hardly knew each other; given a few days, we would have laughed unrestrainedly.

The bike had had twenty-eight inch wheels, but the only replacements Geoff could obtain were twenty-six inch. Once these were fitted, the Grey Ghost began flinging him off on corners, as a pedal touched the ground. It soon gained him an exaggerated reputation for insobriety. I was always grateful to the Grey Ghost; Geoff reserved his worst mishaps for it and vented his spleen on it. It became his personal scapegoat, bearing his worst sins, leaving him shriven before he took to the air.

8

Pupil Crews

In flying it was inexperience that killed, even without the presence of the Germans. Some OTU courses ... lost a quarter of all their members. (Norman Longmate in *The Bombers*, Hutchinson, London, 1983)

On August 1 1942 we five, all newcomers to each other, flew together for the first time. It was an inauspicious start. The intercom became unserviceable; Ted Batten, watching our whereabouts from the nose, could only pass me pinpoints by handwritten notes. Max Burcher, the Australian wireless operator, proved exasperatingly reluctant to provide radio bearings; to him, the flight seemed a bit of a lark; Geoff Maddern had to chide him for moving so much about the aircraft and upsetting the trim. But after we had escaped numerous balloon barrages and had safely landed, I was consoled by Geoff's words: 'Well, I'm only nominally captain of the crew. I didn't realize before that all I would have to do was drive to the orders of others.' They were the words of a natural leader whose task it was to mould four men he had not long met into an operational crew. We were soon to learn he was no 'nominal captain.'

We had six exercises to fly by day from Tatenhill then six by night from Fradley, each averaging five to six hours. The rest of our day exercises went so swimmingly that I look back on them as the pleasantest part of my training. For me it was as if the essentials of the past year had clarified in my mind. Under Geoff we combined rapidly into a crew – though once at least he had to take Max Burcher aside 'for a drink and a talk.' Max had energy and ability and outstanding courage,

but he had set his heart on being a pilot; he lacked patience for
radio work and easily became cantankerous. Geoff's drive
was for efficiency in the air and utter loyalty to each other.
What we thought of our officers or of the rules of Air Force life
were minor matters. If we abused him in tense moments, it
seemed to afford him mild amusement. In Ted we had a man
of equanimity and dedication; in Arthur Browett an eternally
vigilant gunner who, almost over night, had became an hon-
orary irreverent Australian.

The weather favoured us and we completed the required
six flights in just over a week, each one without mishap. Most
of the routes took us into the Irish Sea via Rhyl, with Snowdonia a sombre tumble of mountains off to port, its small lakes
flashing in the sun. We would go out then to the Isle of Man
and on to the Mull of Galloway or Sanday Island, or to the
Skerries, or Codling Bank. As our estimated times of arrival
drew near, I would move forward and look hopefully down
for the expected cape or island or small town. Most of them
appeared rewardingly on time. When these day exercises
were over Geoff wrote in his diary:

*Have done nothing but one six hour trip after another. Nothing
to eat from breakfast until tea time. ... Almost know the east coast
of Ireland, west coast of England and Scotland and the Irish Sea
like the back of my hand.*

Being one of the first crews to finish, we were granted forty-
eight hours leave while the others caught up. I took my bike
by train to Somerset and rode from Nora and Stella's to
Dunster and Porlock, becoming so intoxicated with the beauty
of the countryside that I phoned Harry Wright at Tatenhill to
ask how the land lay. He believed I could safely stay away;
weather had delayed some of the other crews, so that the
whole course was held back. I rode off to Exmoor, into the
Doone country, riding by narrow, deserted lanes, crossing the

tumbling Oare by hump-backed bridges, coming at last to the small and silent church where Lorna Doone was supposedly married. I had vague links with the place: a Lewis great-grandmother had been a Blackmore, claiming cousinship with R.D. Back then to Wells and Glastonbury, where I drank rough cider with the locals and learned that a clear head did not necessarily mean obedient legs – I fell off my bike outside 'The Pilgrims Rest' and was thankful to catch a train home. I returned to Lichfield after four days, my absence undetected.

For one who was a member of a crew, this gamble had been utterly irresponsible. When Johnnie Gordon and his crew absented themselves during duty hours, going no further afield than Burton, their pilot was sent on one of the notorious disciplinary courses; the crew was given a new captain and deprived of leave for the rest of their training.

On my return a letter awaited for me from Max Bryant. He had been last of our men in from the Atlantic crossing and was now on an Advanced Flying Unit at Wigtown, Scotland, an equivalent unit to Bobbington. The weather up there was foul, the accident rate high. The mood of his letter sobered me.

I seem to have been surrounded by the Reaper – there have been three prangs resulting in the deaths of fourteen blokes. One was an Aussie sergeant – Hinton. Do you remember him? a tall, fair, good-natured cove. ... one afternoon he was cracking jokes in class, next morning he wasn't there. The visibility was a hundred yards. Ten crates went out. One landed at West Freugh, one force-landed somewhere nearby (all OK), and Hinton's crate bounced off a hill in the Isle of Arran. ... The other prangs ... one hit a hill, the other hit a Lysander over the sea and dived in. The 'Lizzie' struggled home with a gash in the wing and a wounded pilot. We had the jitters for a couple of days. ... If I buy it have asked Bob Wright to let you know. I should like you to particularly try to extract from the RAF my watch, camera and photos to be sent home ...

I realized that our crew had been immensely fortunate in having good flying weather for our day exercises. We were to return now to Fradley for night flying. Our first exercise was a chill warning: the ceiling was low and a warm front was due through base in the early hours of the morning. Our route was to Cottesmore then north up into Yorkshire, then finally back to Cannock Chase, near Lichfield, for bombing practice on the range there. Geoff was being screened by a pilot more nervous than we were. He wrote next morning:

> *Fl Sgt Johns came with us – was damned nuisance when we ran into some cloud north of Cottesmore and couldn't get any radio assistance. He panicked and took over the controls. He didn't give Don a fair go, was continually changing course. The natural consequence – we became lost...*

I was startled when Ted reported us over the North Sea, then Shag cried from the rear turret, 'Lightning* comin' in, starb'd quarter!' It was soon evident that the fighter was nudging us toward land. There was one desperate procedure we could use if lost, that was to call 'Darkie'. This amounted to a spoken equivalent of SOS and brought quick response from the nearest 'Darkie' aerodrome. We managed to avoid this humiliation; instead we turned back and made undignified progress south, calling for QDMs – radio bearings to steer. In low visibility we found Cannock Chase and there droned back and forth while Ted dropped nine bombs.

These visits to the bombing range were to be the culmination of all our exercises; they reduced everyone but Ted to a state of irritability. We were tired and had had enough of being confined in the vibrating, stinking aircraft. For an hour or more we had to listen to Ted's deliberate, 'Left, left; a little

---

* *Lightning:* the RAF name for the Lockheed P38, a twin-boom fighter/bomber.

right. Hold it steady now, Geoff – Bomb gone! Six to go.' It seemed never-ending. Six, five, four … It worsened when, through a lurch of the aircraft, Ted called, 'Dummy run!' as the target swung out of the driftwires. Good lord, were we going to have dummy runs over real targets, or did we just let the bombs go and get out? What a bouncing, yawing platform an aircraft proved to be when it came to aiming bombs! And this was without flak, without searchlights and fighters!

By the time our first bombing practice was over and we had begun searching for Fradley, the visibility had worsened. Having nothing left to do I relieved the boredom by jotting down crew exchanges:

Ted: *I believe I can see the flarepath through a break in the cloud.*

Fl Sgt Johns [screen]: *Okay pilot; start losing height.*

Two voices: *Hell! that's not our 'drome – it's a railway yard!*

Max Burcher: *There are balloons somewhere ahead.*

Fl Sgt Johns: *Start climbing!* [Longish pause] *Anyone see anything?*

Voice: *Not a bloody thing. We're running into all the muck about the place.*

Ted: *Hey! We're getting very close to the ground!*

Fl Sgt Johns: *For Christ sake climb!*

Geoff: *Curse it! The rain's coming on my knees.*

Voice: *There it is! Eureka!*

Geoff: *Bugger it – they're giving me a red light!*

So it went on until a quarter to two; we got to bed at four.

But these were minor happenings compared with other crews' experiences. Keith Webber wrote thankfully on their return:

Flew tonight on our first night cross-country in 'Wimps', screen captain P/O Pugh ... Turned at Stafford and over that town we lost our starboard propeller. A terrific banging under the machine and my first thought was balloon cables or ack ack. We maintained height fairly well which is surprising in these machines. ... Sighted our own beacon. Came in quickly and touched down near the end of the runway. We finished up near our dispersal in the grass. ... A shaky do. However, all's well that ends well.

In the mess afterwards, I heard Keith's pilot, Ted Laing, express admiration for his screen: 'I saw the propeller go and just sat with my mouth open, then Puggy Pugh exclaimed "I say, old boy, I believe we've lost a prop!"'

Doug Morphett, another Western Australian – a pilot much admired by Geoff – had had to make a forced-landing in North Wales. His navigator, Col Miller, was one of the most meticulous men of our old training course. If maturity and skill were going to get men through, this crew had to be among the favourites. But in a letter to his brother, a fellow navigator on Beaufighters in the Pacific, Col confided forebodings:

I have reached a stage in my operational training when every flight is about as dangerous as an operational trip. That forced landing in North Wales I spoke about in my last letter was a closer shave than I made it out to be ... I have seen a number of chaps I know and trained with disappear one by one either in training or on ops. It makes one wonder when his turn will come.

This all sounds very morbid but it's the way things are. I expect to be on ops before this letter reaches you. I can't say I'm looking forward to them with any great enthusiasm but will do my job like the rest ... After seeing the bomb damage in various parts of England, and being kept awake at night by exploding bombs and gunfire, I'll have no compunction at all at bombing German cities. I hate to think of the loss of civilian life that will

be involved, but that is the curse of modern warfare ...
   I hope I haven't been too much of an alarmist in this letter, but
I think you'll understand my mood ...

The senior intelligence officer at Lichfield was Sqn Ldr
Jimmy James, a popular, accessible man. I was taken aback
when, without prelimiaries, he said to me, 'Why did you join
aircrew?'

As I tried to give an answer, I wondered, 'Why am I being
asked? Is he in the habit of asking this question?' I said,
'Certainly not for adventure. Only because I believe Nazism
has to be stopped.'

'Yes,' he mused, 'Yes.' Then he said, 'And yet good spirit
has remained between the two Air Forces since the last war.'

I wanted to exclaim, 'Then why are we killing each other?
Is there room in warfare for "good spirit"? It's not sport; each
side's aim is defeat of the other; the means don't bear exami-
nation.' In times to come I was to run into this English attitude
again and again, as if the Air Force war were the ultimate
contest in high-risk sports; as if there were a chivalrous
brotherhood of the air. In Fighter Command it might conceiv-
ably have been so, but it did not go with bombing of cities.

Max Bryant reached Lichfield two months behind us. I
watched his crewing up with misgivings. As a trainee who
had gained a commission off course, it was evident to anyone
meeting him that he had done very well; in any case, he was
such an engaging youngster – so open and quick and responsible – that he was obviously a desirable man to have in a crew.
He was approached by a sergeant pilot from Melbourne, Ken
Lay; 'Shorty', as he was known, had already gathered three
RAF men as the rest of his crew. He was to prove himself a very
able pilot, but they had not progressed far before Max and
Shorty had serious doubts about the bombaimer; they found
him to be lazy and an incompetent mapreader. Had such a
situation arisen with us, Geoff would have been quick to act.

In their case action was shifted to Max because he was the crew's only officer. In the air, authority was vested in the pilot; on the ground, the issue was less clear-cut – and Max was the last one to side-step responsibility; furthermore, he was the crew member most affected by the bombaimer's shortcomings. Since he spent his sleeping and eating hours in a separate mess, he had small prospect of speaking to the bombaimer privately in relaxed surroundings. The situation high-lighted the absurdity of separating crews into officers and NCOs when they were so bonded in action. Max and Ken Lay sought a replacement bombaimer, but the flight commander urged the crew to give the man a longer trial. The further training progressed, the more established he became in the crew and the more reluctant senior officers were to take action. Added to this, the crew went through some hair-raising experiences which bonded them further. In one they had an aircraft that refused to climb after take-off; they wallowed around the circuit at 70 knots – below the recognized stalling speed. Max thought it was the end:

> Ken ... fought the thing round trees, chimneys and high ground, with throttles wide and fully fine, about 20 feet up. After about three minutes, I suppose, she started to climb and the grim moments were over. At the time I was not conscious of fear, I was feeling curious, semi-resigned and strangely detached. ... Ken confessed on the ground that he couldn't see much hope, but was too busy to think.

The crew never was to change bombaimers. It was a serious flaw in their composition and something that sharpened my anxiety for them.

I am sure Max confided more in me than in anyone. He asked me during these Lichfield days what I thought our chances were of survival. When I answered I found that his estimate and mine tallied: we both reckoned about four of our

91

eighteen in Bomber Command would reach thirty operations. Half laughing, he said, 'Who do you think they'll be?' With mock prescience, I answered, Tib Barker, Harry Wright, Blue Freeman and – I don't know.' Although Max recognized four as a mathematical probability, he clung to his belief that ours was going to be a lucky flight. I hoped against hope he would prove right.

Our night flying progressed smoothly. Geoff wrote on August 25:

> ... *the boys worked together beautifully. Arrived at turning points dead on ETA.*

But I was acutely aware of not having been really tested. For one thing, the 'weaving', or 'jinking', or 'corkscrewing' recommended by the screen pilots was something we had given only limited trial in training. How would it affect navigation? Again, we had been fortunate with weather. One night when our flying was cancelled because of an approaching cold front, a crew that had already taken off could not be contacted. Their chapter of errors showed what could happen if one were caught. Keith Webber wrote of their experience:

> *They were hopelessly lost owing to striking the cold front in the Irish Sea and the consequent wind shift. They pinpointed themselves at St. David's Hd. in South Wales when actually they were at Lands End. In the gaps in the black cloud this was excusable,... They got searchlight procedure and found they were over Exeter. Even then they got lost again before they touched down at base at 6 o'clock a.m.*

Such debacles were common.

A fortune-teller had told Geoff he would survive the war but 'get his feet wet.' Like most of us he had become superstitious and took this to mean we would be forced to ditch in the North Sea, so he had us practise dinghy drill fanatically. The aircraft set aside for this was a broken-down Wellington in one of the hangars; an inflated dinghy, 'floated' on the concrete floor beside it. On the cry, 'Dinghy, dinghy! Prepare for ditching!' we each went into action, grasping the items of equipment for which we were responsible, leaping then into the dinghy. By the time we got our action down to fifteen seconds, we were cursing Geoff and the fortune-teller roundly.

It always tantalized me when I gazed from the sergeants' mess across the fields to the cathedral and thought of life going on in Lichfield, not as in peacetime to be sure, but at least with semblances of normality. Most of us were glad to escape there. Johnnie Gordon insisted on taking me to Dr. Johnson's house. While Johnnie spoke of Shakespeare and the Greek dramatists with reverence, Sam Johnson sounded like someone he ate and drank with regularly. In Lichfield we could eat at *The Little Barrow*, or walk by those serene sheets of water where Johnson had swum as a boy, or drink at one of a dozen pubs.

To escape the constant roar of aircraft, I twice stayed overnight at the 'Goat's Head' where the kindly Walkers plied me with eggs for breakfast. One of these over-night stays followed a National Call to Prayer. We had marched to a full band under the west front of the cathedral, looked down on by the host of stone apostles and martyrs, each in his niche. The soaring, cool interior was packed, a vibrant, palpable spirit of unity in the air. The organ rolled out an anthem that brought the people to their feet; in an instant their singing swept me away, the words familiar from my schooldays, the splendid air unknown to me. It seemed part of the people's being:

> *And did those feet in ancient time*
> *Walk upon England's mountains green?*
> *And was the holy Lamb of God*
> *On England's pleasant pastures seen ...*

On September 5 I began a letter home that seemed of special significance:

Tonight is to be our last training flight, so I finish training early in the morning of the last day of my 26th year ...

I finished next day:

... a beautiful last flight. ... Harry Waddell was travelling with us to get star shots whenever the astro-hatch was open to him. I used it for half an hour over the sea and he used it for the rest of the time. ... I shot Polaris and Arcturus and fixed our position to within three miles....

My total flying hours were just under 257; Geoff's, 353. Remarkably, our course had escaped training fatalities. Around that time casualties at Lichfield were fewer than most other OTUs. At Cottesmore, earlier in the year, eleven aircraft had been lost in a week. The reasons for training accidents were clear: inexperience, bad weather, crowded skies, worn out aircraft – the only aircraft that could be spared from active service.

Our training over, Sqr Ldr Slade called us together and announced our postings. This was it then, the culmination of the past two years. Four of the Western Australian pilots, Bayliss, Cook, Laing and Maddern, and their crews, were posted to the Halifaxes of 103 Squadron, Elsham Wolds, Lincolnshire. We sought it on a map and found it to be not far south of the Humber, near the town of Brigg. Only one man at Lichfield knew much about the place. This was the laconic Welshman 'Puggy' Pugh, the screen who had so casually remarked on the loss of Laing's airscrew. He had survived a tour of operations with 103 on Wellingtons and regarded it enthusiastically. 'Wizard place! Bang on! I'm trying to get back there for a second tour.' After our time he did just this, but was lost on the first operation after his return.

Our postings announced, Ted set off for London to get married. Geoff and I were to be guests at his wedding, but soon after he left, there was a chilling announcement: there would be a flap next night for all members of our course. We had begun to think we would escape one. Moments we had imagined to be weeks off were on us. I felt incredulous, stunned, my morale suddenly brought so low that I felt it must be evident in my face. It was as if a time of reckoning had come. Now I would pay for the long hours spent in Nell's company at Edmonton when I ought to have been studying. Worse, I might let down four other men. Four? What were we going to do about Ted who had always been so solid in adversity? He proved beyond recall. A replacement bombaimer was detailed to join us, an Australian named Vincent Givney, whom we were to borrow from the crew of New Zealander Mick Sullivan; Mick's navigator was George Loder. They had not even finished operational training.

I was not in a frame of mind to gauge how others felt, though it was not lost on me that most began writing a 'last letter' home with the intention of leaving it with a friend. That night, for the first time in my RAAF life, I was unable to sleep. My mind kept throwing up hypothetical situations: What did I do if – ? If I calculated a wind vastly different from the forecast wind? If Geoff's corkscrewing threw out my estimates? If the ETA came and passed without a sign of the target?

The activity around us next morning was like an extension of my confused mind; the term 'flap' for these so-called 'thousand-bomber raids' had been well coined. All attention was on the operating crews; the rest of the station seemed to be running itself. Set free from flying, Max offered any help he could give me; he even remarked, 'When our turn comes I hope I'm as calm about it as you are.' The truth was, I could hardly articulate anything at all. I wished I had half the equanimity of Harry Wright and Blue Freeman; they were flying together as navigator and bombaimer with the stripling Syd Cook. But I noticed that even these two potential indestructibles had slipped off with the Catholic padre the night before the operation. Keith Webber was silent; Col Miller's voice sounded strained. These were older men, more alert to our prospects as inexperienced crews flying wretchedly old aircraft.

The other navigator of our Edmonton course scheduled to operate that night was Joe Turnbull. Joe, a hearty bucolic chap, had vied with me in Canada for last place on the course. He was flying with Bill Fletcher, another of the Western Australian pilots. I had chided Joe only a few days earlier because he had declared he had only a week to live.

'I'll lay you the odds!' he offered. He was always laying odds, giving amusing imitations of a bookmaker.

I refused to enter into this one.

Geoff had selected A Apple – Wellington Ic 853. We all went out to examine her. She had the usual dim, stinking navigator's section. Here it was then that I was going to act my part. I looked askance at it – at the grubby table, the patched fabric over the combustible cage of geodetics.

We went to our first egg and bacon ops meal at 5.30. It struck me with faint surprise that the cathedral spires rose as clear and serene as ever beyond the mess windows. Looking across the intervening fields and woods, I tried to grasp something of their message, but failed utterly. Instead I began to wonder cynically if this England, which I had always wanted to see, was going to be worth the price of reaching it.

A large classroom had been set aside as a briefing room; on its front wall was a map of Europe fully eight feet by six. Several of the senior officers were already sitting before it waiting for our uncertain entry. When we had settled, Sqn Ldr Jimmy James threaded a length of red wool from Lichfield to a point on the East Anglian coast, then to a point on the Dutch coast, then to a place we feared to hear. He gave name to it.

'The target for tonight, gentlemen, is Dusseldorf.'

As Geoff wrote afterwards:

Briefing wasn't until six-thirty and we had to be down at the tarmac at seven to run up our machines. It didn't give us a fair go. I couldn't study the route, N/F [night fighter] disposition or anything, all I knew was that we were going to Dusseldorf.

As we were driven out to the planes, my extravagant imagination saw the olive-green vans as so many tumbrils. In the event, nothing that night turned out as we had imagined. The sudden change in our crew had unforeseeable consequences. It had been our practice for Ted Batten to pick up the Very cartridges used for firing the colors of the day. No one thought to mention this to Vince Givney. We were already airborne when lack of them was discovered. As Geoff wrote:

... It meant that we had to wait around for them all to get off the deck and then go in and land with a full bomb load and take off again. Not a very nice job landing with 2000 lbs. of bombs.

How flying control felt about an inexperienced pilot landing near them in a bomb-laden, worn-out aircraft, we never heard. We took off again, Geoff thrashing the old machine along, I estimating ETAs again, well aware that we were going to be late on the target. In fact, we never reached it. Geoff wrote next morning:

Right from the outset I had trouble with over-heating on the starboard engine, had to flatten my climb to let it cool down – it was past the danger mark and I didn't want to turn back. As it was, we were running three quarters of an hour late ... I was really concerned about the cyl. temp. [cylinder temperature] over the North Sea, couldn't get it below 230 (20 degrees over max.) All sorts of lights were in the sky, mainly flak and red flares

... passed over a flak ship and up it came beneath us, one burst threw us almost clean out of the sky. Light flak came up as we were going inland, we could see the fires of Dusseldorf away in the distance. ... The temp. had risen to 250 and the motor looked like packing up any minute. There was only one thing to do – put my nose down, cut the motor and turn back, hoping that I could reach home ... had to let the bombs go in the sea. It broke my heart having to turn back. Believe it was a wonderful show. 560 machines participated and 31 failed to return. 6 of our machines had to turn back through engine trouble.

Despite my earlier trepidation, I felt we were completely out of things when the successful crews returned. Young Syd Cook had been coned by searchlights. In the brilliantly-lighted nose Blue had instinctively rolled up like a foetus. They counted eighty-seven holes in their aircraft on their return.

As we listened to all this I felt we had missed a St. Crispian's Day. I was quickly disabused, for again we were held back from leave, this time to go to Bremen. To our relief fog closed in and the operation was cancelled; it looked as if we would at last get away. But no; we were briefed again for Bremen. This time Geoff carefully air-tested two machines.

... chose R for Robert. It was pretty ropey but managed to stay in the air for us.

It was the whole gut-gnawing business over again, but this time we were readier for it. Briefing gave a sudden insight that took me unawares. I wrote bitterly:

... tonight our orders are, 'Bomb the centre of Bremen; make it uninhabitable for the workers.' England! Cricket! Huh! Justifiable? I do not know. I only know that I shall kill women and children soon.

In truth, I was more afraid for my own life than dismayed by what we might do. Nevertheless I had believed till now that every effort was being made to bomb military objectives and, as far as possible, avoid residential areas. I had thought that civilians who were killed were victims of inaccuracies; I did not know that inaccuracy had been accepted because of its inevitability.

From 10,000 feet Bremen was an inferno such as we could not have imagined. It was ringed by searchlights and densely criss-crossed by light flak; heavy flak burst overhead. Suspended there we could hear nothing above our engines, nor feel anything of the searing heat. It struck all of us that to survive thirty trips to such places was scarcely possible.

Years later one may read, in Middlebrook and Everitt's *The Bomber Command War Diaries*, what the results were of this Bremen raid; indeed, what the results were of each raid of the Bomber Command war. In Bremen that night we killed seventy people, while losing approximately 115 ourselves. Additionally 848 homes were destroyed and 371 people injured.

Weather on our return forced us to land at Tempsford, near Cambridge; there we found Harry Wright, Blue Freeman, Keith Webber, Col Miller and all the others of their crews. But we learned that Bill Fletcher, taking off from Fradley after our departure, had lost an engine and crashed. All five men had been killed instantly including Joe Turnbull. His prediction had been right: a week to live. A couple of hours after the crash their bombs had exploded, killing four of the guards placed on the wreckage.

We left Lichfield before the burial of Fletcher's crew in Fradley churchyard. These were always macabre occasions; everyone knew that only token scraps of men could be interred; the weighted coffin was a gesture to the decent life we had left behind. Some of our old course attended, Max Bryant among them:

> *It was a military business, with Union Jacks around the coffins,*
> *Last Post and Reveille. We all walked past the grave in turn and*

99

saluted. ... Even when the coffins were lowered it was difficult to grasp that Joe had really passed on – that never again would he put his foot up on a chair and argue us all down. Poor Joe – you will never know the brightness of Australian skies again; how many of us will follow you?

9

Elsham Wolds

When I arrived in 1942, the squadron had not been very long flying in Halifaxes and already there had been a number of disastrous crashes around the airfield on training flights, often with very few survivors. The cause was eventually attributed to a phenomenon called 'rudder stall' ... There was a strong feeling that if these aircraft performed so badly on training flights, how great were the chances of disaster over enemy targets, so that the morale of the crews was at rock bottom. (Dr. Robert S. Henderson, 103 Squadron Medical officer, 1942-44, from a paper written in 1986)

In London, on my way to Elsham Wolds, I stayed a night at the Strand Palace. The homely, unhurried atmosphere of the dining room at breakfast time, with people reading newspapers and talking quietly across tables, ill prepared me for Australia House and RAAF Headquarters where talk among squadron aircrew was mostly of losses: 'missing'; 'missing believed killed'; 'ditched in the North Sea', all uttered in a matter-of-fact, even jocular way, as if it were best to accept these things lightly since they were unalterable. I went to our northbound train taut and apprehensive.

The great London stations in those years were scarcely places to lift the spirits. In the crowds of uniformed people dozens of parting couples clung urgently, kitbags at feet, faces tense; locomotives nearby released clouds of enveloping steam; announcement after announcement came on the speaker system, each in clearly-articulated female voices – caring voices they seemed. Final announcements drew couples closer; doors began slamming, door after door, the sounds echoing in the vast arches overhead. Then the call, 'Stand clear,' the guard's whistle, the peremptory answering shriek of the engine. Inexorably the train began to move, girls hurrying beside it, men leaning out. Then it was all over and mile after mile, in the compartments, one could feel ruptured emotions. I was never sorry I had no one to leave behind.

That first day at Kings Cross Ted Batten introduced me to Ann, his bride, a small, dark, vivacious girl who barely came to his chest. It seemed much for her to bear that he was being taken from her so soon. I left them to their farewell and found Geoff and Max Burcher. Once our Retford-bound train had drawn out, Ted sat silently. Syd Cook and some of his crew were with us; Ted Laing's crew and Colin Bayliss's sat in compartments nearby. We knew little at all of our destination.

Late in the afternoon, eastbound from Retford, the hypnotic dip and rise of telegraph wires and the flight of smoke from the engine held my eyes as if they represented a flinging behind of our past. At length we followed a valley of woods and sugar-beet fields and red-tiled hamlets to the village of Barnetby-le-Wold. The London and North Eastern Railway called this Barnetby Junction, the rail junction giving the village its small importance. We were twenty NCOs and one ground-staff Pilot Officer who had travelled first class. A small van arrived for the Pilot Officer; its driver told us we were to leave our kitbags at the station and walk to the aerodrome. He pointed to the bare hills, 'It's two and a half mile that way ... '

An Australian responded dryly, 'Tell them we'll stay in the waiting room until we're picked up.'

The driver seemed disconcerted, but went his way without further ado. After an hour transport arrived and bore us out of the valley, past the Waafery, up into open hills sown with mangolds and sugar beet with here and there a wood. Two or three farm houses crouched in a wind which was stripping last leaves from the few trees. Geoff wrote of the new scene:

The station is situated on top of an escarpment and is open to the cold winds off the North Sea and anything that may come overland from the west.

At the gate was the guardhouse and sick quarters; the rest of the buildings – hangars, water tower, watch office, messes – huddled nearly a mile off across a vast airfield. Widely dispersed about the field were four-engined Halifaxes, robust-looking monsters painted the colour of night. They bore RAF roundels and the 103 Squadron identification letters, PM. Though night was their element and bombing their purpose, I could imagine no surroundings that contrasted more with bombed and burning cities than these bleak, empty farmlands.

We were dropped at a long hut beside a wood, a place with concrete floor, thin, wooden walls, high windows; a potbellied stove at its centre had not yet been lit. As it was tea time, no one was in, but many of the folding metal stretchers with three-part 'biscuit' mattresses were made up. Beside these were personal belongings – kitbags, books, a few radios, photographs of girlfriends and wives. The wind outside buffeted the almost leafless wood.

By now we were adept unpackers of kits; within fifteen minutes I had finished and, as a last touch, put a leather folder holding photographs of Nell and my family on a shelf at the head of my bed. Beside me Harry Wright had done the same. He and I still remained together, as if not yet accustomed to the crews into which we had married. I dug out my diary, sure companion in time of change, and closed September 23:

What lies ahead now? It is strange how much happier I feel in barracks among the boys than when contemplating the future alone.

The main part of the camp lay about a third of a mile off. As our bicycles had not yet arrived, we walked there in fading light, pressing into wind. Like most other isolated stations, Elsham Wolds was a temporary village with its own post office, own water supply, own sewerage system, own small hospital and hairdresser and telephone switchboard. In its few streets the youthful uniformed 'villagers' went about their duties, some on foot, some cycling, a few driving. Its low buildings, most of concrete with corrugated asbestos roofs, were camouflaged with swirled patterns of brown, black and olive green; dominating all of them were three large hangars at the edge of the aerodrome. Forty years on two of these hangars would be all that remained of that once busy, purposeful scene.

Outside the sergeants' mess were dozens of parked bicycles. As we went in, a muted roar of male voices greeted us and an odor compounded of beer, cooking, urinals and wet greatcoats. 'Ablutions' were to the left – a place we were destined to go to often for a final nervous pee. Straight ahead was the dining room, about sixty feet by thirty with tables and forms to seat around a hundred. By now it had emptied, so our group sat alone and were served a late meal. We pronounced it not bad; better, anyway, than the perpetual Welsh rarebit of Tatenhill.

The ante-room, home of the NCOs, was full of noise and movement. I had the impression that everyone was speaking in a raised voice in an effort to be heard. Black-out curtains had been drawn across a wall of windows. Part of the opposite wall was occupied by a bar where several men leaned, pints in hand. About halfway down the room armchairs were drawn to a blazing fire. Beyond this was a billiard table and beyond that again, darts boards and a table tennis table. All this we saw through a haze of cigarette smoke. We hovered at the edge of it like so many new boys at school. Presiding over the scene was a florid, elderly-looking man, the Station Warrant Officer. His expression was less than approving as he tried to read his newspaper. He was probably finding all these jumped up young fellows an uncouth wartime intrusion. His breast bore ribbons of '14 – '18. One day before long we would hear him declare that he didn't believe in parachutes; they hadn't had them in his time. Since he was a 'wingless wonder', we doubted that he had ever been high enough to need one.

The majority of aircrew were RAF, but shoulder flashes of others showed CANADA, JAMAICA, NEW ZEALAND, AUSTRALIA, even A.E. SUDAN. Their average age might have been twenty-two or twenty-three; my overall impression was of ebullient gaiety which was highly infectious.

Someone among our group ventured a question . 'How long does it take here to do a tour?' We knew, of course, that many failed to reach thirty, or even twenty; but what we wanted was some estimate of time taken by the successful. We all *hoped* to be successful. The men were communicative on everything else – but not on this. Only in quiet asides did we learn that no one had reached thirty for some time; how long, no one seemed to know – before July anyhow, back in Wimpy days. This three-month run of misfortune was blamed on the Halifax II. No one had got through on them. Years later I read that 103 Squadron's Halifax loss rate exceeded 8% per operation. No one *did* get through on them.

Our tentative questioning did nothing to diminish the clamour. But then we heard something that made high spirits seem bizarre: only a few hours earlier a Halifax had crashed on the aerodrome; everyone on board had been killed; it was said to have been carrying thirteen men – almost two crews. The pilot had been 'Daddie' Fulbrook, DFC, a permanent RAF warrant officer on his second tour of operations. 'Daddie' had been senior aircrew man of this same mess.

We were trying to digest this appalling piece of news when there was a stentorian shout at the door, 'Scunthorpe bus ready!' This was evidently what the men had been waiting for;

for; they clattered out with anticipatory cries, leaving the ante-room to the SWO and ourselves and a few ground-crew NCOs. The sudden quiet heightened my feelings of unreality.

In the morning we found we were still not members of the squadron proper; until we converted onto Halifaxes we were to be attached to the Conversion Unit. This was commanded by Sqr Ldr David Holford DSO, DFC, a twenty-one year old, soon to become the youngest Wing Commander in the RAF. Holford had already completed sixty-three operations; every-one spoke of him with respect and affection. Though only a stripling, he made a profound impression on us. I have never forgotten his sensitive, serene face which lighted occasionally with a boyish smile. His stature in Bomber Command was remarkable. He had been one of two operational Squadron Leaders called to a conference chaired by the Chief of the Air Staff, Lord Portal, to determine the total number of operations that ought to be demanded of aircrew. Their conclusion, as we had learnt at Lichfield, was a first tour of thirty, a 'rest' period of instructional duties lasting about six months, followed by a second tour of twenty.

Holford's life was to prove as bright and brief as a falling star. In December 1943 he returned to operations as officer commanding 100 Squadron. By then he was married and a father. On his first trip his aircraft was damaged and slowed by night fighters on its way to Berlin, but he continued to the target. He was attacked again on the way back, but limped home to his base at Waltham. Fog was forming rapidly and crashes were occurring as pilots attempted to land. Holford held back, giving less-experienced men priority. With his fuel running out and the fog thickening, he finally made his approach. He hit a slight hill short of the aerodrome. He and two others of his crew survived the crash, but by the time the over-taxed ambulances reached them, Holford was dead. His epitaph in Cambridge reads:

Pass not this stone with sorrow, but with pride,
And strive to live as nobly as he died.

Holford introduced us to the group of RAF flight engineers and mid-upper gunners who were to bring our crews up to seven men. This time there was no free selection, nevertheless in our case we could not have fared better. The flight engineer allocated us was a lean-faced, articulate Welshman, Doug Richards, one of the coolest, most skillful men we were to know; the gunner, Frank Holmes, a smiling, brigandish lad of nineteen, was born only a couple of miles away. Frank kept his eye in by poaching nearby on the Earl of Yarborough's estate; he had been a poacher from childhood. All through our Elsham days he was to fight a war on two fronts, one against the Nazis, the other against the earl's gamekeeper. Shag readily joined him on his Lincolnshire 'front.' As far as Geoff and I were concerned, we wished them well; in a meat-starved country it was beyond our comprehension that gentlemen were still permitted to shoot edible game for sport.

At each Halifax dispersal point a team of ground crew men worked incessantly in all weathers, their only shelter small huts. Everything but major overhauls was done out-of-doors. A few days after our arrival Geoff clambered over one of the aircraft. Although he was non-committal to us, he was not much impressed.

... they appear to be very shoddy and rough – mass production I guess. ... four motors producing a total output of over 4000 h.p. ... With full bomb load the weight is something like 26 tons.

There was much for us to learn and pressure was on to learn quickly. While the pilots and engineers went to familiarize themselves with Halifaxes, the navigators were taken to a dimly-lighted room to be introduced to Gee, the RAF's most precise navigational aid, indeed, for some time yet, a navigator's only radar aid. On a circular screen about six inches wide, two parallel horizontal lines glowed bright green; along each a signal precessed in the form of an inverted V. There was something eerie, magical, about their orderly movement. We had only to turn a knob to halt them and another knob to align them one below the other. It was a matter then of reading off indicated co-ordinates. These we plotted on a special chart overlaid with criss-crossing hyperbolic curves; this fixed position precisely.

Our elation over this uncanny accuracy was cut short by the ops. men. 'Jerry's got the thing taped,' they told us. 'He jams it once you've crossed his coast so that you're battling to get fixes at all.' From the appearance of the jamming, they called it 'grass'. Its waving, green pulsations were torture to navigators' eyes. I was left wondering what, then, was the surest way for us to navigate accurately. Or was accurate navigation something attained by few?

There was small time to ponder; we were ordered to report to the medical officers. They turned out to be a most likeable pair. Sqr Ldr John Gauvain, the station MO, was a humane, genial man, married, with a young family. Later he was killed in a flying accident. Flt Lt Robert Henderson, the squadron medical officer, then in his mid-twenties, resembled a good-looking, off-duty commando rather than a doctor. Some months after this he began slipping off on operations himself, at first flying 'to study aircrew stress' but continuing, without authorization, until he had totalled nineteen ops., each with a different crew. These two led us to the decompression chamber, a long, cylindrical tank provided with portholes and entered by a door. Along each side were forms for seating and, every few feet, oxygen outlets and intercom connections.

Oxygen masks were uncomfortable affairs which it was a relief to take off; it was well known that some men took them off too soon. There was a even a degree of male braggadocio in it: real men could do with less oxygen, just as they could hold liquor better than the rest. The masks covered the face from just below the eyes to below the mouth, looking like the snout of a pig. At the end of the snout was a microphone which had to be switched on each time one spoke. The doctors' aim was to convince us of the effects of anoxia. I wrote afterwards:

We were taken up to 28,000 feet, three of us with oxygen and three without. The three without all started well enough, but gradually became like drunks. Watching Harry [Wright] work out simple division was excruciatingly funny…

When his calculations reached the end of the page, Harry continued with supreme confidence down his trouser leg. Noticing my eyes running with laughter, he cast me a glance of hurt indignation. Our roles were soon afterwards reversed. Out of a void 'Doc' Henderson asked if I needed oxygen. Pleased with myself, I answered, 'No thanks sir; I seem okay.'

'Feel for your lead.' I found it to be plugged in. 'You were unconscious till Wright connected you.'

Four days after our arrival Geoff and Ted Laing flew a Halifax with an instructor:

God! they're heavy machines, especially on aileron control, you fairly have to heave on them to do just a rate one turn … They're not so very hard to land, but have a bad fault in the tail-wheel shimmer. It seems as though the whole machine is going to shake to pieces. On take-off it has a tendency to swing to port – not very badly though. … The approach is as fast as a Spitfire … come in at 111 mph. Drag it off the deck on take-off at 100 mph.

Three days later they learned three-engine procedure:

Did a bloody rough overshoot – two bounces and around again. Did a normal landing, the fourth I've done in these machines, and then handed over to Ted. After he had done his three-engined flying, Potts climbed out and away we went solo. Only had two hours dual. Don't exactly approve of it, we know little about the machines ... Doug, the flight engineer, is certainly a jolly good man. It was his twenty-sixth birthday today.

A week later the pilots were reckoned ready to take over their crews. We went up on a local fight on the evening of October 6 and at 18,000 feet I tried the Gee for the first time. 'The black box says Reades Island below, Geoff.' 'Dead over it. Great stuff!'

This was accuracy such as we had never known. We dived into broken cloud.

'Base coming up ahead Geoff, coming up, coming up – should be over it – *now!*'

'Bang on!'

While we became familiar with squadron life, death moved unobtrusively among us. I wrote to Nell:

Two lads who sleep near me failed to return this morning. I woke when the rest came in and heard the news. I saw their belongings still in their places ...It all happens so quietly that one does not realize they have been victims of war. Compared with a soldier's lot, ours is not bad at all.

Such was my first reaction. It changed before long to outrage: did no one care that this flower of youth was passing into oblivion? Did any one know whether the results were worth the fearful price? But, since we, too, were on the same conveyor belt, I had to desist from questioning and go about my duties as if I, too, did not care.

I tried on one of these days to assess for Nell our prospects of getting through:

By each playing our part well during operations, we can gain perhaps 30% safety; but the other 70% – as I see it – is luck or fate or Providence. ... I sometimes think that perhaps you and I will stand together some day and smile over our past fears.

Keith Webber hankered even more than I did to have breaks away from Elsham.

One longs for many things, most of all home and friends. This station is so isolated that we are absolutely penned up. ... If we only knew we had some chance of going home after these ops! ... There was a lot of drivel spoken by Evatt when over here about Australians going back with operational experience. ... The boys had a quiet gurgle the other day when they read in an Aust. paper that Aust. airmen would return home after they had completed their 'post graduate course' of bombing Germany. POST GRADUATE COURSE – that needs framing ...

Two or three times, on nights when ops were scrubbed because of weather, Keith and I escaped on the camp bus to Scunthorpe. Although there was a mixture of nationalities on board, RAF sergeants predominated. They sang together in the dark – ribald, Air Force songs, sung with a sort of defiant gusto.

As we picked up the words, an impression lodged at the edge of my awareness: these men were part of the long tradition of going to war for England; I felt they might well break into bawdy Elizabethan songs; they were Nym, Bardolph and Pistol; they accepted this as their lot. Once it had been war against the French, the Spanish, the Dutch, now against the Germans, daubed this time with swastikas. It was insane; it was not our scene! But as we sang I felt more and more at one with the rest and pushed doubt aside; we, too were sons of Empire!

In Scunthorpe we discovered the Berkeley, a large dancehall on the edge of the town; we came from wet, blacked-out night into smoky light and throbbing music. And at the Berkeley I discovered Betty, a raven-haired local beauty who invited me home. Her mother and sister spoke of hearing our bombers go out and listening for their return ...

Then I found another escape: a Burnham-on-Sea woman had given me the name and address of her Lincolnshire mother: Ada Croft Baker, The Rookery, Cleethorpes, urging me to go there. When I did so, I found myself so welcomed that I knew I had a refuge whenever I wished to go to it. I sat with her by her fire, hearing of her trawler-owner sons, listening to music; I walked barefooted on my bedroom carpet for the pleasure of it.

Our pilots had begun attending pep talks for operational crews at which much was said about inaccurate bombing. 'Inaccurate' turned out to mean a miss in excess of five miles – indication enough of the prevailing failure to bomb the specified target. Geoff wrote in his diary, 'this contravenes all we are supposed to be fighting for.' But if accurate navigation was difficult, how could accurate bombing be achieved? I still had not found the answer to this when it was time for us to transfer to the squadron. I had come through our conversion like so many others – wearing a mask of acceptance.

Jim Riddoch.

Max Bryant.

On the *Monterey* (Chapter Two).
Above: the dining saloon. *L to r:* Max Bryant, Wilf Burrows, 'Johnny', self,
Bill Charlton.
Below: on deck. *L to r:* Max Bryant, self, Bill Charlton, Wilf Burrows.

Lela - perhaps you are the only one to remember me! left this.

Top: Nell East, p.18ff

Middle: Banff, Alberta, New Year, 1942, p.35.
Left to right: Keith Webber, Colin Miller, Max Bryant, self.

Below: Tib Barker, Tom McNeill and Ted (Blue) Freeman at the passing out dinner.

No. 35 Course, Rivers, at the end of training
Left to right, back row: Ted (Blue) Freeman, Keith Webber, Colin Miller,
Johnnie Gordon, Bill Charlton, Tom McNeill, Bob Morgan, Harry Wright,
Tib Barker, self. *Front row:* Harry Waddell, Max Bryant, Ian Heatley, Ron
Wheatley, Tom Cunliffe, two RCAF instructors, Joe Turnbull, Ron
Pender, George `Loder, Colin Cooper. Wilf Burrows was absent.

Harry Waddell boarding the train
at Rivers.

Nell and the author on the rear
platform of the train at Rivers.

3

Above left: The Scottish walking companions, p. 57. Harry Waddell (left) and George Loder.

Above right: Doug Williams (left) and Keith Webber in the bell-tent camp at Bobbington.

Right: Lichfield: Harry Wright and Johnnie Gordon.

Below: Our five-man crew in front of a Wellington 1c, Lichfield, Summer 1942, p.75 Left to right: self, Geoff Maddern, Ted Batten, Max Burcher, Arthur Browett.

RAF Elsham Wolds.
Dispersal points for aircraft show as ping-pong bat-shaped light areas.

Lancaster bomber B Beer

Elsham Wolds, November 1942.
The enlarged crew in front of Lancaster B Beer, 103 Squadron.

Left to right: Arthur Browett, Doug Richards, Geoff Maddern, Ted Batten, Max Burcher, Frank Holmes, self.

Left: The Poachers (p.107). Frank Holmes (left) and Arthur Browett ('Shag'), alongside Shag's rear turret gun turret.

Below: Bill Burchell with other members of our ground crew.

Above: WAAF driver Peggy Forster (p.180f) with (left to right, in front) Geoff Maddern, Ted Batten and Graham Briggs; and (behind) W.F. 'Curly' Jones, a visitor (left) and Doug Richards.

Left: The Stowaway (p.195). WAAF Intelligence Officer Lucette Edwards with Geoff Maddern.

Left to right: Colin Miller, Doug Williams, Ted Laing and Doug Morphett.

Ian Robb and Colin Bayliss

Above: Johnnie Gordon
Right: Bill Charlton in
Cheddar Gorge

The end of the crew, Elsham Wolds, April 1943
Left to right: Geoff Maddern, Arthur Browett, Frank Holmes, self, Doug
Richards. Graham Briggs and Ted Batten had already left. Our barracks
is in the background.

The deserted Sergeants' Mess as it appeared in 1957

10
Noli me Tangere

To be a member of a bomber crew required persistent fortitude at a time and in circumstances when the stoutest mind and heart would have every excuse to show a natural and normal weakness. The average operation was in darkness and in the early hours of the morning; every one who took part in it knew that the odds were against the survival of any particular airman. (W.J. Lawrence, historian of 5 Group, Bomber Command.)

On the morning of October 15, 1942, in half light, the men of our intake paraded with 103 Squadron's operational aircrew. This, then, was the end of our training. For me it was two and a quarter years since I had started the '21 Lessons.' We fell in outside the long, low flight office at the edge of the aerodrome; behind us rose one of the hangars from which came echoing sounds of men working non-stop on Halifaxes.

There was news that morning heavier to the spirits than the cold and cloud: on the night just ending Flt Lt Winchester and his crew had failed to return from their twenty-seventh operation. Although it was an unspoken point of honour that we comport ourselves casually, our eyes were too much open for us to feel casual inwardly. Winchester's crew had been poised ready to show that thirty ops. on Halifax IIs was possible.

All told there were about 120 of us, the NCOs in a large group to the front, officers of aircrew in a small group to the rear. Because of the casualty rate, at least three of the NCO pilots would be commanding flights as Squadron Leaders well before a year was out; most of the others would by then be dead. To say we 'paraded' this first chill morning, or on any other morning, suggests precision we lacked. Officers of other services might have considered us poorly disciplined; in fact the crews' degree of self-discipline in the air was high; on the ground they tended not to bother about it. Aircrew on parade often looked like men under sufferance, assembling rather than parading. Nor would their battledress have borne close scrutiny.

The main purpose of the morning gathering was to ensure all crews were present. Even in this it was not always effective. Sometimes a man answered 'Present!' then 'Present!' again for another member of his crew sleeping in – a favour I was often to do for Geoff – or for a crew member who missed the last bus from Scunthorpe and had stayed the night at Irish Maggie's. It would have been simple to have made a tally of numbers, but I don't remember this being done. The 'parade' was little more than a warning to hold ourselves in readiness. So long as each of us was present for briefing and to climb into his aircraft when the time came, little else seemed to matter. After all, our remote village in the wolds existed for only one purpose and that was to put twenty or so bombers and their crews over targets in Europe. So it was on all bomber stations. For their part, air crew were aware that they were the apex of the station pyramid. Most of their fellow villagers – about a thousand men and women – looked on them with anxiety and admiration, as if the crews were their nightly representatives in a far-off colosseum where prospects of victory were small. The crews, in turn, were borne up by the regard of those around them.

When parade ended – and it was to be the same every morning – the men moved into a large crewroom amply provided with chairs, its walls plastered with aircraft diagrams, warning posters, crew lists. There they lounged restlessly around a potbellied stove, waiting to hear whether ops. were 'on' or 'off.' If they were off, everyone relaxed and looked forward to an evening in 'Scunny'. If they were on, the Battle

Order went up, which was a list of crews taking part and the aircraft each was to take. Then hearts tightened and bellies knotted.

The timetable for the day was reckoned back from one final time: 'time over target.' This dictated set-course time, take-off time, time out to aircraft, briefing time, time of the operational meal, time of navigator's briefing. If take-off was going to be late at night, it even dictated the time crews could go to the cinema.

The crew room opened into a second room, furnished with a very large, smooth-topped table – about fifteen feet by ten. In here crews gathered in their flying kit for final instructions before departure; on this table navigators made last adjustments to logs and charts. From this room crews were called to vans to be driven by Waafs to the widely-dispersed aircraft. These drivers were changed over periodically to rest them from too frequent a sharing of last journeys. Adjacent to this room were the offices of the Wing Commander and the two Squadron Leaders, the adjutant and his lowly minions of the orderly room. All this we saw that first morning as if looking on a kind of open, easy-going prison in which we were to be incarcerated while the gods tossed to determine who lived and who died.

The new crews were split between A and B flights, our own going to A flight which was commanded by Sqn Ldr Fox, senior of the two Squadron Leaders. He had so far done forty-two ops., so, like Holford, was living proof that statistics could be defied. His DFM ribbon indicated that he had first operated as an NCO. These things and his resolute manner and lynx eyes gained our instinctive respect. Before the war he had been a bank clerk; now he was a married man with a daughter. B flight was under the command of a dark-eyed, moustachiod twenty-three year old, Jake Kennard. Sqr Ldr Kennard was as good a pilot on Spitfires as he was on Halifaxes. From time to time he borrowed a Spitfire from a nearby fighter squadron to make mock attacks on Halifaxes scheduled for 'fighter affiliation.' But he regarded all our Halifaxes as fair game. Gunners stooging contentedly back from air-to-sea firing were apt to find Kennard's moustaches bristling at them between a Spitfire's cannons. A gunner of those days wrote that, for him, Kennard exemplified the spirit of 103:

> I think back with pleasure to a morning of fighter affiliation when we were unable to turn inside his curve of pursuit and thus learnt the valuable lesson of timing our turn, which was, on a Stettin raid, to save us ... Kennard certainly saved the lives of many ...*

What distinguished such men as Fox, Kennard and others who were operationally-experienced, was their level of composure. They had survived long enough to measure themselves against the job; they had learnt a degree of detachment that allowed them to push aside each day the fears that welled up in all of us. Some men learned to do this quickly; a majority died without ever learning it.

Above Fox and Kennard was an altogether different type of officer – the Wing Commander commanding the squadron, a dedicated man of proven courage wearing a DSO and DFC, but one who had small rapport with his men. The task of Wing Commander on a bomber station was unenviable; he was a man under opposing pressures: pressure from the Command to get as many aircraft over the target as possible; pressures arising from all the factors that prevented him from doing this. Quite often crews aborted; either they found their aircraft to be unserviceable and did not take off, or they found it unserviceable in flight and turned back. Among inexperienced crews there were undoubtedly those who could have gone on had they been more resolute, or better able to assess their situation.

---

* Flt Lt A.C.P. Gamble DFC, mid-upper gunner.

Our Wing Commander's shortcoming was that he treated many splendid men who aborted as if they belonged among the irresolute. He lacked the patience and understanding to afford them decent hearing; instead, he descended on them with blistering accusations, especially if they were inexperienced NCOs. As a result, some crews were shamed into 'pressing on regardless' next time they struck trouble, when they ought, in fact have turned back. The results then could prove fatal. No doubt it looked better for a squadron's reputation to have aircraft lost than aircraft abort.

As soon as Geoff came to realize the Wing Commander's attitudes, he, too, became involved in a war on two fronts. Resolute by nature, he was also quick to anger; the squadron motto might well have been his own: *Noli me Tangere*, Touch me Not.

Each crew became known by the name of its captain: Kennard's crew; Newitt's crew; Laing's crew ... 'Maddern' became a family name to us. In most cases the pilot was the crew member best fitted to command, both by make-up and the nature of his tasks. Navigators were too much absorbed in their calculations to be involved in it; added to this, they were generally men more inclined to thought than to quick physical response. Each crew member was an extension of the man controlling the aircraft: one tended his engines; another guided him out and home; a third and fourth were ready to direct him in evasive action when fighters attacked; a fifth pinpointed his whereabouts – if cloud permitted – and directed him on the run-up to the target; a sixth listened for instructions from base and was ready to send out emergency messages. But it was the pilot who carried out the manoeuvres on which lives so often depended; also, any decisions made could be sheeted home to him, even if he were an NCO with officers in his crew.

The day we transferred to the squadron Geoff scrutinized our new leaders.

117

Sqr Ldr Fox seems a good scout. Told me that I would be the mug who would get the kick in the pants if any of the crew were missing when required.

Keeping track of his gunners was already proving a headache. When we were not required for flying, Shag would sometimes dash for Nottingham, usually taking Hilda a few tasty items from our Australian hampers, or a plucked pheasant from the Earl of Yarborough's. But once there it was not always easy for him to leave; Hilda was pregnant and anxious. As for Frank, his poaching was not limited to feathered game; he was the 'fancy man' of various local ladies.

Five days after we had transferred to the squadron and were waiting as usual to hear whether ops were 'on' or 'off', Fox came from the Wing Commander's office to address us. Even before he spoke we sensed he was a bearer of good tidings, but just how good, we could not have guessed. I see him yet, standing before us, worn ops cap tilted rakishly, lynx eyes alight.

'Gentlemen, I have an announcement to make: this squadron is going to be the first in One Group to convert onto Lancasters ...'

It was impossible for him to continue for cheering, whistling, stamping, nor could he conceal his own delight. To the men he had become someone exalted, a Moses assuring them of deliverance to the Promised Land. There would be no more high losses, no more crashes on the aerodrome. No moment could have revealed more clearly the state of the crews' feelings.

He regained his composure; the men became intent and eager. The first Lancasters would arrive next week; an intensive training programme had been drawn up which would culminate in an eight-hour cross-country exercise. Our Halifaxes were to go to Snaith, where the lads would be glad to get them – *they* were still on Whitleys! In the meantime, for

118

a few more days, ops must continue on Halifaxes.

Days passed without our crew appearing on the Battle Order; instead we were briefed on October 24 for a five-hour cross country flight. Fox told Geoff we were to deviate at the beginning to take two army officers over Hull; they commanded the searchlights there and wanted to see how effective they were. He himself and the rest of the operational crews were going to Milan; this was reckoned an 'easy' target. Geoff relished our task:

> *Climbed up to ten thousand and got weaving amongst the searchlights. It was quite good fun screaming down in steep turns, skidding and climbing damn near vertically. At 9.30 ... crossing the Humber, Shag called me up to say that flak was bursting behind and coming closer. ... It then dawned on me that Jerry was raiding Hull and that we were being mistaken for one of their machines. We pooped off the colours of the day, evaded the bursts and returned to base for more Very cartridges. ... The army chaps said they were alighting. ...*

Morning brought numbing news: Sqn Ldr Fox was no longer with us; his crew and also one commanded by Sgt Claridge had failed to return from Milan. A third crew, commanded by the Australian, Flg Off Colin Rose, had been badly shot up by a night fighter. Two engines and the hydraulics were put out of action; the tyres were punctured, yet he got home. A fourth Elsham crew lost one engine and flew low all the way home, the first part of it down the Rhone valley. Geoff viewed the night bitterly:

> *This is a real jinx squadron. Only five machines were lost in the raid; two of them from this place.*

The RAF had recognized Fox as an outstanding leader and had specially posted him to Elsham to boost morale during the squadron's disastrous run on Halifaxes. But when such a leader failed himself to return – from an 'easy' target at that – the effect was more than ever depressing.

As far as we were concerned, there was scant time to lament. We were ordered to York to pick up a repaired Halifax from a small aerodrome on the edge of the city. This almost proved the end of us. Four of the crew were taken there by road: Geoff, Doug Richards, Ted Batten and myself. No one told us that the aircraft had been put together from the salvaged halves of two different crashed Halifaxes; it had not been so much as test flown. As Geoff admitted in his diary, a more experienced pilot would have been suspicious.

The chappie who got me to sign for the kite asked me to do a circuit for my own satisfaction. The runway was very short – no more than 800 yards in my estimation. Got her off by going through the gate. The machine was very reluctant about leaving the deck and equally anxious to get down again. The take-off was straight over the town of York – if one or two motors had cut we would have had it. ... Coming in to land, with visibility no more than 200 yds., I missed the runway altogether – it was a blind circuit. The second attempt turned out OK, but damn me I would [try] a three-pointer. She banged and must have bounced at least a hundred feet. The fourth touchdown was OK. Still the workers gaped and said, 'Are you going to take it?' ... they had me sign a form as a test pilot. ... I brought her back here minus intercom, wireless, in fact sweet F/A apart from the motors was working.

It was the hybrid's first and last flight; Geoff's report grounded it. But we could not shake Halifaxes off. The day after our York experience, the new crews found themselves on the Battle Order for Stettin. 'Medieval buildings burn well,' quipped an intelligence officer. We prayed for a 'scrub', for a chance to get onto Lancasters, which now were arriving daily. The operation was very long and fog was forecast for our return; the only part of the country likely to remain clear was

Cornwall. Take off was delayed and we were packed off to the cinema. Fog descended in time to prevent take-off; the operation was postponed until next night. Again we went through the whole procedure; again fog came in earlier than expected – 'Thick grey-yellow stuff,' wrote Keith Webber, 'impenetrable. ... Damp and horrible.' But it saved us. The Wing Commander announced there would be no further operations on Halifaxes. Pandemonium broke out. It was as if we had been given a gift of ten completed ops. The dark days were over.

11

The Coming of Lancasters

The Lancaster bomber was the best of its class which appeared in the Second World War. It had the capacity to lift a ten-ton bomb. It was robust and reliable in action and, on targets of equal risk, suffered a lower casualty rate than its equivalent versions, the Halifax and the Stirling. Like them, it had not, however, the capacity to survive in combat with opposing fighters. (Noble Frankland *The Bombing Offensive against Germany*, Faber & Faber, London, 1965).

With Fox lost to us, Sqn Ldr Kennard moved to A Flight; Colin Rose, now a Flight Lieutenant, was deputed to act in command of B Flight until a new Squadron Leader arrived. This was the second loss of a flight commander in a couple of months, Sqn Ldr Saxelby having been posted missing just before our arrival.

The key man in the conversion programme now became Jake Kennard. Geoff flew a Lancaster with him before I had so much as seen one close up.

After a dual circuit with Sqn Ldr Kennard and two checks with Flg Off Southgate I went solo on them ... They are the most beautiful kites imaginable to fly – they climb like a bat out of hell, very light and responsive to the controls. The main trouble is trying to keep the speed down. ... Quite easy to land – you feel them down like a Tiger Moth.

On October 30 we took delivery of our own machine, Geoff and Doug Richards leading us around her proprietorially, the ground crew happily in tow. She had about her so beautiful a symmetry and promised so much better a future, that I did not pause to consider her real task. The cockpit was thirteen or fourteen feet up, topped by a canopy like a greenhouse; the fuselage sloped back to the tail at about ten degrees, so that we were able to stand on the ground and look in on Shag when he was incarcerated in the rear turret. Her colour was termed 'lamp-black', but large on each side of her was the red, white and blue roundel of the RAF. To the left of the roundels, in red letters about three feet high, was the squadron identification: PM; to the right, the identification of the plane itself, in our case B. The roundel came to be deprecated by mid-upper gunners – it looked too much like a target set close below their turret. On the starboard side, aft of the roundel, was the entrance door; a short metal ladder was already in place for us. Beside the door was B's serial number: W4333.

We soon realized there was a preferred order of entry if we wanted to avoid squeezing past each other inside – it did not apply to the rear gunner since he flew in lonely isolation, further aft even than the Elsan toilet. Of the other six, it was best if the bombaimer, who had farthest forward to go, moved in first, followed by the pilot, engineer, navigator, wireless operator and mid-upper gunner in that order, all of them moving up the slope in dim light – greenish light from the olive-green paint of the interior.

The fuselage had a smell all its own compounded of oil and dope and paint and cold metal. The new aircraft were unsullied yet by odors of fear. Like Jonah, we were in the belly of the leviathan and could view its succession of curved ribs over which its skin was stretched – duralumin skin in wafer-thin panels. All down the sides of the belly sinews of elevator and rudder controls were affixed and arteries for hydraulics and oxygen.

We followed each other along a strip of carpet laid by Cpl Bill Burchell of the ground-crew to protect the shining metal floor from mud. We passed the footrests of the mid-upper turret; the flare-shute; the rest position – a euphemism this, since the bed was really a place for a wounded man, if he could be got there – the armour-plated door, then the barrier of the mainspar from which the wings spread either side. We had to bend to get over it, swinging one leg then the other – a tight squeeze, but not so tight as it would be with flying clothing on. The smooth metal of it was cold to the touch; always cold. Glancing back from there it was about fifteen yards to Shag in his rear turret.

Ted disappeared from sight, taking two steps down into the nose; Geoff, with regal flourish, ascended his throne. Behind his head rose a vertical piece of armour plate to protect him, as befitting one of the royal blood; the control column was his sceptre. Doug unfastened his lowly dickey seat from the starboard side and let it down, so that he and Geoff sat side by side, before them the array of flying instruments, between them throttles and boost, at Doug's right elbow, the fuel gauges. The greenhouse spread of plexiglass gave them clear view through 200 degrees or more. On each side was a blister – they could put their heads into them and look directly below.

Coming next I reached an unbelievable place : a comfortable swivel chair set before a green-topped table measuring about four feet long by two-feet six wide. Over it was the extension arm of an Anglepoise lamp, on its other side an airspeed indicator, altimeter, compass. I sank into the chair and found the Gee screen just below eye-level to my right. How easy now to navigate to Germany – if only they would desist over there from forcing us into inaccuracies!

To my left, scarcely four feet away, Max Burcher sat himself at his Marconi, he facing forward, I sideways. Light, with skylight quality, fell on us from the hemispherical astrodome. When I put my head into the dome I could see along the fuselage to Frank Holmes ensconced in the mid-upper turret. A black-out curtain was there to be drawn across it at night. A second black-out curtain, between my table and the cockpit, was caught back, but by night it was compulsory to use this, too. This lent the office of the navigator and wireless operator an illusory feeling of snugness and security.

There was a drawer to my desk. Among other things I put into it the beret issued at Somers with goonskins. If we had to bale out, at least I would have French-looking headwear. 'Not bad!' we mused to each other, 'Not at all bad!'

'When do we fly?'

'Tomorrow.'

We were small boys with a new toy, nearly ready to play wars with the boys across the North Sea.

Time allowed for conversion was ten days; in thirteen days our first leave was due. For me this was good fortune, as Jim Riddoch was also to have leave from St. Eval; we planned to stay awhile at the Strand Palace. The world was beginning to seem downright bright. It was even brighter next day when we first flew B – Beer as a crew. Geoff was exultant:

Shot up Scunthorpe in vis. no more than 100 yds. These kites steep turn beautifully. Took Shag down to Nottingham. He was so excited he couldn't find the place where he lived. Coming back feathered an engine and flew hands and feet off on three. Cut another engine on the same side and flew on two. It maintains height easily. When we were on three it was climbing at 160 on plus 2, 2200 rpm. They're wizard.

But within the crew we still had a problem. Geoff wrote:

Max Burcher has reverted to his old habits – very rude and not at all co-operative – all the crew were fed up with him, so I had to try and reason with him to pull a little more. He knows his work all right but just doesn't care. He took the talking quite well. Asked him to come out with me in the evening just to show there was no ill feeling.

Max, we knew, was bored and frustrated. He hankered still to be a pilot. His work as a wireless operator by no means absorbed his energies, nor could he accept his category as a misfortune of Air Force life; instead, it soured him. When I called him for radio bearings, he obtained them grudgingly. In the air, there was simply no time to remonstrate with him. In the end the situation was to resolve itself – not at all in the way we had hoped, nevertheless with great credit to Max. But that was weeks off. On the ground, he and Geoff and I contentedly shared our room, dividing our hampers from home, giving part of them to the rest of the crew, cooking weird concoctions on our heating stove.

Life continued to be deceptively pleasant; there were no casualties during the conversion and we were cheered by a succession of happenings. First came the victory at El Alamein. The country's church bells, silent since the threat of invasion, rang out in rejoicing; the bells of Elsham village, rose from a valley hidden steeply below us. Then came the astonishing re-appearance on the station of Sgt Gordon Mellor, navigator of W/O Edwards' crew, shot down a couple of months earlier. When Mellor was followed by Flt Lt Pipkin, navigator of Sqn Ldr Saxelby's crew, then W/O 'Dizzy' Spiller, navigator of Fox's crew, I began to comfort myself with the notion that navigators stood best chance of escape. These men were forbidden to tell us much that we wanted to know, but we heard from the laconic Dizzy that Fox's Halifax had been shot down by a nightfighter; only two of the crew had been able to bale out – Dizzy and the wireless operator, 'Lofty' Maddocks. Maddocks had been taken prisoner.*

November 11 came, the Armistice Day of our childhood. Large numbers of us went to the gymnasium which doubled

---

* In *No Moon Tonight* I incorrectly stated that Fox's aircraft was destroyed by bombs dropped by a higher-flying aircraft. K.J. Spiller's *Ticket to Freedom* describes the fighter attack.

as a church; there David Ratledge, Church of England padre, addressed us. He never exhorted us or made us conscious of our shortcomings; he understood aircrew.

'Let us remember in the silence of our hearts those who fell in the Great War and those who have fallen in this war, especially those of this squadron who have died on operations.'

By November 16 we had flown 11 hours 45 minutes as a Lancaster crew and were ready for the eight-hour cross-country flight. It was to have six turning points, the farthest 150 miles northwest of the Outer Hebrides. When at last we reached there we had long been beyond Gee range and for six hours had seen nothing of land or sea. For me the scene outside was reduced to so many lines on a white Mercator chart: straight lines of tracks I was trying to follow and other straight lines of courses along which we headed. Only once did I go into the outer world of the cockpit. The cloud pile was far down, the hemisphere of sky blue-black; the outer temperature stood at -20 deg.C; the sun was setting ahead over the invisible Atlantic. It was difficult to connect this scene with chart, protractor, dividers. I returned and drew our black-out curtain. In our office Max and I were hot – the hot-air outlet was by the wireless operator's seat – but in the cockpit Doug was massaging Geoff's feet. I had on a pair of fleece-lined RCAF flying boots that gave room enough for my uniform boots. I unzipped them and Geoff put them on. He was to wear them for the rest of our time together; I was never to be in need of more than battledress and street boots.

We got back to Elsham Wolds at 11 p.m., fatigued, but happy, happy with our work as a crew, happy with the prospect of coming leave; happiest with the Lancaster.

12

Moments from a Leave

*God shall wipe away all tears from their eyes and there shall be no
more death neither sorrow nor crying neither shall there be any more
pain. For the former things have passed away. (Revelations* 21:4)

Our first six weeks at Elsham Wolds, with its initiation for us
of steady loss of men, sharpened a sense of urgency in me to
get done on leave the things I most wanted to do. I wanted first
to pass my father information on the places his parents had
come from. He had never come this way himself; was never
likely to. It seemed extraordinary that so little had been passed
to us by the first Australian generation. There was, nevertheless, a family belief that a village of Charlwood existed in
Surrey, that possibly our name had derived from it. In a
postoffice gazetteer I was able to confirm its existence. It lay
three miles or so from Horley; Horley was a fairly short train
ride south of London. As far as my paternal grandmother was
concerned, the search promised to be easier. She had been
born a Lewis and had often told us that she had been baptised
at St Martin's-in-the-Fields.

I was to meet Jim Riddoch at the Strand Palace. His own
ancestral search was completed – a very simple one, since the
home his grandfather had left to establish *Burnside*, Nareen,
still existed and was occupied still by the family. He had
already stayed there and pressed me to return with him. It lay
fifty miles northwest of Aberdeen.

In our search for family origins, we were by no means
unusual; hundreds of Dominions aircrew searched – drawn
perhaps by the permanent nature of the past. There it was;
nothing could take it away.

Given a rail pass to any destination in Britain, it was remarkable how much one could fit into a six-day leave. Geoff had ensured four of us a good start on leave by hitching a ride from Elsham to Lichfield in Colin Rose's Lancaster. Rose had recently relinquished command of B Flight; a new Squadron Leader, Alec Temperley, had arrived. To Rose and his crew this trip to Lichfield was one of those pleasure flights countenanced by squadrons as 'training.'

'J. Colin McI. Rose', as he signed himself, was a willowy, copper-haired Scottish-looking Australian whom I much liked; his manner was easy and courteous. After his effort in nursing his badly damaged Halifax home from Milan the night Fox and Claridge were lost, he had been awarded a DFC.

We swaggered in at Lichfield. No one here knew that we had never operated on a Lancaster. Rose roared away, his Merlins drawing the envious eyes of trainees and instructors alike. Rising above them they beheld the acme of their deluded ambitions.

Doug and Ted set off at once by train for London; like most RAF men, they were heading home. Although in some ways we envied them, there were stresses in their leave that we never had to face. Nothing could have been worse than to take one's place at a family table knowing that in a few nights everything might end on operations. They were men suspended in unreality.

How men from overseas spent their leaves depended on their inclinations, on whether they wanted quiet with families they had come to know, or meetings with girlfriends, or to live it up with other aircrew in London pubs and clubs. London could turn out as exhausting as six successive nights in Scunthorpe – with the bonus of hearing casualty lists daily.

That first afternoon, Jim Riddoch and I walked from the Strand Palace to the National Gallery where Myra Hess was playing Mozart, servicemen lounging about her in scores, drawn almost as much by the warmth of her personality as by her playing.

It was a simple matter to walk from the Strand Palace to St. Martin's-in-the-Fields and seek an 1837 baptismal entry for Emily Lewis, my paternal grandmother. I remembered her as a diminutive, stern, mater presiding at the head of her East Melbourne dinner table, her expression not amused, her eye on our table manners. I grew up with impressions of near-aristocratic origins, but found now that her father had been a 'licensed victualler' in Long Acre. I fancied she might not have been altogether pleased had she seen me walking through Covent Garden in search of their pub.

> ... *everywhere one smells vegetables and sees them piled high in round baskets. Little men wearing scarves and possessing enormous voices, balance baskets on their heads, or sit on the high perches of wagons.*

The pub, alas, had vanished.

Gradually, I had come to love London. It had not been so at first. I see us yet in our Bournemouth days, deposited under the glass roof of Waterloo Station, the vast, echoing place thronged by uniformed men, shoulder flashes showing Guards regiments, New Zealand, Poland, Norway, USA.

As we walked across Waterloo Bridge that day and saw Big Ben, the Abbey, and far-off St. Paul's, disappointment swept over us. These places had been so glorified in our school-day textbooks that there was small hope of them matching expectations.

By night, in the blackout, with street signs removed, London at first confused us utterly. It was relief to go into the underground to seek clear directions. Hundreds of people slept still in bunks along the platforms, seeming untroubled by stale air and the rush of trains and press of passengers. Here and there among them were beings so stunted, so pallid and bent that they scarcely seemed human at all. Each visit now I saw some of them on the surface in light of day, like blanched, curled insects from under stones. They shuffled about lowly tasks, eyes to ground, movements jerky, products of poverty, poor diet, pea-soup fogs and the mysterious class system. But contrasting with them, was the transcendent spirit abroad in London. Whatever our country, we felt ourselves part of the growing force dedicated to restoration of freedom.

Everywhere was bomb damage. Opposite Australia House, St. Clement Danes was a hollow ruin of smoked walls and tower; all around St. Paul's was desolation. I once heard Harry Wright say that the outlook from St Paul's had strengthened his determination more than anything he had seen.

My search for Charlwood village brought me to loveliness beyond expectation. From Horley station I was directed southwest and, within a mile, left the town behind. At a crossroads a man pointed with his pipe to what he called 'the Charlwood lane'. On one side of it were woods, frost still on the grass under the trees. A stream in a narrow valley, he told me, was the river Mole. A narrower, more silent river I had never seen. Two miles on I saw a church tower rising among trees and found a cobbled lane leading to it.

The lane was delightful. By two giant elms golden leaves lay ankle deep … It led me to its junction with a road, at the junction stood a white and green pub, the 'Half Moon.' Opposite me stood the church … Sun slanted between the trees and across the grave-sprinkled turf and lighted the old walls …

This was St Nicholas church, started in 1080. In the village about it the *Cherlewode* family name first appeared late in the thirteenth century. Gradually the spelling had become as we used it now.

I was taken warmly in hand by the rector and his wife. After lunch he and I scraped lichen from two Charlwood headstones, while his wife searched the parish records. Under the lichen were the names of James and Phoebe, my great-great-grandparents whose son had taken his printing press to Melbourne in 1850. Phoebe had died first, died at thirty-nine after the birth of twins, her tenth and eleventh children. The words James chose for her headstone were the words from the Book of Revelations which head this chapter.

Charlwood rectory was to become another home to me. I would knock at the door there one night, sick at heart after loss of a friend, and hear the rector exclaim, 'My dear boy, I *am* glad to see you! It's like having one of my own sons come home.' Their three sons were far off, one of them eluding the Japanese as he made his way from Hong Kong to Burma.

Jim Riddoch had waited for me in London, intent upon taking me to Scotland, to *Tarryblake*, the home his grandfather had left to go to *Burnside*, Nareen.

The night journey to Aberdeen was wearying beyond belief. Uniformed men and women endured the cold with dumb, animal patience. But my coming to *Tarryblake* I have always remembered for it was like my coming in youth to *Burnside*. And my welcome there had *Burnside* warmth. I sat alone in the library, wrapped in peace.

> *Before me is a large window, so carefully polished that it scarcely seems there at all. It looks onto descending lawns which merge into the surrounding fields and woods without interruption of a fence. Beyond the lawns lies the valley of the Isla, a pasture land dotted with homesteads. Beyond the Isla rise remote hills. A fire burns on the hearth behind me. The room is lined with books, good books ...The room is so still that I can hear the minute sounds of the fire. ...*

After two days there my leave was up. I left Jim and made the all-night journey south.

Our crew converged at Barnetby station around first light. Though almost sleep-walking, I seemed in best shape. Geoff was 'surprised ... to find the boys present and in one piece,'

> Ted, Shag and Max looked as though they'd gone through a mangle. Walked ... back to camp through a gorgeous Scotch mist. By this time I was beginning to realize that I had been skating the previous afternoon – hobbled along. ... At 10.0 we were notified we would be on ops that night. Hell, I was tired; hadn't slept for nearly 48 hours. However, later, getting some rejuvenating tablets from the MO and doing all the necessary preparations, I was ready for anything. We were briefed for Stettin. Take-off was scheduled for 5.30. [p.m.] At 5.20 we were in our machines waiting for the OK to take off – bugger it, the op was cancelled.

So ended our first return from leave.

13
Useless Beginnings

Operationally, the idea of area bombing was to attack an aiming point which lay at the centre of a large area whose destruction would be useful. It was, in other words, a method of making bombs which missed the aiming point contribute to the destruction of the German war machine. Since nearly all bombs were missing the aiming point, there was a certain logic about the idea. (Noble Frankland, DFC *The Bombing Offensive Against Germany*, Faber and Faber, London, 1965.)

Doug Richards had already established himself as first man of the crew out of bed and abroad. Before daylight, he and Tony Willis, engineer of Laing's crew, would head off to their respective dispersal points, about a mile away, where the aircraft were maintained by the groundcrew 'erks'.

At our dispersal point Doug talked over B's general health with Cpl. Bill Burchell. On this first day after our leave, he managed to overhear the petrol load ordered for the coming night. He came tramping into our fusty room, sounding from his step a bearer of tidings, waking us with the words, 'Ops tonight!' adding, 'Long trip – maximum fuel load.'

I never learnt to accept these words with equanimity; I doubt that many did. For all the hours of preparation and waiting – eight, ten, twelve – we were taut. That particular morning, the tranquil scene from *Tarryblake* seemed half a life away. I drew back our curtains and saw men and Waafs passing along the road in wet, grey light, each already playing some part in the getting us to the unknown target.

After breakfast we lounged about the crewroom until the Wing Commander confirmed that ops were on, navigators and bombaimers to go early to lunch before their briefing at 1300. The work of these two was so interlocked that they spent most of the hours of preparation together. Ted Batten and I joined the other navigators and bombaimers in the mess, our appetites dulled by Doug's prediction. We confessed thoughts of Berlin as our first op. from the squadron, our first on Lancasters.

After the meal I went, zombie-like, to the locker room where the navigators were getting out their large, green canvas bags. Carrying them they looked like traditional carpenters, but in place of plane, hammer and saw, the bags held Dalton computer, Douglas protractor, dividers, long perspex rule, Air Almanac, star tables.

The navigation centre was a hut little different from barracks huts; in place of beds, it contained rows of plotting tables; on the end wall was a large map of Europe. I was hesitant about choosing a table. Did this one belong to someone else? Harry Wright, who had done a Halifax operation as a replacement navigator and was thus an informed man, believed it to be spare, so I settled at it; Keith Webber took the next. Undoubtedly there were 'lucky' and 'unlucky' tables, but one could not very well ask this information. Next came Jack Jefferies, Australian navigator of Colin Bayliss's crew, then Brian Stoker, hefty young navigator of Temperley's crew – a man destined to survive 67 operations. We gazed with forebodings at the large map of Europe. Nothing was yet shown on it. A long strand of wool dangled from a coloured pin fixed at Elsham Wolds.

In front of the map Flt Lt Austen Magor, squadron navigation leader, waited for us to settle and for the door to be closed. He was quiet and deliberate, a man of long aircrew experience; he doubled on Sundays as organist at Padre Ratledge's services. To me he seemed even more bookish than I was – cast in the mould of a poet rather than of bomber crew. Under his arm he carried a roll of charts which he began handing out to us – that same type of white Mercator projection we had used in operational exercises at Rivers. We looked at once to see the area it covered. It was Southern Europe; at least the target was not Berlin. We pinned the charts to the tables while he picked up the strand of wool hanging from Elsham Wolds.

'The target for tonight is Turin.' His tone was matter-of-fact; he might have been inviting us to tea. 'Time on target 2330 hours.'

From old hands who had been on ops two or three months, there were heartening murmurs of 'Whizzo!' and 'Piece of cake!'

'Your route.' Magor began extending the wool, 'Base to Dungeness, down here on the south coast; Dungeness to point *A*, here on the French coast…'

So it went; out across the Alps, the wool extending over the dark miles, till at last, 'A short leg from Lake Anisee to the target.' I wrote these things down with a sense of unreality; all my training seemed suddenly very brief, as if it had only been last week that Jim Riddoch and I had done the 21 Lessons.

'Now, your altitudes to fly…'

Stooped over the tables the navigators drew in the legs of the route; measured the bearing of each; stepped distances with dividers, their bombaimers checking, crew comparing with crew. All this data – tracks, distances, altitudes to fly, corrected airspeed for each altitude – we entered in the flight plan section on the outside of our folded log forms; inside would go our record of actualities – of winds found, times at turning points, reports of seeing bombers shot down. Magor passed us the met. section's forecast winds at each altitude. Once we had these we could use the Dalton computer to calculate courses to steer and speeds over the ground. My results did not wholly agree with Harry's, nor with Keith's, nor did Harry's and Keith's results entirely tally. But we had been used to this since Edmonton days. We agreed, though, that the operation would take nine hours.

Navigator's briefing seemed an academic exercise that first day compared with general briefing; general briefing, with all crew members attending, was gut-gripped theatre. The operations room was windowless; briefing was conducted under fluorescent lights. There we sat, eighty or ninety of us, restlessly awaiting the entry of the senior officers. As they filed in to take their places on the platform, we stood as if at school assembly. Among the officers were the bombing leader, the navigation leader, the engineering officer, the intelligence officer, our two flight commanders – prefects rather than masters – the Wing Commander, even the Group Captain, resplendent, as Shag pointed out, in tailored battle dress. 'This is the nearest 'e'll get to ops.' Anachronistic in this company was the civilian meteorological forecaster.

The high moment of drama came when the curtain was drawn back on a wall map so extensive that its upper levels could only be reached by a pointer. It covered the whole of Europe. 'Gentlemen, the target for tonight is Turin.' Although most of us already knew it, there were murmurs and comments and intakes of breath.

As well as showing our route, the map displayed the latest intelligence on flak and fighter concentrations, all in colours likely to shake the stoutest heart. The atmosphere of theatre intensified when the room was darkened and an epidiascope projected aerial photographs of the target itself–the city streets, buildings, river, railways. A few more magnifications might have shown us the people whose morale we were supposed to break. Everyone knew, of course, that Italian morale was easier to break than German, but we were warned not to under-estimate Turin; it was believed that the defences were stiffened by German batteries. Slow swirls of cigarette smoke in the beam of light. 'Cloudy Joe' rose to tell a not very convincing meteorological story, illustrating it with vivid pictures of piled-up frontal cloud that might or might not be there, of an icing level that would certainly be there, though probably not where forecast. Of course, the faults were not his; forecasting was a centralised business, but he had to stand derision from the experienced crews.

'Lights!'

Advice, encouragement, exhortations.

'Any questions? None? Very well; good luck chaps!'

The clatter of departure, of mutterings between crews; a degree of relief in movement. This then was 'it'.

As we were due off at 1845, we were due at our aircraft at 1745, due in the crewroom dressed to depart at 1700, due in the locker room about half an hour before that to allow gunners time to don their electrically-heated suits and the rest of us our lesser gear, time, too, for the lot of us to go to the parachute section. Thus the ops. meal of bacon and eggs must be no later than 1600.

The period in the crewroom before being driven to the aircraft, was termed 'final briefing'. We had been warned by oldtimers that a meteorologist could rush in at the last minute with drastic changes to forecast winds that would set navigators re-calculating courses and ground speeds, stooping feverishly together at the large table, praying that their haste would not lead them into error. No one but a navigator could understand this kind of pressure. And we knew that the attack might suddenly be put back an hour or two hours, or so many hours that everyone could take off their flying gear and go to the cinema before eventual take-off. But there was none of this tonight. We merely synchronised our watches; were given pills of various colours by the MOs; wished good luck by the Wingco, who seemed 'not a bad bastard' after all. We climbed into vans that Waafs had backed up to the crew room, some of them small vans for one crew, most larger vans for two crews.

In these we began lumbering out in the darkness. I was filled with incredulity that all this was taking place.

At 1835, nine hours after the morning announcement of ops., we began taxying, moving slowly in the dark toward take-off position, nose to tail, like a caravan of camels, brakes hissing above the roar of engines.

A sudden exclamation came from Geoff, 'What's this ahead?'

Then Doug's voice, 'You're being waved around something. I think there's an aircraft across part of the taxiway – looks as if it's bogged.'

Following waved torches Geoff turned cautiously. All at once a wheel came heavily off the edge of the taxiway. We, too, were bogged.

'Shit! That ends it! And here comes the Wingco's car!'

We braced ourselves, but he shouted, 'Bad luck Maddern! Not your fault. ...'

An hour later we rode our bikes to our rooms. It was too long a time to wait to see if all our aircraft returned; too early for bed. We lit our stove, made toast, spread it with camp pie from home.

I went to see Keith Webber late next morning. He looked wan and tired, but the target had been 'fair enough'. Their worst moments had come over the Alps on the way home, 'Something to do with the automatic pilot.'

We were at 18,000 with peaks below us at 15,000 odd. Suddenly, as the aircraft was flying straight and level, it slipped over straight onto its nose. I was thrown from my chair, the odds and ends in my boxes were emptied all over the table and floor. I reached for my parachute – not that it would have been much use anyway. I looked up to see Ted standing up tugging at the stick. We were still diving. Suddenly the dive changed and we went straight up and stood on our tail ... the four engines cut owing to lack of fuel, as the petrol wasn't getting into the cylinders. Pushed the nose down and levelled out. We were all much shaken...

For some reason Laing's crew was not on the next operation. Sitting by his fire, Keith heard the rest of us take off for Frankfurt – for us our first operation from the squadron; December 2 1942.

'Tis very cold outside, but the sky is clear. I don't envy them their trip. I never do. In fact, who does? I'll bet every one of them wishes he were snugly asleep.

I was not at all satisfied with my navigation that night; I was a zombie still, going through actions mechanically. But somehow we found Frankfurt's concentrated glow of fires through the cloud. I read now, 45 years later, in the Middlebrook & Everitt Bomber Command War Diaries, that even the newly-formed Pathfinders failed to locate the target and so did not put down markers; that the fires we bombed were not in Frankfurt at all but in the nearby countryside – possibly decoy fires. For this, 5.4% of the attacking force was lost – over fifty men.

For our crew the only positive thing about the raid was that Geoff was cheered by the way we worked together: 'Don, Doug, Frank, Ted – all of them were damned fine – wouldn't change them...'

On our return, a landing in Lincolnshire was impossible owing to fog; we were diverted to Middleton-St. George, Bomber Command's northernmost base, home of a RCAF squadron. After eight hours in the air, we landed with half an hour's petrol left. Six other 103 Squadron aircraft presently joined us. At interrogation 'Bunny' Austin, one of our senior captains, reported twelve attacks by fighters; one they had shot down. But word reached us that F/O Cummings's crew from 103 had failed to return. After interrogation we fell asleep in chairs in the mess and at lunchtime were shown to beds.

Next day was too foggy for us to return to Elsham Wolds. We were in limbo – dressed for flying, moneyless, tired. The crews set about finding clothing to wear to Darlington, the nearest town. Some of them left flying boots and pullovers as security on shirts, collars and shoes that they borrowed from the stores.

It was a strange afternoon. We went to *Mrs Miniver*. Geoff's and my response to it surprised the RAF men of the crew – even displeased them. The film opened our eyes to the results of bombing residential areas. The others, having experienced the Blitz, were glad to be hitting back.

The performance over, we stood for the National Anthem. Photographs of four allied leaders were projected onto the screen. Even then they seemed a bizarre assortment to be leading the 'free' world: Churchill, Roosevelt, Stalin and Chiang Kai-Shek.

In the morning the weather cleared and we took off for Elsham. Once landed we were briefed for a 3.30 am take-off. I wrote home after the ops meal:

A strange way of fighting a war this. Here I sit in our cosy room. Max is sleeping like a child; the fire is crackling; the wind is howling outside. Is it possible that tonight we shall roar across the grey North Sea and the miles of heavily defended territory beyond it? Again one looks wonderingly, not fearfully, at the morrow. ...

At midnight Geoff came in; the op was scrubbed. The three of us undressed and turned in. It seemed only moments before Doug was in the room declaring, 'Ops tonight – long trip!'

We began preparations for Mannheim, take-off soon after dark, the round trip to take seven hours forty-five minutes. As Keith put it, 'From ten in the morning until you come back from an op it is in the vicinity of 18 hrs. flat out.'

This time there was cloud cover all the way; identification of the target was impossible. Again we bombed a concentration of fires seen by their glow through cloud; again, as Middlebrook and Everitt have shown, we bombed open country on the outskirts of the target. On the ground no lives were lost – apart from twenty-five sheep and four lambs. For this about sixty aircrew lost their lives.

For Max and me the journey home became nightmarish:

...our wireless transmitter went U.S.: splashers* were jammed and the Gee was jammed. We turned north on our D.R. position at the French coast, but at ETA on the English coast we could not tell where we were. Max by now was trying to repair his set, while I struggled beside him – ineffectually – to get some star shots. On and on we went – and still saw flak! The crew was convinced that we were still over France, though probably the flak was from ships. We called Darkie, but there was no reply. On and on; God, it was awful. I felt responsible for the lives of six men and there was naught I could do... Soon after, in answer to Darkie, the most wonderful Waaf's voice said, 'This is Thorney Island.' Max and I nearly wept tears of joy. We both felt responsible for our predicament.

Finally, in low cloud over England, our fuel running out, Geoff decided to land at Waddington. By the time we taxied in, twenty minutes was left in our tanks. Not everyone got down; four aircraft crashed in various places.

As we settled with many other aircrew to sleep in a small, foetid room at Waddington, I knew utter dejection. What *ought* I have done? Ted and the rest of the crew had not been able to see anything of the ground; I had been able to get only one astro sight before clouds veiled the stars, whereas I needed two; anyway, flying straight and level for star shots left one a sitting duck for fighters.

---

* *Splashers*: the code name of long-range radio beacons in Britain.

In retrospect I see these operations to Frankfurt and Mannheim as typifying winter raids on distant cities at that time. Our navigation was strained to find our way to the target and back; given a cloud-covered point of aim, there was small prospect of also achieving accurate bombing. The most that can be said is that reports of our efforts boosted British morale and tied down German troops, guns and 'planes.

The operation to Mannheim had exhausted Keith Webber:

The worst part of the trip was coming up through England. Cloud closed to 800 feet which we had to break through... I almost decided in the 'plane that I couldn't carry on this job. It seems to be wearing me down. I was really exhausted half way through the trip and was quite a case when I landed. I don't know what the matter is but I'm very weary. Must be my age. We haven't had a stand down for 7 days...

When our crew reached Elsham from Waddington Geoff found himself in trouble because he had failed to attend parade the previous morning.

...they expected me to do a cross-country run as a penance. ... Told Rose to go dip his eye in s... Guess the Wg Cdr will be on my wheel tomorrow morning. He too can visit the sanitary depot. ...

Nothing more came of it. I escaped to Scunthorpe and took Betty to see Robert Donat in *The Young Mr Pitt*. I insisted that we be 'pals only', that I had a girl in Canada... But neither of us seemed adept at keeping to this restriction.

In the morning a few crews, ours among them, were briefed for mine-laying. Eighty aircraft were to go from the Command to various points along the German and Danish coasts; our own particular 'gardening plot' was to be in Copenhagen Sound.

Geoff reckoned our journey out 'a piece of cake'.

We were first off the deck – 5 p.m. 'George' did nearly all the flying over the North Sea – flew at 2000 ft. – clouds were at about 3000.

Approaching the Danish coast, we went down to 1000 ft. and then, when crossing the mainland, I took her across almost at ground level with about 200 mph on the clock.

To that point navigation had also been a piece of cake, but once the mapreading search for our 'plot' began, it was a different matter. As Geoff put it:

East of Denmark the clouds were right down to 800 ft. – it was as rough as hell. With no Gee or wireless we had to rely entirely on pinpoints. It's exceedingly difficult in the Baltic with the maze of islands and isthmuses. We were unable to locate our allotted plot – must have been over Sweden for some time. Came back on a reciprocal and let them go...

Where we let them go was far from certain, consequently we set course home from an unidentified point. In the search for our 'plot' we must have edged south, for eventually we were caught by flak on the west coast of Denmark at a point I later calculated to be Esbjerg. This was confirmed years later when Ted Batten met a Dane who had been in Esbjerg that night and had seen a Lancaster flying close to the ground, leaping over and diving under searchlight beams while being cannonaded with flak. Geoff told us afterwards that the altimeter had read a hundred feet, the airspeed indicator 300 mph. He flew superbly.

I could see [flak] coming closer and closer and found myself ducking all the time – it's a hell of a feeling. Bang! There was a metallic clang. I knew that the machine had been hit very close to myself – thought, well, either Max or Don has been killed. Intercom went – the silence in the machine was terrifying. ...I sent Doug back to ascertain who had collected. Max [had been] trying to get loops* at the time. He was blown from one side of the machine to the other. ... The wireless, intercom and IFF** all

---

* *loops*: radio bearings.   ** *IFF*: Identification Friend or Foe *went unserviceable. How we got clear without any further damage is a miracle. Don dressed Max's wounds and then got busy on his job of navigation – he did a wonderful job and was as cool as a cucumber – the only aid he had was Gee. He couldn't keep Max back in the rest position. He was continually coming back to see if he could repair the set.*

Although Gee was functioning, it was not directed our way, the 'southern chain' being in use. But I had kept its readings outbound and, even without a chart to cover our area, it was simple to compare these with readings obtained on the way home. Far from feeling I had done 'a wonderful job', I was dismayed by the night's happenings and blamed myself for them entirely.

With our IFF not functioning, Geoff was anxious to identify us as 'friendly' to anti-aircraft batteries south of the Humber:

Put on nav. lights, downward recco and flashed off the colours of the day. Don brought us back right over base. Fired off emergency cartridge and came straight in to land. Experienced trouble getting the undercarriage down. Max was taken straight to hospital – the MO said his wounds were only superficial. Our starboard mainplane was holed badly just to the rear of the aileron. Max has plenty of guts – he never complained once; all he was concerned about was getting his set going so that we would be sure of getting home. I can't speak highly enough of the boys – not one of them panicked. ... Reaction set in with me once we were on the deck. My stomach was all churned up and then, when in bed, the room seemed to spin.

Max's wounds might have been 'superficial', but, as Geoff wrote next day, 'He's just a mass of stitches.' Doc Henderson had spent four hours extracting shrapnel from him while he drank egg flips. His right arm was put in plaster as he had lost about a third of the muscle above the wrist. His prospects of recovering in time to re-join us were nil. He left our crew high in our esteem. No replacement wireless operator was available so we were sent on three days leave.

On the morning of Sunday December 13, less than 35 hours after Max had been wounded, I hitch-hiked along the Horley-Charlwood road, over the last mile sharing the passenger seat of a lorry with a whippet. At 11.00 a.m. the driver dropped me near the 'Half Moon' and I walked along the flagged path by the church. The opening lines of the morning's first hymn drifted out to me:

> *The King of love my Shepherd is*
> *Whose goodness faileth never…*

It was hard to believe that Esbjerg, or Elsham existed.

14

Winter

During those years '42-'3-'4 but especially '42 and '43, I was deeply conscious of living through great days ... It was as if a sublime tragedy was being enacted ... In addition I learnt ... what amazing possibilities there are in men ... I was never very interested in people's failures – they seemed so unimportant against their successes. (Canon David Ratledge, Church of England padre at Elsham Wolds, 1942 – 44.)

From my upstairs room at Charlwood rectory I looked onto lawns and elms and the ancient church. I felt absorbed into the place at a level even ops. could not touch. Since my earlier visit, the rector's wife had done further research for me. I wrote that night to Nell:

> *She has traced Thomas Charlewood who was begetting vigorously in 1680. A good idea, this begetting, don't you think?*

But as I joined Doug at Kings Cross next evening for the journey north, begetting seemed a remote prospect. On our platform the usual urgent farewells were taking place. Light cast from high, hooded globes touched cheeks and chins, leaving eye sockets and lips in shadow. Words were overwhelmed by amplified announcements and giant hissings of steam and a final slamming of doors, all echoing, echoing.

It was cold and black when we reached Barnetby. Fortunately Doug had left his car in the village, so we were spared the walk up the Elsham road. I sought Keith Webber out as soon as we arrived and heard there had been no further losses. The squadron had been again to Turin and again Keith's crew had experienced a hazardous return. Crossing the Alps they had lost first one engine, then another and had had to skirt the higher peaks at an airspeed of 140 mph. As soon as they reached England Ted Laing put down at Tangmere under a low cloud base. 'A shaky do', wrote Keith.

Nearly piled ourselves up ... Made a long low approach. We had a hundred feet of height when suddenly the trees were on our wheels. It appears a hill came between us and the flarepath. Got down with a screeching of brakes. Cut the tyres somewhat.

We still lacked a wireless operator. Max Burcher was up and about, reconciling himself slowly to loss of the crew and delay to his ops. He was about to go to the RAF hospital at Rawby for physiotherapy. It was to be six months before he joined a crew on 460 Squadron. After all his efforts to build up his morse arm, he was lost with them at the end of July 1943.

The day after our return was Geoff's birthday.

15 Dec.: 26 today. As a special present from the RAF, I remained in bed until 10 a.m. The Air Force have taken a dim view of my action – I have to appear on a charge tomorrow morning.

16 Dec.: ... My hat was removed – prisoner and escorts, quick march, left turn. Halt! Hell, it was all I could do to suppress my mirth. The Wg Cdr went through all the usual bullsh; asked me if I had anything to say. Considering that I'd only attended two parades in the last sixteen days, I had no alternative but to reply in the negative. ...

His punishment was a spell of duty in the control van at the end of the runway. The prospect left him impenitent; he wrote later the same day:

We're supposed to go on a cross-country run. It was too bloody cold. All the Aussies got out of it with plausible excuses.

For my part, I escaped the run not because of weather, but because Max Bryant had hitch-hiked over from the conversion unit at Lindholme. We welcomed him to Max Burcher's empty bunk and I lent him my uniform so that he could join us in the sergeants' mess. Our talk was mainly of the possibility of his crew coming to 103 Squadron. Much as I hoped it would eventuate, I had irrational feelings of responsibility for him. He was still the delightful young enthusiast. He knew the odds well enough, but could not bring himself to apply them to his friends. The fact that Keith, Blue, Harry Wright and I were alive was confirmation of his belief that ours would be a lucky flight. He began asking awkward questions about my faithfulness to Nell. I assured him she was the only girl I wanted to marry.

'But ... ' I prevaricated.

'But what?'

'Well, to stay sane here a man needs the company of women – I do, anyway.'

'I know what you mean,' he granted.

I saw him off on a gravel truck, my feelings about his proposed posting very mixed.

Next morning our crew appeared on the Battle Order; we were to borrow a wireless operator. At briefing I could sense Geoff's concern, but he confined his comments to a later entry in his diary:

The idea was to bomb a little village south of Cologne (of no military importance) from below 2000 ft., shoot up anything or anybody you saw, irrespective of whether they were women or children. In fact, the whole raid was in contravention of the one thing we are supposed to be fighting against – barbarism. ... It's entirely against my idea of the just conduct of war. ...

We waited in B under low cloud. At the last moment 103 Squadron's part in the operation was cancelled. We were dismayed that one aircraft – that of P/O Harry Smith – was dispatched alone: minelaying to Denmark. We were disturbed to see them go off into the murk we had escaped. In the morning we heard they had not returned. Forty-two years later I received a letter from a young Dane, Peter Lund, telling of their fate:

On the evening of December 17 1942 a Lancaster was shot down over South Jutland, Denmark, by a German night fighter. The Lancaster, on a minelaying operation in Danish waters, came from 103 Squadron and had the serial number W4786. The 7 man crew was killed ...

From my father and neighbours around I've often heard the stories about the crash which took place only 2 miles from my father's and later, my own home. ...

On their way to the target the bomber was engaged by a German night fighter in the area around Esbjerg. During the fight the Lancaster turned west and started to burn. ... A few hundred yards from the farmhouse the Lancaster, by now almost enveloped in flames, turned slightly to port and seconds later hit flat ground about 100 yards west of the farm buildings. It seems as if Pilot Officer Smith saw the light from the farmhouse and managed to steer his crippled Lancaster away from the buildings ...

About one and a half minutes after impact the mine load exploded and spread the wreckage and its contents over a wide area. ... The bomber crew was buried at the cemetery in Abenras with attendance from the Danish police and other authorities. A German Guard of Honour saluted at the funeral.

The writer listed the dead crew. Although there were seven men – the normal complement of a Lancaster – the crew composition was unusual. Two non-aircrew W/T operators of the RCAF were carried and there was no bombaimer. I could only conclude that minelaying had been the crew's secondary role, that primarily they had been involved in radar or radio detection and jamming, work of which the rest of us knew nothing. It may well have been that they were making early investigation into V2 developments at Peenemunde.

Although Smith's was the only aircraft lost of fifty sent mine-laying along the enemy coast, the night had been very costly in other operations. According to Middlebrook & Everitt, forty-nine additional aircraft had been sent to bomb small German towns in the manner we were to have done – this included a well-warranted attack on the Opel works at Fallersleven; seventeen failed to return, a loss rate of 34.7%.

Briefing next day promised something equally disturbing. Political pressure was being exerted – by Churchill we were told – to mine the mouth of the Garonne. It lay roughly as far away as Berlin, but we knew that at the end we would be groping at low level, in bad weather, trying to locate the river mouth. Navigators had joined four charts vertically to cover the route. Visibility at Elsham as take-off drew near was fifty yards; added to this, final briefing became a scene of confusion because of last-minute route changes. In the crewroom, as navigators were urged to finish their work and be ready to leave, indignation came close to boiling over. Suddenly the operation was cancelled; instead of being urged to the aircraft we were told we could go to the cinema. But the confusion seemed to have infected even the movie projectionist; the sound-track was impossibly garbled. All our pent-up indignation burst out in catcalls and a shrill blowing of dinghy whistles*. As it was still early, I walked out, caught a bus to Scunthorpe and took Betty to a dance at the Crosby and forgot about being 'pals only' .

That Sunday Ted Batten and I went to church with Jack Jefferies and Ian Robb, navigator and wireless operator of

---

* Whistles carried on the battledress collar. If a crew survived ditching in the sea, these could be used to attract rescuers' attention.

Bayliss's crew. We flung ourselves wholeheartedly into Christmas carols, Magor at the organ; toward the end of the service we were called to navigators' briefing for Duisburg.

For us this operation was a turning point; it was as if the crew had come of age. We took as wireless operator Flg Off Nicholson, an experienced man we would have been happy to have kept. The whole flight was in brilliant moonlight, so brilliant that it exposed the scores of attacking aircraft. Geoff reckoned the traffic like Piccadilly Circus.

We sighted six nightfighters, most of them I'm glad to say, were going in the opposite direction. ... During the whole of the trip Don's navigation was superb, we were on track all the way. ...

Navigationally the short trip had been undemanding, but, after Esbjerg, it put heart into me. The Command's losses were 5.2%, among them the crew of a popular 103 Canadian, Flt Sgt Moriarty. His had been one of the crews already at Elsham when we arrived, so that we had thought of them as old-timers, less vulnerable than we were. Flt Sgt Johnnie Roper, one of the more experienced RAF pilots, had failed to get off; he had reported his engines to be over-heating. The Wing Commander refused to accept his excuse and, in the morning, ordered Geoff to test fly the aircraft, a task he found thoroughly repugnant.

... we took it to the end of the runway with motors running abnormally hot, turned into wind, opened the throttles, but instead of cooling off, the radiator and oil temps. rose and the oil pressure dropped. I taxied the machine back to dispersal. In my opinion it [would have been] foolhardy to take off, especially with a bomb load. There was something radically wrong. ... It was a downright insult to Roper.

There was a sequel to this. When we went out next evening to take our own plane to Munich, we found technicians working feverishly on the blind-flying panel. We waited for them to finish, then Geoff did his run-up. The panel was still unserviceable. We hastened to the spare aircraft; it turned out to be Roper's J Johnnie. It had no guns in the turrets, nor had it been air-tested since Geoff had reported its deficiencies. As there were only five minutes left until last permissible time of take-off, there was nothing we could do but go back to the crewroom.

Next day, the Wing Commander ordered Geoff and Doug to his office to explain the aborted operation.

> ... [He] hauled me over the coals for not taking off. My blood boiled. To think that anyone with an atom of sanity should condemn me for my action. It is impossible to fly without instruments when we had so much cloud to contend with. I looked the swine up and down and then said, 'Excuse me sir, but are you suggesting that I and my crew are lacking in moral fibre?' He hummed and hawed and gave me no satisfaction. ... I'm not going to let the matter drop at this. No man, no matter how many rings he may carry on his arm, is going to cast any aspersions on my name and get away with it. I'm going to ask for an interview with the Group Captain tomorrow. Doug was a real brick. He ... endeavoured to explain the technical side of the defect. It still didn't sink in. ...

When Geoff demanded an interview with the Group Captain to seek redress of grievance, the accusations were withdrawn.

All this was insignificant compared with the outcome of the Munich operation. Geoff wrote:

> Only one machine returned to base last night, the remaining seven landed all over England. Col Bayliss and Col Rose are missing, in the two crews four good Aussies have gone – how, nobody knows – weather most probably. All the crews had a rough time from both fighters and flak. Jock Greig was shot up, to return

153

*on three engines. Douglas shot down an ME 110 over the target.
They had the same trouble as last night – could see far too much;
it was like daylight.*

We heard of the night's losses first thing in the morning.
Bayliss, like Cook and Laing, had been on the same pilots'
course as Geoff in Western Australia. Jack Jefferies, Bayliss's
navigator, had a wife in Australia; their wireless operator, Ian
Robb, an enthusiastic young perfectionist, a heartbreak among
the girls, had lived near my family. I decided to pick up his
more personal belongings.

When I crossed to the barracks, men from the Committee of
Adjustment were already at the door. I did not envy them their
task of bundling up belongings of missing crews, but knew
full well that most Australians preferred friends to look after
personal possessions – diaries especially. So I asked if I might
send Robb's diary to his mother. This they agreed to, provided
I handed it into safekeeping if I went on operations before I
could mail it. When we then went together into the barracks,
there came a moment like an episode from a second rate
movie: at Robb's bed one of the men switched on his light; his
radio also came on – Richard Tauber singing 'Just a little love
a little kiss.'

Loss of Ian Robb made me realize how foolish I had been to
send my mother the names of other mothers – seven or eight
of them – whose sons were operating while I was. My thought
had been of the mutual support I imagined they would
provide each other. In the end only two of their sons survived.

It came as a relief to be ordered to Topcliffe, northwest of
York, to pick up Greig's crew; they had crash-landed there
after the operation; a night fighter had set one engine on fire
and shot away a tyre.

Munich had proved a bitter experience on many squadrons; overall losses ran to 8.8%. Middlebrook & Everitt show
the attack to have been a virtually useless; the force of 137

aircraft had bombed open fields, probably misled by decoy fires.

Months after the raid we heard there had been one survivor from the two crews lost from 103: Colin Bayliss. Their aircraft had been fatally attacked by a nightfighter. Bayliss was one moment straining on the control column; the next, falling through the air amid burning wreckage while he groped for his parachute release.*

On Christmas Eve we were briefed again for Turin. When the operation was cancelled, a madness descended on the station. On Christmas morning the sergeants were entertained in the officers' mess, then a mildly inebriated group went on with the next part of the tradition – the serving of Christmas dinner to 'other ranks' by officers and NCOs. Down the full length of their mess, beery jollity reigned, faces flaming like Christmas puddings. The ORs linked arms, swaying to the station band as they sang 'Bless 'em All'.

When we left to entertain the officers in the sergeants' mess, we were a sorry lot; our mess became a shambles. In half an inch of beer a sergeant wrestled a Flight Lieutenant to determine whose crew was the better; someone was baling out off the mantelpiece; the singing had become tuneless and maudlin.

By evening I was glad of clear, cold air as Frank Holmes led me on our bicycles down moonlit lanes to Brigg, where Ted and Ann Batten were ensconced for a few days at the 'Black Bull.' The rest of the crew were already there and looked incapable of return. But depart they did, Black Bull tankards with them. I wrote on haggard Boxing Day,

---

* Many years after the war, Dr Colin Bayliss wote of his experiences with the French Underground and his eventual capture for the book *Aircrew for the Duration, WWII,* edited by Bruce Gaston, Harry Horner and Raymond Storer, private issue, Perth, W.A.

This life is a grotesque mixture of comedy and tragedy. At one moment one is laughing; at another one is afraid and, worst of all, there are moments, as last week when Ian Robb went, when one would find the gift of tears a blessing.

Over Christmas week dense fog set in; twice operations were announced then scrubbed. By now we had accumulated more scrubs than completed operations. I put in hours playing table tennis against Keith Webber, never once beating him, always envying him his effortless footwork and timing.

28th Dec.: How interminable these ops seem! Yet we always hope there are plenty before us. This one has been another rush for navigators, as Command decided that we'd prepare two areas in case of one being scrubbed. ... Later: Once again – scrubbed. So it goes on. ... I am sitting in Keith's room – we have been talking Air Force life. ... [He] gets pretty down about things.

Keith wrote that night:

We are still fogbound – thank Heaven. It at least gives us a respite from ops and briefing. Everything wet and clammy. Visibility about 50 yards – no more ... How I wish I could get to the Middle East in the warm sunshine ...

At our Christmas dance in the sergeant's mess, I met a Waaf whom I had wanted to know for weeks past. We danced together and I found her easy to talk to. I began taking her after that to the station cinema and would walk her home to the Waafery, a five-mile round journey. I only knew Joan – as I called her in *No Moon Tonight* – for a matter of months, but they were months that became a life within a life.

I wrote home on December 30:

Snow is falling quietly, filling every crevice and corner outside this warm mess. ... It blankets the world so unobtrusively and so peacefully. The crunch of it underfoot today has reminded me of many an exciting moment shared with Nell. Sharing anything with her was always something of an adventure. ... Odd that I should be writing fondly of my Canadian memories when tonight I take Betty to see 'The Great Mr. Handel' and tomorrow night go out with Joan to a New Year's Eve party. Geoff tells me I'm going to the dogs.

The party was at the Waafery. In the girls' mess the dining tables had been folded, the forms pushed to the walls; they had decorated the place with streamers and sprigs of holly; most had invited a partner from our RAF village on the wolds. There was snow to the very door – not a night for escape to haystacks, let alone to Gallows Wood, stripped bare of leaves. An orchestra had been hired; it sobbed out, 'I'll be Loving You', 'Jealousy' , 'Wish me Luck' . We not only held partners, we held the permanence they represented. Like the country-side around us, they would see out 1943, see out the war.

At the end we clasped hands for 'Auld Lang Syne' , surging forward, reeling back. The glances men exchanged said more about the incoming year than they would ever put into words to each other. Only to Joan could I mention the shadows.

In our room Geoff speculated in his diary on the new year with a spirit more resolute than mine:

Will I marry? I would like to – perhaps it would act as a deterrent for my insatiable desire for action – it engulfs me like a huge ocean wave. And yet I won't be sorry when my ops are over. We all have some fears when the words, 'The enemy coast is coming up now navigator' , come to our ears over the intercom. I have no illusions as to what 1943 may bring ...

Across the room I was writing home:

Geoff is a splendid room mate. He is a real man and has tons of courage in everything he does. ...

I always felt positive in his company, even when afraid. At twenty-seven I was one of the older aircrew, sharply aware of all that hung over us in the days ahead.

157

15
Nineteen Forty-Three

And so another year unfolds. New Year's Day. At home the Show Ground will be skirling to the sound of the pipes, races I suppose at Randwick, surfing at the beaches – cricket, tennis and what have you. Ye Gods! We have had incessant rain, low clouds and high wind. Everything is wet and muddy. (Keith Webber: letter to brother)

In our room Geoff and I were writing New Year letters beside our stove, taking breaks for sustenance – hampers had reached us from Australia. Outside, rain and wind buffeted the long, flimsy building.

> *Geoff is now making the toast … During these days we eat, sleep and do little. Consequently our morale – at least, mine – suffers. Life is easy and ops appear very black. The best thing for morale is a successful op.*

The bare boards of our floor were swept and our daily quota of coal and coke brought to us by a Leading Aircraftman, an 'hasthmatic' member of the lower orders whom Geoff, with his propensity for derogatory nicknames dubbed 'Buggerlugs'. We took it in turns to give him half a crown. Geoff would shake his head, murmuring, 'Some of them in this country would sell their grandmother if they were tipped enough.' But he conceded that their pay was wretchedly low.

Officers quarters were not much more comfortable than ours, but there were certain social distinctions between us: their beds were made, rooms tidied, boots cleaned by batwomen, whereas we did our own and our standards of tidiness were subject to weekly inspection.

January 3 came without so much as a briefing. Over Lincolnshire the weather had cleared; we could only conclude that over Europe it must be bad indeed for 'Butch'* not to send us out. Nevertheless, it was not bad enough to stop the Luftwaffe from making the short hop over the North Sea from their aerodromes in Holland to the mouth of the Humber. At the cinema that evening we heard gunfire over the soundtrack. No one moved to go out. Keith Webber was just leaving the mess when the attack began.

Flares were dropping over Grimsby. Searchlights in dozens probed the sky and flak burst spasmodically. Over the thump of the guns we could hear the bombs. After a while the flak started bursting over the 'drome and going off with a crump. ... I wish our targets were such a piece of cake ...

In the morning I met our replacement wireless operator, a permanent RAF Flying Officer who had already logged forty operations and wore a well-merited DFM. I looked on him with admiration and was glad it fell my lot to teach him use of Gee. I soon found his attitude arrogant. However tactfully I phrased my instruction he accepted it reluctantly. I expressed a doubt to Geoff that would he would fit into our crew; Geoff's reply was that we would soon 'straighten him out.'

His first operation with us came on January 4th, which was also our first experience of a new form of attack on the Ruhr; the target was Essen. It was explained at briefing that Pathfinder Mosquitoes would mark the target accurately through use of a navigational aid code-named Oboe. A system of pulses transmitted from Britain, then re-transmitted back from the aircraft would allow precise positioning. The Mosquitoes would drop either red markers on the ground, code-named Parramatta, or, if the ground were obscured, sky

---

* Air Marshal Sir Arthur Harris. He was sardonically nicknamed 'Butch' for his demands on aircrew, rather than his area bombing of the enemy.

markers, code-named Wanganui. Whichever marker was used we must bomb with the greatest possible accuracy at a pre-determined heading and speed; our altitude on bombing was not to be below 20,000 feet. 103 Squadron's altitude en route was to be 23,500.

We were unaware that the Pathfinders, under Air Vice-Marshal D.C.T. Bennett, had been experimenting with Oboe on operations for nearly a month. Ultimately its use would bring accuracy to the bombing of nearer targets, especially to the bombing of the Ruhr. Obviously such accurate marking would be wasted if main-force crews failed to bomb the markers. Although the range of Oboe did not extend much beyond the Ruhr, we were witnessing a great turning of the tide in the Bomber Command war.

Briefing was more than usually tense. We were told frankly that the technique was still experimental, that nineteen 5 Group Lancasters had gone out to Essen the previous night; they had bombed markers put down by three Mosquitoes and had suffered 16% losses. In our case, twenty-nine Lancasters were going out; again, Mosquitoes would be marking. The meteorologist warned us of icing – we would be in cloud most of the way; the target would almost certainly be marked by sky-markers. The forecast wind at cruising level was a west-erly of 110 mph. We had never before planned for such a wind. When the Group Captain uttered his usual, 'Good luck chaps', I fancied he was looking at us as if we were condemned men.

Take-off was early – soon after 5 pm. Two of our aircraft failed to get off, then, outward bound, the experienced 'Bunny' Austin had to abandon the operation when M mother iced up badly over Holland. As I wrote next day, our own fortunes were little better.

Over the Zuider Zee, dead on track and on time, Shag's oxygen supply failed through a break in the line. Our altitude was 23,500 feet, so he went out like a candle. When Doug was trying to get him our of the rear turret, his guns started firing, so there we were over the Zuider Zee, one of the worst nightfighter areas, minus a rear gunner and our guns blazing ... As we could not bomb below 20,000, we just had to clear out. We went out the way we came in and, crossing the coast, dived down to 12,000 feet. Shag revived quickly – fortunately, for a fighter followed us. ... The Group Captain approved Geoff's decision and the doc. said Shag could have lasted only half an hour and got away with it. Our temporary wireless op ... proved of no help at all and was confoundedly high and mighty. He wanted us to drop our 4000 lb. bomb on an aerodrome in Holland. We wouldn't consider doing so.

Despite these individual setbacks – in our case rotation of the turret had somehow cut off Shag's oxygen – the raid had been a success; the Battle of the Ruhr had begun. If any targets could be morally justified, these could be, especially as there was now a much better prospect of achieving accuracy.

Next morning, while I was taking my turn under the ray lamp – Doc Henderson's remedy for lack of sunshine – Blue Freeman came to tell me he was organizing a get-together of our Canadian training course; it was to be at 'The Elephant' in Doncaster that evening. Since there was a stand-down, we would be able to stay the night.

Eighteen of our twenty had begun training for Bomber Command. At this stage, four months later, our one casualty was Joe Turnbull, killed on take-off at Lichfield. Nine of the remaining seventeen were able to meet. Our quartet from Elsham booked into 'The Angel': Freeman, Webber, Wright, Charlwood.

It was like a reunion of brothers; not a moment was wasted as we caught up with each other's news. The big, golden-hearted Tom McNeill had come with Max Bryant from the Conversion Unit at Lindholme; three others had come from

161

460 Squadron at Breighton: George Loder, companion of my walk through Scotland; the gentle Bill Charlton, who was still airsick on nearly every flight, and Ron Pender, soon to become our only prisoner of war after being shot down over Berlin. The 12 Squadron men, Wilf Burrows and Col Miller, had not been able to get away, but we learned that Wilf, with thirteen operations, had logged more than any of us. Nor had Tib Barker and Johnnie Gordon been able to get up from 467 Squadron, away south in Nottinghamshire.

Max Bryant was elated by the gathering:

The talk was fast and furious, everyone gabbling at once. ... The tankards were on the move. Bill C. even had one to celebrate the occasion!

Several times the men asked after Nell. Were we still in touch? How was she? What news was there of Edmonton? Max listened to my answers, with an amused, sceptical air. He and Tom McNeill decided to stay the night, Tom with Blue and Harry, Max with Keith and me. When we three left for the Angel, the other trio showed every sign of 'pressing on' beyond closing time.

Keith and I pushed our single beds together to fit Max in. For an hour we regaled him with ops tales, while he confided the discords still plaguing his crew. We were becoming drowsy when a din began outside; it sounded as if a party of huntsmen were urging reluctant horses up the steps of the hotel, hallooing as they came.

The voices were unmistakably those of Tom, Blue and Harry, all in high good humour. But their tone all at once changed and we heard a scuffle. Harry's aggrieved voice rose above the others, 'I don't like being pushed around!' And a warning from Blue, 'Take your hands off him – he's my mate!' And Tom's bass, 'Get your hands off me – I'll give you three – one, two, three!' followed by a *thud*. Doors along our corridor were opened uneasily, but after a crescendo outside everything subsided and we heard crestfallen footfalls past our door. I must have looked at my watch every hour for the rest of the night as I had undertaken to wake our party at 5.30.

When I made my way in the dark to the other room I was surprised to find the light on. Tom and Blue were lying under it, trying to share a single bed. There was no sign of Harry; in his bed was another Australian whom I recognized as Frank Falkenmire. All were asleep.

Shaking Blue's shoulder I said, 'Where's Harry?'

Without opening his eyes he replied, 'In gaol on four charges', as if this were not an untoward place to be.

Taking a few seconds to digest the news, I said, 'Well, we'd better get going – the train leaves at 6.15.'

'Can't,' replied Blue, eyes still closed. 'Tom and I have to appear in court at 10 o'clock.' 'Oh well,' I replied uncertainly, 'good luck.'

I switched off their light and left them. Tom and Frank Falkenmire hadn't so much as wakened.

Max saw Keith and me off at the station. An hour later we began the walk from Barnetby to Elsham in a chill dawn, Keith setting a cracking pace uphill on a road frozen at the centre, slushy at the edges. Dyspeptic he might have been, but his balance was much surer than mine. I arrived at our room breathless and irritable. At least there were to be no ops.

Harry made his entry to the mess at lunchtime to a chorus of boos and hisses. As a ten-ops man he was an old identity and affectionately regarded. He was oblivious to the fact that someone had stuck a piece of paper on his back: CONVICT 99. Frowsy from the past night, he looked the part. His story was demanded, but all he seemed to know was that they had been involved in fisticuffs with the local police. Their charges were to be heard the following week.

Relationships with our new wireless operator worsened; he regarded us with disdain. Admittedly we were not remarkable for our polish. Geoff complained to Kennard and the Flying Officer was transferred to another crew. It was their misfortune to be lost three months later. Our replacement this time was Flt Sgt Graham Briggs, DFM, whose Leicestershire accent and idiom left him safe from RAF commissioning. He was a quiet rebel with challenging eyes who fitted easily into our crew. He made one request of us: when we met Gwen, his wife, would we avoid letting her know he was back on ops? He first flew with us on January 9, the target again Essen. I found his composure and helpfulness a tremendous boost.

> I have never worked so hard as on this trip. The met. wind was wrong and we quickly blew north of track. I had to get Geoff to raise all the speed he could. We crossed into Holland on time. The whole Ruhr was ablaze with searchlights and flak. I had to admire Geoff and Ted. Our aiming point was surrounded by a box of flak, but they got their bombs home. ... Geoff was an inspiration. When things are really bad he is very calm, even though fighting the controls every inch of the way. Ted, lying face down in the nose, said it didn't seem possible that we could get through. He was watching the flashes of the guns and counting, wondering when our shell was coming. It wasn't possible to see the ground detail for searchlights, gun flashes and fires. I was coldly afraid ... waiting, waiting, waiting for sudden oblivion. But soon the flak was behind us and before long we were winging over the North Sea unscathed. Navigationally it was my best trip yet. Missing ... was Sgt Reg Morris a 'pretty' lad of 20 ... Such news on our return is more shaking than the Ruhr flak.

By 'pretty' I did not imply lack of manliness; Morris was still a callow English schoolboy, his body slight, his complexion fresh, his manner deferential. The Wing Commander had censured him for an earlier failure to get off. Noticing his dejection at briefing, I had urged him to back his own judgement.

According to Middlebrook & Everitt, Essen reported 'concentrated bombing in or near the centre with 127 buildings destroyed or seriously damaged and 28 people killed.' Twenty-one aircrew were lost.

There are lots of new faces in the mess. It does not do to pause and remember that we are veterans now – and only quarter way through our ops. But somehow one learns to shrug at such things.

Not long after our return heavy snow began to fall and much of next day passed in inter-flight snowball battles, the flight commanders leading, Jake Kennard urging us on like Harry at Agincourt. Next morning, January 11, we were briefed for a new approach on Essen – we were to come in from the south.

This time cloud cover was so complete that we bombed on Pathfinder sky markers. Inexplicably, the Gee remained clear to 5 degrees East, facilitating our way as we passed between Cologne and Dusselfdorf. I was by now beginning to know the flak dispositions and to find them useful pinpoints, sometimes the only pinpoints. We returned to a jubilant station; not one our crews was missing. Laing's F Freddy had suffered partial oxygen failure. Keith Webber wrote:

The rear gunner gradually became less and less clear until, at the rendezvous, he was practically out. I was horribly sluggish and panting. I knew what I had to do but couldn't do it. Decided to turn back. In the meantime Doug [Williams – bombaimer] had fallen asleep ...

Our B – Beer had not long been fitted with a device called 'Mandrel'; what its purpose was we were not told, but Geoff made the observation that searchlights seeking us appeared to 'fall all over the sky'. On the other hand, we suspected that night fighters were homing on it. We heard long after that its purpose was radar-jamming.

To everyone's relief the charges laid by the police on the night of our course reunion were dropped. Max rejoiced,

> The Goddess of Luck seems very partial to our old 20. Somehow I've always felt we'd be a lucky crowd. Poor Joe's passing was the worst of bad luck.

None of us thought the fracas mattered much. Tensions so built up that lightning flashes in pubs were inevitable. As a CO of 460 Squadron put it, 'The boys who get into scrapes in pubs are the ones least likely to crack up.' Tom and Blue, accustomed to the hurly-burly of their differing codes of football, were quick to leap into physical action. If clashing with policemen was not a civilized pastime, neither was bombing civilians. Harry had been an easier mark. He was thin and elongated and had not the physical attributes to back his verbal attacks; on the other hand – as his operational career soon proved – he possessed extraordinary courage and staying power. His main outlet in our Elsham days was to immerse himself in *War and Peace*, which he carried down his battle-dress tunic. All of us had our differing outlets. I wrote voluminously, but could no longer settle to read. I enjoyed nothing more than to walk Joan back to the Waafery after the cinema.

> Often I have shuddered at the emotionless clear sky that has afforded us little protection on ops; but one becomes curiously volatile in this life. At 6.0 pm a clear sky may appear cold and heartless, then ops are scrubbed and one sees the beauty of the stars and life seems enjoyable. ... Walking to Barnetby [tonight], the skies were friendly and the world seemed pleasant. It was not necessary to think of the war till tomorrow. Underfoot the road was glassy with ice, ... We went to the Station Hotel. It was packed with warm and singing humanity. ... At 10.0 the pub was

cleared, but as Joan did not have to go in till 12.0, we walked on.
She said, 'I shall show you the Saxon church.' We walked on
through the village streets. They were dark and empty and very
quiet. We passed a farm and smelt the pungent smell of cow yards
and stables. A dance band throbbed somewhere. Our road led up
a hill between bare, black trees and on the hilltop stood the church.
We saw only a square black tower against the expanse of stars.
The churchyard was white with snow. ... I left Joan at the
Waafery and walked on alone ... at last a voice called, 'Halt! Who
goes there?' The guard recognized me – I being a veteran of four
months on the squadron. As he said, 'Goodnight sarg,' I felt that
sergeant was a pleasant sort of rank. ...

On January 12, with leave two days off, we were briefed a
fourth time for Essen, take-off 3 am next day. After this long
wait we failed to get off; B had an unserviceable port inner
engine. Geoff and Doug put up arguments for a new one, but
were over-ruled and we went irritably to bed; four and a half
hours later, we were called for briefing – again to Essen. The
ground crew were working hard on B's doubtful engine, but
we found we were not listed to take it; it was to be flown by Sgt.
B. E. Atwood of 12 Squadron; for some reason his crew was
attached to 103 for one night. We were to take L. It was a
measure of our superstition that we preferred to risk B than
take L – Max Burcher had been wounded in L. The Wing
Commander probably believed he was giving us the more
reliable aircraft, nevertheless, Geoff confronted him.

Had a row with the Wg Cdr about B. He had us down for L. I
refused point blank to take her ... we had been shot up twice in this
machine. Eventually the Wg Cdr came my way. ... On run up
everything was beautiful; taxied to the runway and still the
gauges were normal. On take-off I noticed an unusual big swing
to port; corrected it the best I could and hauled her off the deck at

120 mph. Shag called up to say that bags of smoke was pouring from the port inner. A moment later the motor caught on fire. Doug feathered it immediately. We weren't a hundred feet off the deck, indicated airspeed less than 120. Things looked black. I levelled out, trimmed for the swing and built the speed up for climb. Once I had her up to 1000 ft. I knew the danger was past. As a matter of fact, with a full load of bombs and petrol she performed remarkably well. Jettisoned our cargo at sea, came back and made a perfect landing. Compliments were thrown at me from right and left, even from the Wg Cdr. He said we'd earned our leave. They all thought we were going in when they saw parts dropping off on the runway. Atwood in L failed to return. Greig had a shaky trip, shot up by flak and a night fighter. Dave Lowther had a cannon shell through his leg. ...

Poor Atwood's crew seemed fated either way. Had they taken B, it is unlikely he would have been ready for loss of an engine on take-off. Doug's log entry read: 'Piston trouble causing con rod through sump.' Frank Holmes young sister, who delivered newspapers to the camp, told us that Brigg fire brigade had turned out and were heading to the point where they expected us to crash.

If our threat had been sudden oblivion, Kennard had experienced more protracted tension. He had taken Laing's F Freddie and struck the same partial oxygen failure as Laing had experienced. He tried limiting the supply to himself and the navigator, but was forced to fly lower than the main stream of bombers. His petrol cocks froze and all four motors cut over the North Sea. He was preparing to ditch when the engineer succeeded in hammering the pipes free of ice; the engines picked up and they reached home.

This was the last tale we heard before going on leave.

16

Laing's Crew

Outpaced, outmanoeuvred and outgunned by the German night fighters and in a generally highly inflammable and explosive condition, these black monsters presented an ideal target to any fighter who could find them, and it was the night fighters which caused the overwhelming majority of the losses sustained by Bomber Command (Webster and Frankland: *The Strategic Air Offensive against Germany, 1939-45*)

Doug, on his way home to Penarth, ran me by car to Bristol and I went on to Burnham-on-Sea. During that leave I did little more than sleep and eat and linger in hot baths and yarn with Nora and Stella of Australia, of my parents, of anything but war. But while I luxuriated, there were two raids on Berlin. Losses on the second were 11.8%; among those missing from 12 Squadron were two from our course of Edmonton – trained navigators. Max Bryant heard the news of them well before I did.

> *Both Wilf [Burrows] and Col Miller are missing from the second trip to Berlin. Their passing is even more unreal than Joe's; it just isn't possible to realize they have gone on. I dread the thought of Don or Bill going; every time we hear on the news that so many aircraft are missing, the hateful query pops up in our mind.*

Wilf Burrows, from our table on the *Monterey*; Col Miller, school teacher of Coleraine. Col's pilot was Doug Morphett of Geoff's course. According to Middlebrook & Everitt, no important damage was done to Berlin.

On the way back from leave, Doug picked me up in Gloucester. Having heard percentage losses on the second Berlin raid, the same thing was on both our minds: how had 103 fared? Mostly we were concerned for Laing's crew. To our relief we found them safe, though, for unwell Keith Webber, it had been an exhausting week:

Jan. 16th: ... the target was Berlin. ... Took off in shocking weather; low cloud and visibility about 500 yards. Everyone thought it would be scrubbed. ... What shook us was the vapour trails we were leaving – and in bright moonlight. The most amazing thing – we didn't see a fighter. ... The whole way we encountered Lancs. ... We had 8 legs before hitting the target. ... We ran through some fierce flak and dropped our incendiaries. On the way out we ran into some fearful muck – very accurate. One burst under us turned the machine into a dive and the engines cut for a moment. I reached for my 'chute but couldn't put it on for the centrifugal force. It was minutes before we got clear. ... I was feeling sickish besides, ... I feel so tired that I could throw my pencil down. In this game you just can't afford to relax.

When they arrived back they turned in at 3 am.

... wakened at 11:30 ... by the Tannoy telling all navigators to be in the nav. room for briefing at 12:30. The game was on again – the same place. ... Another rushed briefing. We got out to F but it wasn't ready. ... We were switched to W ... There was a lot wrong with this job, too, but it was being rushed through – rear turret, front turret etc. When the engines were started there was a mag. drop of 300 revs. Definitely US so we didn't get off. The only one not to out of a dozen. When they took off tonight it was raining with low cloud about 300 feet and visibility of 500 yards. ...

The weather deteriorated so badly for the return that 103 aircraft landed wherever they could get in; by daybreak there were only three crews on the station, Laing's included.

... we were horribly shaken when told that eight aircraft were going on a nuisance raid. ... No one in authority was unduly concerned where the bombs were to be dropped, ... so long, we were told, that a noise of aircraft was heard over enemy territory giving them the idea that another raid was on the way. ... It had been thick fog here all day. ... We were to be diverted to a place in the north of Scotland... were just about to go out to the aircraft when word came through that ops were scrubbed. ...

Laing's crew were packed ready to go on leave when our crew returned; Keith in particular looked ready for it. I slept alone in our room that night; Geoff was due in from London first thing in the morning. When he arrived, he did not look exactly refreshed – and there were to be ops that night. To our dismay Laing's crew was also shown on the Battle Order, this to make up numbers, as one crew had still not reached Elsham after the second Berlin raid. Geoff was ready for bed rather than ops.

Just as well it was only to Essen; if it had been a long trip, I don't know how I would have coped. Had no sleep last night and besides, a week in London is no rest, not the way we did it at anyrate. Shag hadn't returned from leave. ... we had to borrow a Canadian gunner from another crew. ... clouds right up to 20,000 ft. The moon was very bright – a good night for night fighters. ...

Three separate interceptions were made on us. One, an ME 210, I think, was down below and in front. He spotted us and was about to turn and try to effect an attack from the beam. I kept on his tail and went into a steep turn with him; by doing this I got behind where he couldn't see me and then did a steep diving turn the other way, into cloud. The second one came as I was orbiting. He got on our tail and chased me north. I turned in towards him and lost him by going into cloud again. I think it was either a Focke Wulf or an ME 110. The third attack was made from

171

beneath. I turned down towards him, and luckily for us, another Lanc came along and nearly collided with the fighter. ...

Navigationally I found the trip straightforward, but had no doubt we were fortunate to have eluded the fighters:

Geoff's splendid flying shook them off and cloud over there helped us. We picked up a bit of ice, but not sufficient to be dangerous. A Canadian rear gunner flew with us – his first op – and did a really good job. On landing one engine cut, but Geoff brought us in safely.

All this seemed of small moment when we got back. Two crews were missing. One was Burgess's, on their second operation; the other was Laing's. Always on our return from ops Geoff listened for Ted Laing's deep, husky voice in F Freddie.

Tonight I listened in vain. I feel rotten about it as Ted was one of the whitest men I know. They were supposed to have gone on leave at lunch time, but no! the bloody fool of a Wg Cdr ... must send them. Keith was sick and reported the fact, but still they were sent. Somehow I had a feeling they wouldn't be coming back, even before we set out. Ted's crew was the most popular on the station. ... Out of the four Aussie crews in our intake, there's only 'Cooky' and myself left. ... Ted took off over half an hour after us, and even then I believe one of the motors was shaky. If that was the case, he shouldn't have gone.

But Ted, having been censured for failure to get off on the second Berlin operation, flew on, though he knew stragglers were easy prey for night fighters. It was their eighth operation. If loss of them was a blow to Geoff and me, it was even more so to Doug who roomed with Tony Willis, their engineer.

When we came away from interrogation, Geoff went to Ted's room and I to Keith's to pick up their more personal belongings. Keith had roomed with Doug Williams, the crew's RAAF bombaimer.

Their fire was burning cheerfully, closed up so that they would have a warm room upon their return.

In the morning a friend of Keith's handed me a note from him asking me to do what I already had done. His last diary entry was on January 19:

We are trying to hang out until Thursday when we go on leave. Living from day to day bears one down. The whole business is just sheer strain. ...

In 1946 a letter reached Keith's mother from a citizen of Enschede, Holland:

[Your son] was killed while his plane was shot down by a night fighter abt. 10 miles from this town, while flying into Germany. This happened at 1930 in the evening of January 21st 1943. I was present at the place where this happened. ...

A local family took over care of his grave:

We can assure you that we shall watch over it as if it was that of our own son. In this way, we, the Dutch people, can compensate a little bit of our thanks towards our allied friends who gave their life for the liberation of our country. ...

The father of Stan Brewer, F Freddie's mid-upper gunner, wrote from England to the Webber family:

... I wish it were possible to thank you all personally for sharing with the old country its sorrows and trials. To those of us who think, we know the enormous efforts put out by Australia during the time when her sons were so badly required near home and real danger was near.

For us, life on 103 Squadron could never be the same.

Shag returned a day late from leave and was on the mat. In the crew we did not ask reasons for his absence; we felt sure it concerned his wife. She was intensely anxious, nor was all going well with her pregnancy.

The triple loss from our old training course in as many days left me stunned and bewildered. As well, Geoff had lost, in Laing and Morphett, two of the pilots he most admired from his own training course. There was unreality about it. In groups of seven, crews vanished from what was otherwise an almost normal life. We were not like a battalion, a company or even a platoon. In action *esprit de corps* existed between only seven men, who were mostly out of sight of each other. In off-duty hours we talked with others; even so, the composition of the squadron was changing so constantly that we tended to mix only with our few contemporaries, or listen to the fewer surviving stalwarts who had begun operating before we had reached the station; to us they were like older boys at school.

It seemed to me in those winter days that even the gramophone records most played in the mess reflected our mood. There was a popularized version of Chopin's *Fantasie Impromptu* beginning, 'I'm forever chasing rainbows -'; another from the first movement of Tschaikovsky's *Pathetique* beginning, 'This is the story of a starry night.' And always the sombre *Warsaw Concerto*. More haunting than any of them was the Chopin Etude we knew as *Deep is the Night*. They were pieces without hope.

17
Hours of our Days

Looking at the blackboard in the flight office you see that your name and the name of your crew is down for operations that night and you feel as if someone has hit you in the stomach. After that you live through the day in a comatose state, you are neither really alive or dead, you wander around, doing the daily inspection of the aircraft, you wait for your briefing, you are waiting subconsciously to go there, get it over and get back. (Geoff Parnell, quoted by Norman Longmate in *The Bombers*, Hutchinson, London, 1983)

Gradually we became accustomed to the pattern of operational days. I see us in the plain hut Geoff and I shared, the half-light of dull morning in our room. After ops we sleep late, but by the time Doug comes in with his cry, 'We're on again tonight,' I am already half wakened by voices and footfalls and the radios of ground crew men nearby and the hiss of occasional cars passing on the wet road outside. Doug's words bring a hollow, taut feeling, but I'm learning to accept it; it will remain till we take off in six or eight or twelve hours. It eases once we set about our tasks in the air. Should the op be scrubbed, as half of them are, this feeling fairly explodes in us, then we want only to rush off to Scunthorpe.

Our stove has long gone out. I stand on my bed to dress, avoiding contact with the chill floor. Geoff shows no inclination to move; he asks me to look at the weather. I draw back our blackout curtains on a scene opaque and melancholy – low cloud, its underside touching the bare tree tops of the opposite wood; snow slush on the narrow road; the breath of each muffled passer-by rising into the general mistiness. I still have moments after waking when I feel we have been caught in a

175

situation monstrous and unbelievable. Sometimes I see the eyes in my family photograph on me and my mind swings to Frankston, to beach scenes, bush, to sanity.

Ted drifts in, already dressed and scarfed against the cold. He sniffs, blows his nose. 'They've allowed a half-hour early lunch for navigators and bombaimers. ...'

At lunch I sit with Ted and Harry Wright; Blue Freeman is far removed in the officers' mess. As we eat, we avoid talk of Laing's crew. We speculate on the target; mention every-day things like haircuts, books, laundry. We ride our bikes together to navigators' briefing. Most targets are in 'the Valley' just now. In a room occupied mostly by strangers I compare distances, courses and ground speeds with Harry, conscious that we used also compare results with Keith.

'See you at main briefing. ... '

The large claustrophobic room again, packed with crews; cigarette smoke rising between us and the curtain-covered map of Europe on the end wall; the line up again of principal, vice-principal, master, prefects. Kennard calls each captain by name, asking if all members of his crew are present. Our gunners, with their poaching obsession, are a constant worry, but today they have graciously arrived on time.

The curtain is drawn back from the map. 'The target for tonight, gentlemen, is Essen' – or Dusseldorf, Cologne...

Intakes of breath; restive stirrings; murmurs between crew members.

'All right met.' The fluorescent lights go out. The Waaf we call 'Epi' because she operates the epidiascope, projects a synoptic chart with isobars as tight as our knotted stomachs. No doubt about what that means – high winds which will suddenly change direction as we pass through that blue-spiked frontal line; cumulo-form clouds. A section then of the route weather: a daunting picture of fronts with piled cloud

SEVENTEEN : HOURS OF OUR DAYS

and icing levels. It always looks as if the forecaster has allowed himself full creative expression of these terrors, as if in this he finds his substitute for reality.

'Conditions here at base are likely to be deteriorating around the time of your return, but aerodromes to the west should remain reasonably clear.'

'To the west?' What might that mean? Devon? Cornwall? 'Intelligence please.'

A donnish-looking young man with the VR letters of the Volunteer Reserve on his lapels, a young man given to quips we are in no mood to laugh at.

'The Command will be attacking tonight in two waves. You are in the first, due on target 0015'

To Geoff and me that means hanging back. Someone else can light the way. We aim for a buffer ahead, a buffer behind. If, on the other hand, we are in the second wave, we keep well to the front.

Detailed target pictures then – streets, buildings, railways, a river – the point of aim marked in red. I am becoming better at shutting people out of my mind. But not ourselves, not these men around me; may we all survive. I know we shan't, of course, but it doesn't do to abandon hope.

We are to climb over base to fifteen thousand feet and rendezvous at point *A*, here at Sheringham – or Mablethorpe, or Cromer – setting course from there for point *B* on the Dutch coast at 1815. Then it's across Holland and into Germany to point *C*. 'And from point *C* a short run to the target.' It always sounds so easy – 'a short run.'

Next the Pathfinders' marking technique; the estimated numbers of light and heavy flak guns and their location; the importance of the target to German industry. Once, when we were briefed to get the ballbearing factory at Schweinfurt, VR quipped, 'Let it be said Germany was defeated through lack of balls.'

Warning now of fighter tactics.

Beside me Geoff emits an occasional 'Gawd!' to himself. He has 'Nickel' the ops. room cat, on his lap, stroking her, drawing good luck from her. She has become part of his departure routine.

The bombing leader. 'You will be carrying a 4000lb. cooky' – a nice homely name, 'cooky'; no harm to anyone in cookies – 'and ten cans of incendiaries.' He reminds us of the importance of approaching the point of aim in straight and level flight; the value of getting a good photograph. ... Admittedly we sometimes photograph fields; more often cloud covers everything. Not many get the point of aim with regularity.

The signals leader next. Graham Briggs takes notes assiduously. Flying control... So it goes on until the Wing Commander announces the times of ops meal and final briefing and utters exhortations, his face fretful, as if he anticipates aborted take-offs. Once a message came to us from the Commander-in-Chief, from 'Butch' himself. He urged us to 'bomb the black heart out of Germany!'

We have a new Groupie, Group Captain Dickens, survivor of Fairey Battles during the Battle of France, as far back, surely, as Mafeking. He wishes us good luck and we feel he means it; we like the old chap. Old? Thirty-five, perhaps.

Before we leave we are issued with flat packages about six inches square. We know what is compressed between their perspex surfaces: a map printed on silk, a small compass, wax matches, concentrated chocolate, even a fishing line, in case we bale out and become evaders in enemy territory.

Dark outside. We go to the mess and sit at tables in crews. I am sure I do not imagine the affection bestowed at ops meals on our transient group by cooks and serving staff. So soon, they know we are to pass into the dark. If we have eggs and bacon now, there might not be sufficient for another lot on our return. Better have them now. Words come unbidden to my mind, 'The condemned man ate a hearty meal...'

We drift into the ante-room, to the open fire, to read or play snooker or talk, or even sleep. There is none of the usual hilarity. Mostly I write – there at that table by the window. Always someone winds the gramophone. Why do they play pieces so full of forebodings? The mood of them is the mood of the night. I hanker for something cheering instead of sombre, tumultuous chords.

A visit by each of us to the urine-smelling ablutions. The men are engagingly frank about reasons for it: 'Better have a nervous pee!' It is comforting to know we are all feeling much the same. In one of the cubicles are a few lines of Air Force graffiti: crew rivalries; the advice, 'Don't come to 103 – you'll either crash or go missing.' Bit late to heed.

Out into the dark buttoning greatcoats, cold and rain assailing us. Geoff and I ride cautiously through the blackout to our room and there empty our pockets of personal belongings, loosen our ties in case they strangle us in the sea, Geoff dons his heavy, white, polo-necked sweater. I have no need of mine. I slip the small folder of photos – my family and Nell – down my battle-dress, then make a few last notes in my diary...

Words form in my mind at such a time – not very coherently; prayers that, in a way, transcend words. It is unreasonable to ask for survival – or so it seems to me. We are caught in too vast a web of cause and effect, spun by everyone from Hitler and Churchill to Geoff and me, by thousands in the past who have made wrong decisions. Instinctively, though, I seek strength, strength not to disintegrate, not to let the others down.

I drop my diary at Padre Ratledge's office. Regarding me with concerned eyes he says, 'Good luck, sergeant.' 'Thank you, sir.'

179

Outside the locker room I park my bike until our return, placing it in exactly the position it was in during our last trip. Since that was a 'good' trip, I must follow the same routine precisely. Inside, thirty or forty gunners are struggling to dress. Already they have on wool and silk long-sleeved singlets and 'long-johns'. They help each other into neck-to-ankle electric suits, electric foot-covers, a couple of pairs of woollen socks, the heavy aircrew sweater, fleece-lined flying suits. For Graham and me there is nothing more to do than put on Mae Wests and parachute harness and take flying helmets, ours being the only warm section of the aircraft. Geoff and Doug both wear Irvin jackets and flying boots.

A few steps through the dark to the parachute section. Each day the girls here inspect and dry and re-pack our 'chutes. Pipkin, Mellor and Spiller, who have baled out on ops and come back to us, were saved by 'chutes from here and came in to express their gratitude. Others saved are prisoners in Germany. Geoff's is a seat-type 'chute – uncomfortable to sit on, but a life-saver if a plane is blown apart. The rest of us, should the moment come, have to clip 'chutes onto our chests.

As we go to the crewroom we see the vans backing up outside. Waafs in greatcoats and driving gauntlets move about them in the dark. That chubby youngster is Peggy. Even on her days off, she comes to drive us. She feels and we feel that a break in such continuity might bring disaster. She has become sister to us and mother and wife.

The crewroom is filled with men clothed ready to leave; there is a sound of flying boots scraping the linoleum floor and of murmured exchanges. There is bulky sameness about men's garb; perhaps for this reason faces seem more vivid – eyes and mouths particularly. If the op is scrubbed, expressions will all at once change. But it won't be scrubbed – not tonight. There is no badinage. The only loud voice is that of a corporal calling the crew roll. The navigators, loaded with canvas 'bag of tricks', cluster at the large table in case of last-minute adjustments to logs and charts. Magor calls for attention: 'Synchronize watches please ... '

The Wing Commander hovers about us, fretful still. Are we all going to get off? Will some fool get bogged or abort? What will Group have to say about it?

The corporal begins calling crews to vans. As the crowd breaks up our farewells to each other are always the same laconic words 'Have a good trip.'

At our van there is a mock struggle for the right to sit beside Peggy, but it's all part of our ritual; invariably the seat is conceded to Geoff. We put in the green food box; the yellow pigeon container, the pigeon's innocent head protruding from the hole at the front; my navigator's bag; our parachutes; we clamber in ourselves.

'Take it away, Peggy!' Frank's voice; that's his role.

As we sway in the back Graham starts the song that is also part of our ritual; no word of it must be omitted:

> *Do not trust him, gentle maiden,*
> *Though his voice be low and sweet –*

We sing with religious fervour as we enter the perimeter track. We begin passing other aircraft, each dimly lighted – Berry's K Kitty, Kennard's A apple, Austin's M mother, Newitt's L London, crews shadowy about some of them.

Here, looming up, is B. As ritual requires, Frank shouts, 'Back up to 'er, Peggy. We aren't walking. Back; back – Whoa! Don't run into 'er! All out!'

The black shape hangs over us, her ground crew around her, Bill Burchell, Oscar, Henry, 'Misery' ... The night is very cold; within us we, too, are cold. Peggy fusses over us, handing out parachutes, food container, pigeon. She must return to the crewroom.

'Now don't keep us waiting when we get back, Peggy!' I

fancy she's near tears. These drivers are the last women many a man will see. They know it; we know it. 'Have a good trip,' she says.

There is a story concerning an Elsham crew left waiting at their aircraft after return. Exasperated, they wrote a note demanding transport, fixed it to the pigeon's leg in the approved way, released the pigeon. This was probably the only Elsham pigeon ever to return. Frank is our pigeon-handler. Despite his poaching, he converses gently with the pigeon before we go, stroking its head as he speaks. 'Ah pigeon wants t' know what's the sense in goin' out like this at night? We want t' know, pigeon, too.' Sometimes I wonder what happens the pigeon when we are twenty thousand feet up. Does it pass out through lack of oxygen, then revive? Does its small brain suffer damage?

If we come down in the sea, we must try to get the pigeon-container into the dinghy with us, then release its occupant with a message. 'Wouldn't like to depend on it gettin' there,' Frank muses.

With torches Geoff and Doug accompany Bill Burchell on an outer inspection of B. There is an hour to go. Apart from our voices and the sound of distant vans, the night is silent, solemn. I walk with Ted under the open bomb bay. Here is what it is all about – this monstrous black cylinder of the euphemistically-named 'cookie' and these containers of incendiaries. 'A Lanc is only a bloomin' flying bomb bay,' Doug sometimes says. 'They only send us along to get this lot over there.'

True enough, but I'd as soon not be reminded. The bombs extend from underneath Geoff and Doug almost down to Frank – pretty well half our length. If they're hit it's oblivion. It is part of our ritual to pat the cookie, each one of us. At the edge of my consciousness are half thoughts of victims, but mainly I want us seven to survive.

Shag and Frank go to great trouble with layers of zippers and buttons so that they can piss on the tailwheel. This gives them protection from fighters, they claim. Though the barrels of their machine guns are black and sinister, they are mere peashooters compared to nightfighters' cannon. Ted climbs the short metal ladder and vanishes into B's belly, making for the nose. His circular window there is angled downward; he lies face-down to the inferno.

It is quite a moment, stepping onto the ladder. Will these be our last steps on mother earth? Geoff and Doug glance about them as if imprinting the outer scenes on their minds. They climb in. I put in my navigator's bag, then my sextant and parachute, clamber in, walk the metallic way uphill to the mainspar, lift my gear over, feel the cold metal under my hands, squeeze over the spar, my parachute harness catching annoyingly.

Graham comes after me bearing our food box. He settles under the small light at his Marconi. He and I are scarcely three feet apart, he facing forward, I port. I begin pinning down the night's chart on the large, green table. Over the table is an astrograph which, when switched on, will project star curves onto the chart. But who dares fly straight and level long enough for star shots? I take out log form, dividers, computer, protractor ...

Bill Burchell squeezes behind my swivel chair, a Form 700 in hand for Geoff's signature of acceptance. As he presses back, he wishes each of us luck. Doug follows him, sees him drop back to mother earth, stows the ladder, fastens the door. We are sealed now within the wafer-thin fuselage.

Below B's nose the Wing Commander's car pulls up. 'You all okay, Maddern?'

'Okay, sir.'

'Good luck.'

'Thanks sir.' To us, 'He'll have our balls if we don't get off'

Another car – Gauvain and Henderson. Our hearts warm to them. 'Everyone okay Maddern?'

'All okay thanks Doc.'

'Have a good trip.'

Stillness then, silence. Time is nearly up. The accumulator is being plugged in. Geoff begins his check: trim, mixture, pitch, fuel, flaps … Aloud to Doug, 'No.2 tank?'

'Selected – booster pump on.'

'Master fuel cocks?'

'On.'

Then, from his window, calling to Bill Burchell: 'Ignition?'

'On! Okay for starting?'

'Okay for starting!' 'Contact port inner!' These are the last words we'll hear from earth. After them comes a giant cough, then the roar of a Merlin engine. Now we become voices on the intercom. What is it that we are doing? Why are we here? No, no; no good asking. Just get them there and get them back.

Hand signals for the other engines. When all four are running our very entrails vibrate to their beat. The French and Dutch will rejoice at this sound; the Germans will steel themselves – except those children too young to know. Trundling, close together, nose to tail – a camel train. It's a long way – too long; let's get it over. A scrub at this stage would tip us into a kind of insanity. Graham is tuning his set; voices babel in from other frequencies, phrenetic – sounding, mysterious. A pause for run-up, all of us silent except Geoff and Doug. No radio instructions can be given by control – the enemy is listening, always listening. There they go, one up, two up, all on the green flash of an Aldis lamp from the van at the far end of the runway. We can get each off in just under a minute. From Doug: 'You've got your green, Skipper.' I breathe deeply; the game is about to begin.

184

18

Journeys into Night

It never was and never could be a mode of warfare to be conducted in hot blood; the bomber crew was engaged throughout a flight in a series of intricate tasks ... calculations and minute adjustments of machinery had to be made all the time with a clear head and a steady hand. (W.J. Lawrence, historian of 5 Group, Bomber Command.)

All targets differed. There were 'easy' Italian targets, but they were dauntingly far off – occasionally crews ran out of petrol trying to reach home from them and had to ditch in the sea. And there were German targets, both distant and ferocious. There were no easy German targets. There were also widely differing weather conditions – nights when there was icing all the way to cruising altitude, when many aircraft fell out of the sky, encased in ice. And clear, moonlit nights when vapor trails streamed behind each of our four airscrews like chalk on blackboard.

We watched on those nights for the sinister single vapor trails of fighters. They waited high up for us, seeing us as clear as flies on a tablecloth.

A crescendo of engine noise; a frenzied, straight race between runway lights. All is quivering, shaking. On the airspeed repeater dial I watch the rising needle: eighty knots, ninety knots, a hundred, a hundred ten, a hundred twenty, a hundred thirty. A navigator – after the war – told me he said the 23rd Psalm to himself in these moments. Up, up, straining over blacked-out buildings, over Barnetby, over the red flash of base beacon. The game has begun.

In our lone thundering down the runway there is subtle transition of spirit among us. By some alchemy seven men are lifted among peaks of high endeavour, each sustained by the others, yet each clasping his own store of inner resources. The whole of our day has been a winding up to this pitch; we will remain at it through all the hours of flight. Sometimes I even fancy it to be a state induced by the hypnotic rhythm of the engines, the pounding that penetrates body and brain, urging us on, on, on ...

Up into cloud, earth obliterated. We might remain in this all the way to 15,000 feet, the usual set-course altitude. On better nights we pass through it quickly and emerge into a zone of second sunset and see those who are climbing ahead of us, sun glinting on turrets and canopies, while others below emerge from cloud and soar like eagles on updrafts, sometimes near enough for us to read their identification.

Each of our planes climbs back and forth on base beam; this holds us from drifting with the wind. It emanates from base radio beacon and is picked up by the pilots through their headphones. Occasionally Geoff cries, 'Bah! bah! bah – it sounds like a bloody sheep!'

About now I check the functioning of the Gee. Its small green signals precess reassuringly. I halt them, read off the co-ordinates, plot them on the lattice chart, tell Ted, 'Position over Barton-on-Humber', or wherever we might be. If the cloud breaks sufficiently he replies, 'Ah yes; I see it below,' his voice detached, deliberate. This will be my only slack time during the operation. I take advantage of it to check my flight plan, well knowing my proneness to error. Ahead of time I give Geoff the course to steer to the rendezvous point. This done, I switch out my Anglepoise lamp, draw back the black-out curtain and stand behind Doug. My intercom cord is long enough to reach these few feet. In the cockpit all is concentration. If it is already dark, the luminous dials of the instrument panel gleam green and, outside, the exhaust stubs of the four engines glow. Geoff and Doug are swaddled in their fur-lined Irvin jackets. Up, up. It's a wonder we don't have collisions here; we are only separated by our brief initial take-off intervals. For some reason we don't worry much about this; we delude ourselves by thinking these chaps are friendly, anyway.

Doug's voice: '9000 feet; oxygen on.'

We each acknowledge and clip on our pig-snouts. My oxygen lead of corrugated rubber is long enough to reach the cockpit. I check my wrist watch – issue Longines, rotatable seconds ring. 'Five minutes before we set course Geoff.'

'Thanks navigator.' The course is already set on the P4 compass by his right knee.

I return to my desk; draw the curtain; turn on the lamp. We are nearing 15,000 feet and will continue climbing to 20,000 on the way to Sheringham or Mabelthorpe, or even Dungeness if we are going south. Not that we will see much of the other aircraft at the rendezvous point – only occasional dark shapes with glowing exhaust stubs.

'Two minutes to go Geoff.'

'Thanks navigator.' Soon each crew will make its individual way to the target; there can be no formation flying on night operations.

Graham switches briefly from Marconi to intercom. 'Windin' out trailin' aerial, Geoff.'

'Okay Briggy. Could you turn up the heat a bit – it's starting to get cold.'

'Okay.' As the hot air outlet is near Graham's seat, he and I will inevitably be over-warm.

I keep an eye on my watch. 'One minute to go, Geoff ... Half a minute. Set course *now*. ETA Sheringham ... ' or wherever it may be.

'Thanks navigator.'

I begin following our progress on the Gee, marking on my

chart how far we are drifting from our intended track. Climbing as we are, it is not possible yet to calculate an accurate wind for our ultimate cruising level, but at least our general tendency can be determined. We say little to each other; intercom channels must be kept clear for essentials. When we do speak, we articulate more clearly than in daily life and are more forbearing – well, most of the time. Graham is 'listenin' out on base', as he puts it, chiefly in case a recall signal comes. It would be disastrous to miss it, to go on alone. Already the gunners are rotating their turrets, watching as much for our own aircraft as for intruders, watching with poacher-sharp eyes. Geoff can feel the rotation through the controls. The front turret, above the bombaimer's position, is seldom manned; the field of vision it commands is already watched over by Geoff and Doug and its rotation upsets the plane's aerodynamics.

Graham and I will seldom move now from our 'office'. Behind Graham the armour-plated door cuts off vision aft, just as the black-out curtain cuts off vision forward. Everyone in B's outer world stares into darkness; here, we work under lights,

Propped below my instrument panel is my photo folder, Nell on one side, my family on the other. Incongruous to have them here, yet they form a link with that other life. Sometimes I fancy they look at me reassuringly. By the time we reach the rendezvous point we are at cruising altitude – 18,000, 20,000, sometimes higher – being tossed by slipstreams. Geoff usually makes the same remark, 'Shit! – it's like Piccadilly Circus!'

Below, in the houses of the town we have never seen, people's morale will be lifted by the sound of our strength. Probably this does more for them than news of hitting targets. We are about to pass out over the North Sea, part of an invisible armada. For as long as the Gee remains readable I must establish position frequently to check and re-check the wind. All the unseen navigators about me will be doing the same thing, for over Europe there can be no certainty of determining wind accurately, no certainty indeed of anything.

From Graham, 'IFF on Geoff.'

'Thanks, Briggy.'

Although its signal shows us as friend, not foe, is it true, we wonder, that fighters are able to home on its transmissions?

'Okay t'test guns, Geoff?'

'Okay.'

Shag and Frank leave their microphones on and we hear the sharp rattle of fire. Often I wonder how it is we don't shoot each other down – or does this sometimes happen and we don't hear of it? Now our routine tasks are all over; we are poised on the brink of the unknown.

'Going to start weaving navigator.'

My body detests it. Riding side-on, I am rolled over the chart, then slowly plucked back; pressed down within myself, opened out. But at least I can be sure the gunners are getting a look below, that we are presenting a difficult target. From past experience I know I can trust Geoff to average out courses I give him.

Sometimes out here the cloud breaks and the dark face of the sea is revealed. Nearly always the outside crew puzzle over lights down there that move and flash and fade. Theirs or ours? We never know. Our main concern is to avoid straying over convoys – whether ours or theirs doesn't matter much; both fire on us.

As I work, I listen. There might be sudden cries that must be logged. 'One of ours going down!' 'Explosion dead ahead!' 'Flak ship firing below!'

From the Gee I know when the sea crossing is almost over. If cloud allows, there is confirmation from Ted – 'Enemy coast coming up navigator.'

Time is approaching to change course from point A on the coast to point B near the target – a long run and always costly; fighters want to get as many of us as possible before we bomb. And it is easy to stray over defences that lie waiting in darkness. Sometimes, to keep the enemy guessing, there are additional changes of course as we move eastward. All the flak concentrations along our way I have marked in red, copying them from the large wall map in the ops. room – 'The ops room', that far-off place in the other, the predictable life.

On the Gee screen jamming has begun – waving 'grass' that mounts higher as we move inland, mounts until the signals are obliterated. Nothing is predictable now. The gunners must watch the skies; Geoff must be ready to fling B into evasive action; I must plot accurately. Whatever violent interruptions come from fighters or flak, we must try to cling to precision.

The gunners cries are full of defiance. 'ME 109 port bow up! See 'im Shag?'

'See 'im Frank! Prepare to turn star'bd, Geoff … '

So it goes on – sudden searchlights and flak, each mile of the way uncertain, till, somehow most of us reach point B. 'From there,' the operations officer had said, 'it's a short run to the target.' Had he any real idea of this scene ahead? of these hundreds of searchlights and skies blotched with shell bursts?

The advice given navigators is to remain in their 'office'; not to look at targets; it is reckoned too distracting for men supposed to work accurately. Nearly always I obey. When I do look, I am appalled. With no preparatory lead-up and no task to perform, the scene clubs my mind. If I remain, it exerts hypnotic power. Square miles are alight, not just with steady fires, but with pulsating explosions and thousands of silver-winking incendiaries that change as we watch, to red. Over this cauldron the hundreds of bombers are silhouetted, insect-like, some banked, some under attack – for fighters follow us even here. Only the nearby shell-bursts are audible to us; they toss us like a canoe in rapids and leave drifting entrails of black smoke.

Suspended here Geoff must decide when to make our run to the red Pathfinder markers – that mortal, gaping wound in the city's body. If he can manage it, he waits till the nearer searchlights grasp one of the attackers, grasp first with a bluish 'radar-predicted' beam, then with a score of others.

'I'll duck in now Ted.'

'Okay, Geoff.' I always find it difficult to take my eye from a stricken aircraft, brilliantly exposed, unlikely to escape. Always they remind me of a harpooned whale, beating the sea to red.

'All your's Ted.'

'Okay. Left, left Geoff.'

A rattle of shrapnel, a smell of cordite, a blinding sweep of searchlights.

'Further left.'

In the sea of flame there are detectable patterns of streets; sometimes glimpses of buildings. These are the only semblance of human life.

'Steady; steady. Coming along nicely now Geoff.'

How can anything 'come along nicely' in this hell! Each op Ted directs us as if this were a film set, as if the inferno were not real, as if we were not about to make a personal kill. 'Steady; steady.' We cease breathing. How long can this go on without violent disintegration? But this is what we were selected for, what Bomber Command, Somers, Edmonton, Rivers, Lichfield exist for ...

'Bombs gone!' B leaps like a horse. 'Hold her steady, Geoff.' Now it's ten seconds straight and level so that we can photograph the place where our bombs strike; they are curving on their way below. As if *we* really want this photograph! At the end Geoff's cry never varies, 'Let's get to hell out of here!' It's like riding back now after the Charge of the Light Brigade – except that there will be another charge tomorrow night and the next.

Clearing the target, we are at our most vulnerable; an unwary joy assails us. We are more dependent than ever on the gunners' vigilance. As the target recedes weariness possesses us. We drag over my chart, usually bucking a westerly wind, moving across the white glare with intolerable slowness. I get rough bearings on the flak dispositions, but there is little else to go by. If I feel really unsure of our whereabouts, I can ask Graham to transmit a seven-second dash for a fix, but this is a rare step.

'What's the ETA at the coast again navigator?'

I repeat it wearily. 'Hell! another hour' or half an hour or some other interminable period.

I check my figures, ' ... seven eights are fifty-six ... '; I am in the third grade, chanting tables. After school I shall swim. No, no; I must not sleep ...

The 'grass' on the Gee is diminishing. Peering at the signals while we corkscrew is sure recipe for airsickness. Occasionally I dry retch, holding up my pee tin just in case. 'Coming up to the coast navigator. I'll start losing a bit of height.'

The odds now are shifting; we are likely to come through, likely to see cottages and women and children. Mysterious lights again on the North Sea. There could be men from ditched planes down there, drifting in dinghies. The fear of convoys. We descend below 10,000 feet; remove our oxygen masks; rub our faces. Graham is quartering a couple of white onions. All of us except Frank are raw onion eaters; it is Frank who procures them for us.

'English coast coming up navigator.'

'Thanks Ted; ETA base 0231' – or 2230, or 0215, or even 0800.

If dawn has come I draw back the black-out curtain and see

dim lines of waves curving to the beaches, then Lincolnshire villages, red-tiled, asleep, breathing. Flocks of sheep; haystacks; farmhouses; families stirring, listening.

Because the raid is now over, we can call control; no matter that Germany is listening.

'Hazel control, B beer; over.'

If we are first in, a girl's voice rises with that sweetest of instructions, 'B beer, this is Hazel control, QFE 1012,* pancake, pancake!' which is 'Clear to land.' But, by inflexion, she is saying more than that, much more; no woman's voice in all our lives will welcome us more warmly home. We hear other voices calling her; to each she is a shepherdess.

If it is still dark, enemy intruders might be among us even here; we land without lights, then follow blue-lit taxiways until, at our dispersal, one of the ground crew appears, torch in each hand, moving backwards, waving us in. The engines redouble their roaring as Geoff pivots about. I begin packing my canvas bag.

'Switch off!'

'Switching off!'

Deep and wonderful silence; most blessed moment. Geoff and Doug kiss 'Nunc Nunc', their grubby little rag doll upon whom our safety has depended. We are alive and have come home. A homecoming to Australia could not be more wonderful than this. And we have regained normal voices. My helmet off, I hear Doug checking the petrol gauges. Even now, I can't resist transcribing dialogue:

Doug: *Good consumption tonight, Skipper.*
Geoff: *Let's get out of this bloody thing! Who's seen my cap?*
Doug: *Who's seen old Maddern's cap?*

---

* Prevailing barometric pressure reading which, if set on the sub-scale of the altimeter, results in it reading height above the aerodrome.

Geoff: *Is it down there, Ted?*

Ted: *How the hell would it get down here?*

Geoff: *Well have a look, can't you!* (Change of tone) *Here it is – down my battledress.*

Like attendant midwives the ground crew help us from the womb into the fresh night, out of the odor of fear. Bill Burchell, Oscar, Henry, 'Misery' ... They look clean and elated and are regarding us as gods, their own personal gods, begrimed, weary, proud, relieved. In the morning they will paint one more bomb in the row below Geoff's window showing another op done.

How good the earth is! Peggy's van appears out of the darkness, its headlights reduced to the regulation dim slits. If ever a girl had a comradely role, this is it. She is beaming on us, sister, mother, wife, friend.

'Good trip?'

'Fair enough, Peg.' We sound laconic, but inwardly are not so. How could we be?

'Give me some of your things.'

We pile parachutes, pigeon, food box, navigation equipment into the back of the van. No singing this time, only fragmentary talk.

In the locker room Frank and Shag help each other out of sweaty layers of clothing. The room is crowding with crews agog with release of tension; friends exchange congratulatory glances.

'Let's get to interrogation.'

Our footfalls echo along the dim corridors of the ops block, till we enter under bright fluorescent lights as if coming onto a stage set. This is the room where we were briefed six or eight or ten hours ago, the chairs now cleared back. Tea and sandwiches and cigarettes are pressed on us. The doctors circulate, the padres, the Wing Commander. Pilot relates experiences to pilot, navigator to navigator.

'Good trip?'

'Yes thanks, Doc.'

Usually we aim to be interrogated by Lucette Edwards, pretty WAAF intelligence officer who once came on a flight with us. We feel unashamedly important before her. She is gentle and thorough and unfailingly patient.

Did we follow the route as briefed? Did we see the Pathfinder flares? At what time did we bomb? At what height? Was the target heavily defended? An argument between us here as to whether 'heavily' or 'very heavily'. From the next cubicle, where Cook's crew is being interrogated, comes Harry Wright's raised voice, 'Don't believe you ever got there Charlwood!' I retort, 'Rotterdam Wright!' He blundered over it once on the way home and hasn't lived it down.

'Did you see your cookie burst?'

We are always asked this. In that mass of fires and bomb bursts, is it possible to see it?

'How intense were the fires?'

'Very intense,' answers Shag. 'I could still see them for a hundred mile.'

Were fighters active? Where? What types? Did we see any aircraft shot down? Invariably we have seen several.

It's all over now; we straggle through the ops room to go to breakfast. Further crews have come in – crews late because they had become lost, or been shot up by flak or fighters, or lost engines. Some faces have not yet appeared – probably will never appear.

Outside the night is silent. Instinctively we listen for those others. Once in the mess we wash our hands, comb our hair. A moment of incredulity descends on me as I see the face in the mirror. Is it possible that tonight you were over Germany? that you killed? that you have lost friends since you were last here? Insane! Insane! I have an impulse to wash. But water won't do.

Already a few crews are sitting to breakfast. We wander into the forbidden kitchen and sit about the stove, chatting to the girls as they break eggs into a huge pan. We are scoring two lots of egg and bacon this op! – eggs enough for a village's monthly ration. The girls smile indulgently. We take our plates to a table, sit together, talking desultorily. There is something unreal about this scene, this domesticity after destruction and death.

Eventually we drift out, each going with room mates. Geoff and I stop and listen again as we step into the dark. We walk, wheeling our bikes, exchanging few words, listening, listening. As we reach our barracks Geoff articulates what is in both our minds, 'No hope now.'

As we undress I take the photo folder from my battledress and put it on our chest-of-drawers, glancing at family eyes with feelings of unreality; between their world and ours a great gulf is set. Will we ever cross back over it?

We go to bed and, despite everything, sink deep to sleep.

19

Plateau of Efficiency

Early in 1942, No.5 Group produced figures showing that crews were most vulnerable in their first five trips. A later study, however, also showed a rise in the loss rate for crews between about half-way through their tour to the twentieth operation. ... it was argued that by the middle of the tour crews had reached a plateau of efficiency that drifted into fatal overconfidence. (A Last Call of Empire, by John McCarthy, Australian War Memorial, 1988.)

Like all Bomber Command squadrons, 103 was constantly haemorrhaging, not as evidently as Western Front armies had haemorrhaged, but quietly, steadily. The transfusion from Training Command was equally steady; numbers of men never diminished; only faces changed. A few remained familiar to us; these were the faces of men who had done fifteen, twenty, even twenty-five ops. We watched them closely. The others we never really came to know, we saw them arrive, caps jaunty, faces ashine. They appeared a moment on stage then were gone. We never saw them die, just as we never saw the victims of our bombing die. I knew that before long Ken Lay's crew would arrive among the newcomers. Much as I looked forward to Max Bryant's company, it was going to be like having a young brother at risk.

Such news as we had of missing men was almost wholly bad. Word came from the Red Cross that Flt Lt Colin Rose and all his crew were dead. Later the same day we heard that six of Colin Bayliss's crew, lost on the same operation, had also been killed. The fate of the seventh we did not know; at that stage we did not even know which man had not been accounted for.

197

Somehow five senior crews were hanging on inspiringly, all of them having done between twenty and thirty operations: Flt Sgt Berry's crew; Sqn Ldr Kennard's; Flt Lt Douglas's; Flt Sgt Austin's. and Flt Sgt Newitt's. I realize now that they were not much more than senior schoolboys. Douglas was an Australian, Newitt a Canadian, the other three Englishmen. Because of their experience they were in a realm somewhere above us. Their nationality mattered nothing at all – we had long since shed chauvinism – nor did their youth matter. It only mattered that they had proved themselves by surviving nearly twice as long as most; they were our assurance that survival was possible. Geoff wrote:

Berry has completed 25 trips. They asked him yesterday if he would like to be screened – he refused. His crew weren't too pleased over his action. With three married men in my crew, I know what I would do – I wouldn't tempt providence.

On January 23 B was unserviceable; with uneasy feelings, we took Sqr Ldr Temperley's T Tommy to Dusseldorf. Geoff was half-amused, half-exasperated by the demands Temperley's crew made of us:

They have a hell of a ritual before taking off. First of all, every member of the crew rubs the belly of Yohodi, a little devil painted on the tail near the rear turret. Don's job was to rub a horseshoe over the navigator's table. It's kept in the kite for that purpose.

Geoff soon lost confidence in Yohodi.

... we climbed up to 15,000 ft – everything was icing up. For a time I had visions of abandoning the sortie because the tail trim froze up – however, between two of us we worked it free. ... An ME110 came at us but we lost him by turning in towards him. Above the clouds it was as clear as day.

Despite this unpromising start we returned unscathed. We

were in high spirits not only because of this but because a hoodoo had been broken: for three successive operations three successive new crews had shared our van on the way out for take-off; each had failed to return. We tried at first not to think of them, then we began joking of our malevolent powers. This night, as we approached Elsham, we listened for the fourth crew. At last a laconic voice called, 'X X-ray – landing instructions.' Cheering broke out among us. This relatively new captain was Sid Burton, a twenty-one year old RAF sergeant. The meting and doling of fate were beyond all understanding: three successive crews who had travelled with us dead, yet Sid was destined to complete two tours.

Next day we were briefed for Dusseldorf. While we waited at the aircraft the Roman Catholic padre drove out to wish each crew luck. After he had gone, Bill Burchell remarked dryly, 'He gives you a holy blessing to do some unholy work!' We were all sick of the Ruhr; added to that, over the North Sea, homeward bound, my oxygen connection caught on the edge of the table during Geoff's corkscrewing and became unfastened. The margins of my field of vision began closing in before I discovered the dangling connection. I was left with a ringing headache, and longed for Geoff to cease corkscrewing – I was opening and closing like a concertina. Instead he began pestering me until I blew up:

> Don tore me off a glorious strip. He said that we would make landfall down in Norfolk. I hounded him about the convoy down that way. He was up to his eyes in work – turned on me and said, 'You fuckin' bastard, what do you think I'm doing. I'm going south to dodge the fuckin' thing.' I was dumb-founded; he is usually so quiet. … Trouble was, we were going so fast that it was all he could do to keep up with the machine … Of our twelve [ops.] nine have been to Happy Valley. I would like to go somewhere else for a change. Three machines crashed in this neighbourhood tonight …

According to Middlebrook and Everitt ten industrial firms in Dusseldorf were destroyed or seriously damaged; also we demolished 456 houses. Such were the inevitabilities of area bombing.

It was announced next day that Berry, Newitt and Douglas were all to be screened after the next operation. None of them had reached thirty, but they were given no choice in the matter. Four-engine instructors were needed and this was the only way to get them. Also, operationally-experienced men had to be saved to lead the oncoming flood of novice crews, not only lead them, but to bear witness that survival was possible.

I remember looking at Berry once and wondering what opportunities postwar England would offer such a splendid man. He was a big, genial Yorkshireman, lively, open-countenanced, positive. A year later he came back to 103 Squadron as a Flying Officer, but he and his crew were lost on February 15 1944.

Keith Douglas, twenty-one year old son of a Tamworth doctor, had risen to Squadron Leader on 103. Like Rose, he was quietly-spoken and looked more a scholar than a warrior; he fitted easily into the English scene. Only three crews who had started at 103 with him in August '42 were alive the day he left. He was to return to operations as a Wing Commander commanding 462 Squadron, the youngest RAAF squadron commander. He was killed not long after D-Day. Only Roly Newitt, the Vancouver Canadian, survived two tours – a sergeant on his first, a Squadron Leader on his second. The potential of such men was unlimited.

The last operation for these three screened crews was Hamburg. The day leading up to it had been full of uncertainties. We were briefed first for Berlin, then for Berlin with Hamburg as a possible alternative, finally for Hamburg alone, taking off at midnight. For its savagery Hamburg had been dubbed 'Chopburg', derived from 'Got the chop', an expression often uttered by aircrew of missing friends.

I was feeling distinctly unwell and cared little which target we went to, though I knew that once in the air I would work like an automaton. It did nothing for anyone's tension that the take-off runway was badly out of wind. We began an unnerving swing, but Geoff managed to correct and pull away. Behind us, Roper's swing was worse; he wiped off his undercarriage and starboard wing. Somehow they all got out unhurt.

Luck also turned against us. Over the North Sea our rear turret guns iced up. Doug helped Shag try to free them, but to no avail. At 6 degrees 18'E we decided to return, as the sky had cleared and we were easy prey for night fighters. We were away four and a quarter hours and returned at 4.30.

Having got that far, it was not a happy decision, but it was accepted even by the Wing Commander. Not surprisingly, it contributed nothing to our tally of ops. Next morning 'Doc' Henderson ordered me to sickquarters.

For the first time Geoff and I were split. To make matters worse, Ted was also admitted; indeed the number of aircrew in bed with upper respiratory tract infections and fatigue surprised me. One was Blue and Harry's twenty-one year old skipper Syd Cook. He was discharged the morning after I came in, but returned later in the day 'for company,' as he put it. 'The mess is full of strangers; I only know the chaps in here.'

I slept twenty-three hours straight, then woke so refreshed and optimistic that I began writing to Nell of our future:

I wonder what we could do if I managed to get through ops? Wonder what it would be wise to do? Have you any ideas? ... Perhaps the opportunity of fulfilling such hopes are so remote that it is untimely to discuss them; but, just in case fate is kind to us, it may be wise to examine our wishes and think over any courses we may like to take....

201

Even as I wrote, I realized I was posing unanswerable questions. It was improbable that I would be able to return to Canada; less probable that Nell could reach England. Even if we did get together, there was her father's attitude to confront. All we could reasonably do was wait and see what circumstances presented themselves. In the meantime I had to remember I was not halfway through a tour.

Over at Lindholme Lay's crew had received their Elsham posting. Although it pleased Max Bryant, the rest of the crew let him know they were deterred by 103's reputation. Max felt confused and despondent:

> *Can't account for my feelings tonight; a mixture of restlessness and sadness. Probably a combination of gladness to be with Don, yet apprehension for the future ... uneasy feelings in case I can't cope – all combine to render me at the moment not worth a sneeze in a bottle.*

To my surprise he turned up as a sickquarters visitor next evening, full of questions, torn between eagerness and forebodings.

In the morning I heard there were to be operations to Essen and that someone else had been briefed as navigator for B. The news troubled me; I knew Geoff would be equally uneasy. Before I could importune Doc Henderson, word came through that the op. had been scrubbed.

Next morning ops were on again, this time to Cologne. Doc Henderson peered into my eyes, looked down my throat, tapped me, became distinctly dubious, but let me go. Ted Batten he kept in bed. As bombaimer we were to have the best possible stand-in: Blue Freeman volunteered to go with us. Fed up though Geoff was with the Valley, he was buoyed by Blue's gesture.

> *We took off in weather they described as good. Climbed on the beam over base up to 15,000 feet. We were still in cloud; every-*

thing was icing up inside the kite, ... Don brought us right over the rendezvous dead on time. ... Over the North Sea we were in cloud at 21,000 feet – hell it was cold – minus 40 degrees. ... [Blue's] bombing run was the longest and most nerve-wracking I have yet done. For once it was I who was yelling to let the bloody things go. In all we were 30 seconds straight and level. ... Silhouetted by the searchlights and fires I could see the Halifaxes and Stirlings jinking violently to evade the ground defences. We wasted very little time in making our exit. Saw two fellows going down in their parachutes. On the way out an ME 109 came at us – a steep diving turn fixed him. He was blinded by the fires over the target. ... Saw one poor blighter crash and explode in Holland. At that moment we damn near cleaned up another Lanc. It passed about ten feet beneath us. ... We were dead on track throughout the whole journey. We still have the blue riband – we were first back again.

That night I stood behind Doug during the bombing run and felt the spectacle's distracting, hypnotic power:

It was a hellish but wildly beautiful sight. I felt that some earth-bound giant was down there, lashing at the wasps above him. Searchlights swept everywhere and sometimes silhouetted struggling aircraft. Flak burst below and above and all round us and on the ground were the constant flashes of the guns. Huge fires glowed through their own smoke. As I looked it swept over me, 'We have done that!' But then a shout broke in, 'Stand by! ME 109 astern! ...'

I caught a glimpse of him silhouetted against the inferno as Geoff dived away – some unknown young enemy defending his city. Were we breaking German morale or were we steeling it?

In RAF vernacular Cologne was 'a wizard prang'; the city appeared overwhelmed, but according to Middlebrook and Everitt this was not so at all. 'Damage was caused right across the city, but was nowhere serious.' Fourteen people were killed compared with thirty-five men of the attacking crews.

The brief stay in sickquarters had recharged me:

The weather is very grey and drizzly, a cheerless day. Somehow I'm 'warm inside.' It's odd that at times one's morale is high and at other times low. A lot of waiting when one is tired is something that hits me hardest. When I'm fresh and kept busy, I can face ops without many qualms.

Although it did not strike me then, I realized years later that Doc Henderson had saved many of us from gradual deterioration by judiciously resting us. By no means all medical officers were as perceptive and far-sighted as he was; many were bitterly criticized by aircrew for their lack of understanding. Few, I am sure, matched Robert Henderson's willingness to go out himself and observe crews by flying with them on operations. But they could hardly be criticized for that!

On February 2 a break came from the Valley; the target was Turin. Max waited in the officers' mess for our return.

While we sit here and loaf in luxury, Don is somewhere over the other side twisting and diving twenty-thousand feet up. ... It's a strange existence. ... The thought of him going is quite unreal to me – perhaps the wishful thinking I do on his behalf and Nell's has something to do with it.

At first sight Geoff assessed Turin as much more formidable than we had been let to expect:

A huge cone of searchlights was formed with heavy flak being pumped up into the centre. As we approached we saw the PFF drop the arc of normal flares around the aiming point. We orbited outside the target area waiting for the red marker ... to be dropped. They were about four minutes late. It was apparent as soon as the main attack developed [that] the personnel manning the searchlights and AA guns considered the shelters the safest place while the blitz was in progress. ... Never before have I seen so much ground detail – the aiming point, railway station, racecourse and river were as visible almost as in daylight.

As the target fires fell behind and we came again over the Alps, I found we were drifting steadily south of track. As Geoff had not yet resumed weaving, I decided to try astro and stood with my head in the dome selecting from the brilliant host of stars. The fix showed us eighty miles south of track. If this were so, we were lining up for eventual emergence into the northern reaches of the Bay of Biscay. I doubted such an extreme wind-shift and decided to halve the distance; we altered course accordingly. The fix – the only astro fix I took on my entire tour – had been correct; when the Gee cleared I saw we were about to turn for England over the Channel Islands. In a trice we were boxed by their flak. Geoff broke away, diving at high speed toward the Bournemouth we had known so well in the days of our innocence.

The Turin flight had lasted eight hours forty minutes; for five and a half hours of it Geoff had persisted with corkscrewing. 'Don, Doug, Ted and Shag all complained of sickness through the jinking I did.' 186 aircraft had set out, Middlebrook and Everitt estimate that 156 reached target; the damage was 'serious and widespread.' In terms of lives, twenty-nine people were killed; twenty-one aircrew were lost. All Elsham crews returned safely.

Having next night off we took the ground-crew to Scunthorpe – four of them, seven of us. After a rowdy return the eleven of us jammed into our room.

... we stood the boys a feed, a horrible mixture of onions, chocolate, squab, fruit salad, Horlick's tablets and biscuits! They feel wrecks today. ...

'What a crew!' Geoff lamented. 'Shag and Frank are in the poop now. They were pinched this morning for poaching ...'

The Earl of Yarborough secured their release on the grounds that they were 'fighting for their country.'

'After the war, come to Australia,' we urged, 'then you'll have something worth fighting for.'

The target next night was confined to fresher crews; it was Lorient. The bombaimer over whom Lay's crew had expended so much worry, was ill. Blue Freeman volunteered to take his place. To a crew on their first operation, this was a tremendous boost; it was especially so for Max. He wrote afterwards that the moments before take-off had them all on edge.

Ken ... turned off onto what looked like a perimeter track, only to find it a dead end. We had to cut the engines and be towed out. The Wingco did his little bit towards making us feel happy by coming out and blowing our heads off. Finally we got airborne and climbed straight out on course. We were belting her along to try to get to the target before 2200, though it looked impossible ...

By the time they reached the Channel, the attack on Lorient was at its height – they could see it 150 miles off.

... Blue said, 'You can give up navigation, Max; I can see the bloody target from here! ...' There could not be any mistake about it being the target. Over 300 heavies had been there before us and it was a terrible mess of fires. There was little flak, and only 2 searchlights. Blue directed us in in masterly fashion – 'Weave port – weave starboard – steady up – steady – bomb gone – get weaving – 1,2,3,4,5,6,7,8 – incendiaries falling – straight and level – camera working – flash gone – OK, let's go! ...' Blue flew most of the way home.

Blue often volunteered to help a crew short of a man – a spirit that deserved recognition; but it never came. Decorations on 103 at that time were confined almost wholly to pilots.

Whether raids on Lorient could ever be a success was doubtful; the targets were U-boat pens, so deep under concrete that bombs could not reach them. But it was reckoned an 'easy' target; on the night of Max's first op losses were only 2%. What we did not know was that the 2% included our loved Harry Waddell, the 'Cheerful Pessimist' of my journey in Scotland, George Loder's flying partner in Edmonton. No trace was ever found of their aircraft nor of any body other than the pilot's. They would appear to have been shot down by a fighter over the sea.

Lay's crew, having brought leave credit from Lindholme, had only to survive nine days to get the benefit of it. On four of those days we were briefed for Wilhelmshaven. By the fourth briefing everyone felt uneasy – such repetition seemed a gift to German intelligence. On February 11 the weather improved and we got away. Once over 12,000 feet Geoff began to report heavy icing:

> *Could hear the ice breaking off and clanging against the fuselage. With warm air and icing we couldn't get above 15,000 feet or more than 150 mph on the clock. At the first turning point, 6 degrees E, we were orbiting to kill time. Shag called a stand by – an ME 109 had passed us in the opposite direction; turned and came in dead astern, then went into a vertical climb and delivered his attack from the port quarter. At the critical moment I went into a screaming steep diving turn, at the same time jettisoning our 4000lb [bomb] to give us added manoeuvrability. The Hun's fire passed under our tail. Both Frank and Shag gave him a long burst from their six guns. They claim to have got him – he went into a vertical dive and straight down into clouds. We saw nothing more of him. We carried on and bombed the objective with our incendiaries ... Whilst over Wilhelmshaven we observed a terrific explosion which for a period of about three seconds, lit up the sky like daylight. Must have hit a mine dump ...*

Geoff's speculation was not far wrong: the naval ammunition depot at Mariensiel, to the south of Wilhelmshaven, had been blown up. According to Middlebrook and Everitt it devastated an area of nearly 120 acres, causing widespread damage to the dockyard and the town. Of 177 aircraft only three were lost. For us it was our halfway point – operation fifteen.

The day Lay's crew went on leave, the squadron was briefed again for Lorient. I wrote afterwards, 'Our best trip yet – and to top it we took the squadron's best photo.' But as a contribution toward winning the war, it was probably useless and the cost was over forty aircrew lives.

In the morning Australian mail came; at the same time we were called for briefing to Milan. I managed to read a letter from my brother Ian who had turned twenty-one in appalling conditions in New Guinea – this shortly before his battalion – the 39th – went into action at Gona. Anything seemed better than what they had gone through; nothing could have contrasted more with it than our journey that night over the Alps.

... snow-covered peaks and ridges looked unearthly in the moonlight. We watched and watched, marvelling over the enormous valleys and the great razor edges spread far out into the moonlit night. Tiny villages and chateaux were perched almost at our own level. The target was reasonably hot. We actually took an overlap photo of a section of the city – 3 in a row. They were Group's best effort. Coming home we just missed Paris-we were eating raw onion at the time! I skirted Rouen and Le Havre on the Gee ... To bed at 7 am.

Bed between sheets, I thought, no fox-holes, no sniping, nothing hand-to-hand. After German targets, Milan had been a relief; for all that, 103's Sqn Ldr W.H. Powdrell had failed to return. All the crew were killed – one of only two crews lost that night from the whole Command.

'Easy' targets bred false optimism. When next I wrote home, I was unaware of a growing over-confidence:

Ops. have lost fully 90% of their old sting. Certain aspects of them are even enjoyable. I wouldn't swop my job for anyone else's ...

The last of the easy targets came on February 16 – again Lorient. By now the town had been obliterated. To guards down in the U boat pens our bombs were probably no more than rumblings overhead. Only one aircraft was lost, but again it was from our squadron, its pilot, Sgt. J.C.H. Young, an Australian; other Australians were in his crew.

I walked back to our billets alone in the moonlight. A few chinks of light showed from various rooms as new and excited crews went to bed. New crews; new voices. I stood out in the pallid light awhile, remembering last week, last month, last year ...

There was a lull next day. I started a letter home before turning in:

... I took Joan to a dance in Barnetby tonight, a real country hop. We meandered along the moonlit road afterwards, going as far as Gallows Woods. The aisles of trees were magically lighted and very quiet. Then back to camp and deep to sleep.

In the morning it was briefing for Wilhelmshaven again. I added on our return:

A good trip. The met, promised us cloud, but there was not a shred of it. Fighters were about, but they did not molest us. Navigationally the trip was very enjoyable. All our boys returned.

Lay's crew returned from leave next evening. Max had had one of those breaks that made return to ops seem hideous by contrast. He had gone back to Lichfield where he had a Land Army girl friend. His days had gone helping her on a farm.

It was very pleasant to be working in sunlight and, more especially, in such charming company. We took a few minutes off here and there to sit in the sun, steal a kiss or two ... England on sunny days has a beauty which seems to catch you by the throat, so intense is it ...

His sixth day brought the inevitable parting.

The train came, stopped and I hopped in. A whistle, a long kiss – and Brenda was gone again. I could not help thinking as I watched her grow smaller, 'Shall I see you in six weeks, or never.' ...

He returned to a tough target: Bremen. Again his crew was away to a bad start: a ground staff man accidentally pulled Ken Lay's parachute and a long delay ensued while another was brought out. Then the pilot's compass proved to be at variance with the navigator's by 200 degrees. Max's was correct, but before the error was discovered, Ken had headed inland instead of out to sea. They recovered the situation, skirted Hull balloons, set out twenty minutes late, cut corners, risked undivided attention from fighters and still bombed only a minute after the time limit. At the end, all the rest of us were back and there was no sign of them. Harry Wright and I waited anxiously, then heard a plane droning overhead. It droned on for half an hour and we feared it must be damaged; in fact Lay's radio-telephone had become unserviceable and they could not attract attention.

For us this Bremen trip was number twenty. Geoff had been unhappy about it from the outset, having vivid memories of the city as we had seen it from a Wellington IC. He found it no better.

For at least half an hour we were subjected to an incessant barrage – damned hot and accurate. I didn't think it possible to get through unscathed. The strange part is that all Bomber Command's machines returned.

Over the North Sea, homeward bound, Geoff treated us to unintended comedy. Needing to relieve himself but wanting to avoid the long walk back to the Elsan, he handed over the controls to Doug and attempted to use the starboard window. I heard him mutter, 'Jake Kennard says it's possible.' In the next second Frank cried from the mid-upper turret, 'Maddern, y' pissin' all over me tooret an' it's freezin' on!' Geoff moving back hastily, put his left foot on two of the throttles. There was a dramatic swing to port. The experiment was never repeated.

I had never really let my expectations reach as far ahead as twenty ops. Geoff wrote:

Is it to be another five or ten before we are screened? Bunny Austin did his 25th tonight – nothing has been said about screening him.

I navigated for Bunny next day on a cross-country exercise to Glasgow, his own navigator being unavailable. Bunny was a black-haired fellow whose battledress looked too big for him. I was impressed by his alert manner and by his assured crew – silent unless it were really necessary for them to speak.

… We came home very low … just skimming village churches. The white upturned faces fascinated me; especially those of children going home from school.

How could we have bombed them!

Three days later, just before we started leave. I wrote home from the deluding 'plateau of efficiency':

[The days ahead] hold a fascination, for we have something to meet them with – experience. If we survive them, life will seem very strange when the excitement subsides. I never imagined there were many aspects of squadron life that I would learn to love. We are now veterans and are known to every man and girl with whom our lives bring us contact.

211

20
Spring

...all the skill and dedication of the experienced crews was statistically undetectable. Experienced and inexperienced crews were mown down as impartially as the boys who walked into the German machine gun nests at the battle of the Somme in 1916. (*Disturbing the Universe*, by Freeman Dyson, 1981. Dyson was a scientific adviser to Bomber Command)

Setting out that leave, Shag approached the camp gate carrying a suitcase. The guard demanded that he open it, but at once exclaimed, 'For God's sake shut it!' It was packed with partridges.

This was the beginning of the gunners' 'game racket'; even the officers' mess became a beneficiary. Geoff and I, on the other hand, were kept much in the dark. The two gunners began drawing shotguns and cartridges from the armoury at the clay-pigeon range. This saved Frank trying to conceal his folding .410 under his battledress. Not that it went entirely out of use. During his leave he put it under the mattress of his infant niece's pram when he volunteered to take her for a walk. The baby came back riding high on pheasants.

By contrast, my leave at Burnham-on-Sea was quiet and uneventful. I went for a day across to Wells to meet Bill Charlton, that gentlest of *terrorfliegers*, and we walked together in Cheddar Gorge. His crew had finished nine operations, Bill suffering airsickness on nearly every one of them. He refused to make much of it and would not contemplate seeking release on medical grounds. There was about him a faintly incredulous air, as if, even yet, he could not believe he was navigator of a Bomber Command Lancaster. We talked about men gone – a quarter of our training course, and only three of us beyond the halfway mark. We were silent awhile, unable to put words to feelings.

Bill was staying at Frome, his girlfriend's town. I was glad a girl had discovered the reserved, correct, loveable Bill. As with Max and his Brenda, I guessed it to be a painfully chaste relationship.

We parted at the station, Bill holding a large hand to me, each of us uttering the usual, 'Look after yourself', intending no irony. Next day I left for London.

... At Kodak House I inquired ... about the outlook after ops – over-optimistically perhaps. There are chances of going home after six months with Training Command. I am going to see if it's possible to get to Canada.

I went down to Charlwood for my last two days, cycling through the countryside, talking late over the rectory fire, dropping into 'The Half Moon'.

Breakfast in bed! – porridge, egg and bacon, toast and marmalade. Then I cast my conservative eye over The Times *while the Rector's wife discoursed on their huntin', shootin' and fishin' family and the classes of England. Fascinating; distasteful; puzzling. I like these people, though.*

I more than liked them; the Rector had become like a father to me; his wife still researched our family history. They expressed little of their anxiety for their own absent sons.

At Kings Cross I met Harry Wright and Blue Freeman; Cook's crew's leave had coincided with our own. Our train was due out at 4.0; by then shadows wrapped the clinging couples, steam billowed, doors slammed, the cargo of aircrew moved into the voracious north.

We walked up from Barnetby in the dark, speculating on the squadron's fortunes during our absence. They were worse than we could possibly have imagined. Geoff turned for relief to his diary:

... Bunny Austin is missing on a Berlin trip – it was his 29th. Flt Lt Stanhope went on the same raid ... Jock Greig hasn't come back tonight. He was on his 24th. It's bloody awful. They're all going one by one – it makes you wonder when it will be your turn. ... Besides all this Flt Lt Stubbs was up with Crouch and Lee-Brown and crew giving them the gen on skid turns for fighter attacks. He said 240 wasn't fast enough – they stepped the speed up to over 340 then tried. Damned foolish in my opinion. The result was that one of the rudders came off. Everyone baled out but Stubbs – he had no parachute. He flew the machine back here and seemed to have full control. His first attempt at landing was unsuccessful. When turning to do the second circuit the other rudder came off. He went straight in. They discovered afterwards that there was a spare 'chute in the machine – bloody shame.

It was a measure of Geoff's spirit that he finished:

It's not worrying me. I have faith that we are to see Aussie again.

I was by no means so confident. If Austin's crew could go, anyone's could. As for Stubbs, he was a decorated two-tour man. On that night of our return I waited for Lay's crew to arrive back from Hamburg and, having greeted Max, hung about fruitlessly for Greig and Peter Bailey, his navigator. Max wrote before bed:

Greig went from here tonight, on his 24th trip. Makes me realize how slim are the chances of getting through.

He added in the morning:

... What a long road there is to travel. I shall never believe the boys of the old flight have been killed, not till after the war and everything is cleared up. It is not possible that such real, vibrant

personalities should suddenly cease to exist. ... — If only one of our twenty survives, all his life he will have around him the laughing shades of nineteen other blokes, of the most congenial bunch of lads ever to leave their homeland. Don has only to keep alive for three more weeks. It all feels so unreal.

Geoff reported another blow next morning.

B crashed last night, and is a complete write off. It happened somewhere in Shropshire. The pilot, a Yugoslav, was killed; all the rest of the crew baled out. As yet I haven't heard full details. Apparently an engine caught on fire; they put it out and restarted the engine – a bad mistake. [The fire] started again, That is all I know so far. ... It's like losing a member of the crew. ...

We had done fifteen ops in B; she had been our major talisman. That day, March 5, we were briefed to take U-Uncle to Essen, our first operation there since loss of Laing's crew. Geoff confessed uneasiness, but for us the raid turned out well. He reckoned it the most devastating we had seen:

... We saw hundreds upon hundreds of searchlights – they covered the whole of the Rhur. ... I shall never forget the sight that confronted me – we were in on the kill, so saw the fires at their best. Smoke was pouring up to 7000 feet ... one huge blazing area of over a mile square. It was a wonderful concentration; only two dropped their incendiaries outside. In the midst of this veritable hell could be seen the red TI* markers. You must hand it out to Jerry. He sticks to his post in the face of all odds. ...

This was the enemy whose morale 'Butch' was confident of breaking. Fourteen aircraft of 386 that reached the target were lost. Middlebrook and Everitt have it that fifty-three of Krupp's buildings were hit, though the main damage lay between there and the city centre; 3,018 houses were destroyed; be-

---

*   *TI :* Pathfinder Force 'target indicators'.

tween four and five hundred people killed. I wrote home in the morning:

No town in the world has suffered as German cities are suffering now. Though they started the business, it is a dreadful state of affairs. There is some justice in our high casualties. ...

We were briefed for Essen again next day. Max had the uneasy feeling before take-off that the defences would be ready for our return.

It was a very still evening and we were waiting in the dispersal for take-off just as the sun went down. Spotting a couple of vans on the horizon we cocked our ears and found it was a scrub! It was like the lifting of a great weight – we all yelled with relief. We presented some of our chocolate to the people on the farm near our dispersal, salvaged what coffee the ground crew had left and departed in high glee to get undressed. I did not realize just how strong had been the strain until sudden and unexpected relief showed it up. We had a special bus put on to carry us to Scunthorpe and about half the squadron descended on the 'Oswald.'

The weather was improving; foggy mornings followed by clear days, with horizons extending far beyond their winter limits. The feel of spring in the air fostered hope that we or Kennard or Cook or Roper would soon reach thirty. On March 8 the attack was suddenly switched to distant cities, the first to Nuremburg, a return trip of over eight hours. I recorded it as 'a mild target and a poor prang', but Middlebrook and Everitt give 600 buildings destroyed, including the M.A.N. and Siemen's factories and over 300 people killed. RAF losses were eight aircraft.

This turned out to be Jake Kennard's last operation of his first tour. Although the crew had not reached thirty, the need for instructors was still pressing. Everyone was sorry to see

216

them go, for Jake himself was lively and gregarious and a born leader; each of the crew was an identity. This outstanding combination was to be lost from Elsham seven months later, early on their second tour.

Geoff wrote the day after Nuremburg:

We're on ops tonight. Target Munich. … Quite naturally we're all very tired and moaning because it will be another trip of eight hours. …

Before take-off Doc Henderson was liberal with tablets and powders, Lay's crew, on their eighth operation in ten nights, receiving maximum attention. Max wrote:

… a spoonful of pink mixture to settle my stomach, five B1 tablets to give me a bit of energy and two caffeine tablets to keep me awake, so I felt like a walking chemist's shop.

On this Munich operation we took a Lancaster III for the first time, but it turned out to be incompletely prepared. We were still over the aerodrome when I discovered that the Gee wasn't functioning. Later on Geoff recorded its other deficiencies:

There was no quadrantal correction card for the loop and no IFF. We carried on. Don did a wizard trip navigationally. Couldn't have been better. These IIIs are dreams – they climb and fly beautifully. … There was a hell of a concentration of searchlights when the first TIs went down. I stooged around outside and waited for some mugs to break them up. They did, and got coned into the bargain. … As we were coming out there was a tremendous explosion beneath us. Must have been a petrol dump. …

Max recorded it as 'a lurid flash.'

Immediately afterwards a fiery red billow of flame rolled up to a thousand feet turning night into day by the intensity of its light. Every detail was clearly lit up – clouds, kites – we felt naked. For

217

five seconds perhaps it burned then died as suddenly as it came,
leaving a pall of white smoke.

We returned home to numbing news: Johnnie Roper, on his
twenty-fourth operation, had failed to return. Those of us who
had come to the squadron when his crew did, felt for them
deeply. Roper was married and had a small son.

According to Middlebrook and Everitt's analysis, our
bombing of Munich had been haphazard. The BMW aero-
assembly shop was put out of action for six weeks and 293
other military buildings were hit, but also we hit eleven
hospitals, the cathedral, four churches and killed 208 people.
Eight bombers were lost – over fifty men. What the explosion
had been, we never heard.

Roper, Greig and Austin had been men lighting the way to
thirty ops. They had been our familiars ever since we had
come to the squadron. It didn't do now to think of them. With
Kennard and his men off the scene, only Syd Cook's crew and
our own were within striking distance of thirty. Syd and
Harry Wright teamed well, contrasting pair though they
were. Syd, a tall, fair, clean-cut youth, was now commissioned
and wearing a DFM. He was the youngest of the West Australian pilots yet was to go from sergeant to Squadron Leader in
six weeks. Though ambitious, he was also shy and sardonic.
Harry was lank, unshorn, untidy, his expression often lugu-
brious and oppressed. I suspected this to be a persona culti-
vated with Irish perversity to mislead the RAF. He, too, was to
go far. A great strength of their crew was the versatility of
Blue Freeman who could take over almost any role – navigator, bombaimer, gunner, even emergency pilot.

One night off, then return to southwest Germany, this time
to Stuttgart, Geoff with a heavy cold,

I coughed all the way there and back. Not very nice when you're
at oxygen height. I was as weak as a kitten and it was all I could

*do to keep the weaving up. Don did a jolly good job navigationally.
… We were the only A flight crew to get to the target. … This was
our 24th trip. Went to bed feeling fairly ill. Told Wg Cdr not to
expect me to operate for a day or so.*

It had been another journey far beyond Oboe range. According to Middlebrook & Everitt most of our bombs fell in open countryside, even so over a hundred houses were destroyed about 200 people killed. Eleven aircraft of 314 attacking were lost.

In the morning Doc Henderson sent Geoff to sickquarters and prescribed treatment every two hours, nevertheless the Wing Commander made sure Ted and I attended navigator's briefing 'in case Maddern is discharged.' To my relief, he remained where he was, as the target was Essen. I had no desire just then to return to Happy Valley. The loss rate on the distant targets had averaged 3%; the attack that night on Essen brought it back to 5% and this included one of our new crews. I found I could not even visualize the missing men.

On one of the distant targets we had experienced a disconcerting take off. Above the cockpit was an escape hatch – often the pilot's only hope of getting out – unless he was blown out. This hatch itself blew out as we gathered speed on the runway. A cold gale swept papers off my table. Then I saw Doug ripping the lining off his side of the fuselage. Holding a piece to the empty hatch, it was sucked into place and the gale ceased. It was an action typical of his quick thinking and ingenuity. By the time of our return we had forgotten about it. As we slowed on the runway the piece of lining landed on Geoff's head – fortunately without much force.

Lay's crew went off on leave, Max assuring me cheerfully that we would be finished by the time he returned. In fact, we were to do no operations at all. Twice we were briefed for Augsburg, twice it was scrubbed because of forecast fog. I was glad of it, as it was my turn to feel off colour. 'Don has a nasty cold,' Geoff mused in his diary, 'but still he persists in his study of haystack formations.'

On those chill evenings haystacks held almost as many aircrew and Waafs as they held mice, but had I been living up to all Geoff suspected of me, I would have been beyond flying altogether. He was confident still that we would reach thirty and was beginning to lament the prospect of losing his crew:

> ... it's going to be tough when we're screened. If you see one of the boys, you can guarantee that the rest are waiting around the corner. In the mess they make more noise than the rest of the NCOs put together ...

With six operations still to do, the prolonged run of fog left us restless; we and Cook's crew had now had thirty scrubbed ops. I escaped on March 15 to Mrs. Baker's:

> ... did not even feel like writing home ... just lazed in front of the fire. I listened to music from Germany. Jerry came over and there was a warning of 1 1/2 hours. The drone of planes was very distinct and guns close to us were firing. I'm afraid I was hoping the raiders would get away – quite futilely tho', I think.

Next day the sun broke through and shone warmly enough for us to lie out in it in an attempt to get rid of our colds, but by evening fog closed in again and ops were scrubbed.

During the period of evening fogs Lay's crew came back from leave. There was soon unanticipated news for them that I viewed with forebodings: they had been posted to Pathfinders. All through his Air Force life, Max Bryant had been a young enthusiast – articulate, dedicated, personable. This and the fact that he was commissioned, meant he was bound to be noticed by senior officers. These things, probably more than any other crew factor, led to the sudden change in their fortunes. Max wrote on March 21:

About 11am Ken gave me a great shock; we were posted to Pathfinders without any choice at all. This was a blow to all of us, as we had settled down in Elsham and came to like the place. To me especially it was a bitter pill, for it meant leaving Don after seven short weeks and moving right down south out of 1 Group. The Wingco had conveniently absented himself and there was nothing we could do about it.

Ken, a sergeant still, had built himself a good reputation as a pilot, but it was doubtful that anyone at Elsham knew of the rift that still existed in his crew, a rift that would hamper them in the exacting task ahead. On the day they received their posting, 103 Squadron had a stand-down. Our crew had elected to go on a cross-country flight for the fun of it, so I was glad when Max decided to come with us as far as Breighton, base then of the Australian 460 Squadron. Chiefly he wanted to see Bill Charlton for whom he always felt special concern and affection.

Loaded with several ground crew, including two Waafs, we took off. After dropping Max we went low over Lichfield, North Wales and the Lake District, everyone relishing the sight-seeing. When we returned to Breighton Max told me that Bill Charlton, despite his airsickness, was up to fifteen operations. Other news was that George Loder's crew had been posted from 460 to 156, the same Pathfinder squadron as Max. Although glad that two of our old Edmonton family were going to be together, I was concerned even more for George than I was for Max. As a married man and a father, I had hoped he would reach thirty and finish.

Lay's crew left Elsham in the morning; we waved them goodbye, then went to briefing for St. Nazaire, glad of an easy target for our twenty-fifth.

Geoff's corkscrewing that night was more vicious than ever; I can still see those strong hands on the control column and the rhythmical movement of his shoulders.

221

Made the evasive action pretty violent. Don was sick ... [He] got his new Gee right down to the target. We were coming back at a good speed when word came through about a diversion to Pershore. Two squadrons were to put down there, so I opened her up even more – were second to put down. Some of the lads were circling for two hours.

The other diverted squadron turned out to be 460, I cast about for Bill Charlton. There was no sign of their crew. We learned later that they had been badly knocked about. During a fighter attack an engine had been knocked out and their 4000 lb. bomb had hung up. Efforts to free the bomb failed, so there was no option but to land with it on. Dave White, their twenty-year old pilot – a handsome, slight lad who looked as if he ought still be at school in Colac – nursed the aircraft back to England and landed successfully in Cambridgeshire. He received an immediate award of the DFM.

Geoff likened our packed accommodation at Pershore to the Black Hole of Calcutta. It was midday before we landed at Elsham. Any prospect of rest vanished when we were ordered back to Pershore to pick up two crews whose aircraft proved too damaged to fly home. By bedtime Geoff was determined to have a morning sleep-in, but the RAF had other plans.

The station played at war this morning. Not me. I slept in until 10.45. At 8.45 the adjutant came around and caught me. He made excuses to the SWO* and saved me ...

Through some misunderstanding, Geoff was not saved at all; he was put on a charge for 'failing to attend parade' and 'being in bed two hours five minutes after reveille.' As a nice touch of irony the charge was heard the day after he had been interviewed for a commission. He had already written about his interview:

---

* Station Warrant Officer

My conscience pricked me when [the Wingco] asked me to define the responsibilities of an officer. Afraid I'm not exactly an example for discipline. Only this morning, when we were supposed to make our beds up for inspection, I left mine down, locked the door and hid the key. ...

Despite his setback, he and four others of our crew were interviewed by the Group Captain for commissioning: Doug, Ted, Graham and myself. The gunners knew the uselessness of applying; Graham, though he was close to completing two tours and had a DFM, would have needed the coaching of Shaw's Professor Higgins to stand a hope of being accepted as a 'gentleman.' The rest of us were well received by Groupie Dickens, Geoff included. That night there were ops. to Duisburg. The nearer we came to thirty the more Geoff corkscrewed.

Laid the evasive action on thick and heavy coming home – Don was sick. ... The taps were well open on the sea crossing – averaged 220 all the way home and cut the corner to Mablethorpe ... That's our 26th behind us ...

I had now been sick three times and was beginning to get some idea of Bill Charlton's sufferings, but it was small insurance to pay for survival. It seemed reasonable to suppose that fighters would first attack aircraft flying straight and level.

Cook's crew and our own were now the only two remaining of our intake and the only ones on the squadron close to thirty. We were level pegging at twenty-six, but next night Cook's crew passed us. We had both been briefed for Berlin, but for us it was to prove an 'abortive.' Geoff wrote next day:

Went out to take off in B. On the run up we received no joy from the supercharger – did everything possible in the limited time to

223

remedy the defect. Take-off was at 8.10 pm. At five past we realized that we would have to take the spare aircraft, G for George. We did a record changeover – ran her up and were airborne at 8.26 pm. By set-course time we had 5000 ft. on the altimeter and were well on time considering the trouble we were confronted with at the outset. Over the North Sea at 14,000 ft. the starboard inner engine revs. began a 200 fluctuation, also the boost by 2 lbs. The fault was the mixture control not operating on Stromberg carburettors. We had no success in overcoming the trouble but continued to climb. Round about 16,000 ft. the port outer began exactly the same thing – surging continually. Doug cut one motor, exercised the blower, exercised the constant speed control, changed tanks and we even tried her in hot air. It was all to no avail. Being a technical matter, I asked Doug's advice. Due to the resultant detonation and the possibility of fire breaking out, as well as the consequent loss in power and over-heating and damage to the engines, he advised me when 50 miles from the enemy coast, to abandon the sortie. I didn't like the idea, but considered it the wisest action to take. We came home. The front turret draught stops were missing – I nearly froze. Shag's rear panel fell out – he froze, too. We landed at 10.30 pm – seven very disappointed men.

In the morning the Wing Commander called Geoff and Doug to his office and demanded their reasons for turning back.

First of all he maintains that B was OK. Secondly, on ground run this morning, G was OK. They forget that this trouble with the Stromberg carburettor is prevalent at altitudes above 14,000 ft. We outlined our reasons for turning back, but … he said he was putting the reason for abandonment of the sortie down to lack of determination. However I controlled my temper I don't know – I could have killed the bastard there and then. When Doug explained the technicalities, he said that he knew too much and

*was a bad influence on me. Bloody ridiculous thing to say ...
There and then I told him I was appealing against his decision.
I've stood up to too many of his insults. We saw the station
Engineering Officer afterwards and were told that we were quite
justified in our action. In Command anything up to 4 machines
a week are turning back through this defect. Through insults such
as these I have seen many good crews thrown away. Finest chaps
in the world ... If he thinks I'm to be influenced by what he says,
he has another think coming. ...*

*29th March: ... Proof has come to hand that B was definitely U/
S. The pressure relief valve was sticking. We're on tonight. I pray
the Almighty Father that we get off. ... It's to be the Big City
again.*

He added after our return:

*What a mess it all was. Met was far from good. Were to take off
at 7.15. It was cancelled till midnight. We all went back to the
mess. A tannoy message came through at 7.30 to say that we had
to be back in the crew room at 7.45. Take-off was to be 9.15. The
rain was pouring down, a driving gale was blowing and the cloud
base down to 800 feet. ... We taxied around to the take-off point
– more hold up. Three machines had to stop their motors because
of over-heating. We had the sense to turn into wind while
waiting. I had to skirt around on the grass in front of two. We took
off 20 min. late and climbed through icing clouds on the beam up
to 10,000 ft. before setting course. From Mablethorpe to almost
5 degrees E. we were flying in severe icing conditions; the clouds
were right up to 20,000 ft. The blue flames of static lightning
could be seen jumping all over the machine [which] was sluggish
on the climb with the added load of ice. ... the first machine we saw
go down was on our starboard at Flensburg. It started off as a dull
red glow in a glide, gradually brightening as the fires took hold.
It disappeared in cloud and then – a terrific explosion. Poor*

blighters, they hadn't reached their target. ...

We arrived well on time. As we approached the outskirts [of Berlin] hundreds of searchlights began their sinister search for stray machines. One was picked up. A few minutes later we saw him go down and explode on impact. Did a number of orbits outside the city waiting for the PFF to drop their target indicators. They went down at 0049. We made our run in ... and unloaded our cargo – waiting, of course, for someone to break up the tremendous searchlight concentrations. To the north of the town there was a cone of over a hundred beams trained on one of our machines. Another machine was caught in the same cone but higher up. The lower of the two received the undivided attention of almost a hundred heavy AA guns. He went down – a brilliant explosion in the middle of the city marked his end.

We were one of the first to bomb ... We must have been ahead of the PFF on the way home – the yellow track indicators came up behind us. Ran across the outskirts of Magdeburg and had a willing few moments with searchlights and AA. At this stage Shag's rear turret went U/S. Doug went down and spent an hour and a half trying to build up the hydraulic supply from the mid-upper turret. Ted came up and took his position as engineer. Don did a wonderful trip navigationally. ... Saw one machine go down just north of Osnabruck, another down near Zwolle. ... Don ... brought us out five miles south of Texel. ... All our kites returned. ... we learnt that all times had been put back a quarter of an hour. In that case, we must have been stooging in with the PFF and quite possibly it would account for the heavy losses. 21 failed to return. ...

On this raid 460 Squadron lost Tom McNeill, golden-hearted warrior of our Edmonton course. He had been too badly wounded to bale out. Two others of the crew perished with him. Middlebrook and Everitt give the losses as 6.4%. It adds to the poignancy of such heavy losses to read that ' – most of the bombs fell in open country 6 miles south-east of Berlin

... ' Over 2300 men strove against bad weather, inaccurate wind forecasts and long distances to little avail. When news of Tom McNeill reached Max he wrote:

> ... that is the sixth [of our course] and not one yet finished a tour. No wonder one becomes a little bitter and cynical at times. ...

The same operation had cost him a room mate:

> ... the third ex-room mate of mine to buy it. I wonder what plan it is that picks one chap and leaves another? Every time one of the boys goes, it makes you wonder whether you'll see another dawn yourself.

Sqr Ldr C. O'Donoghue had come to 103 Squadron as Jake Kennard's successor. We heard – with what truth I don't know – that he had been accustomed to daylight operations. At all events, on March 20, after operations the night before to St. Nazaire had been cancelled, he went out alone in daylight and attacked the town of Leer, just over the German border, southeast of Emden. Despite the great risk incurred, he returned.

Middlebrook and Everitt report his next operation – again by day – this time on April 1:

> A lone Lancaster of 103 Squadron, again piloted by Squadron Leader C. O'Donoghue, set out to bomb the town of Emmerich just over the German border, but the Lancaster was shot down over Holland, the crew were all killed.

At Elsham we were unaware they had been shot down. As a distress call had been heard from them, we were sent over the North Sea to search for them – six aircraft in pairs. I wrote later:

> Gale weather still persists and waves 30 to 40 feet high were running. It is almost needless to say that we found nothing, though we scanned the sea for two hours through binoculars.

Close now to thirty, we could have done without extra risks, but Geoff was asked to test A Apple, Kennard's aircraft after it had been fitted with two new engines. We all flew with him.

On take-off the port-inner nearly came adrift – it vibrated like hell. A bent crankshaft. We feathered it as soon as we were airborne. Prepared to come in to land on three ... On making final approach control gave us a red when we were about to touch down. The second circuit was wizard. Came in and made a perfect landing. The starboard inner packed up on the runway – lack of fuel pressure. We had two armoury sergeants with us – poor blighters, they were scared to death.

A letter from Nell was waiting for me in the mess pigeon-holes.

She is jubilant to hear that my ops are so close to 30. I shall not be jubilant till 30 are over. One has either finished or not finished ... Tonight we are to go to Happy Valley again – Essen it is. I think this will be our seventh trip to the place and it seems to get progressively worse. I am sitting by an open window in the mess, a soft spring breeze drifting in.

In Geoff's view this was the most menacing operation of our tour.

The air was alive with night fighters and bursting shells all along our route. Seventy miles from Essen we saw four machines go down in the space of two minutes. One in the target, one a few hundred yards away on our starboard; the third northwest of Essen and the last behind us as we made our way in. Others could be seen going down all around us. The searchlight cones seemed well occupied, so in we went. Hell! it was like hell in there. Fingers of light were feeling for us; shells bursting very close, bumping and rattling on the fuselage. Even their night fighters were in there. About a thousand yards away I saw one kite cop a packet.

He burst into flames and started going down. A fighter must have been on his tail – he kept pumping tracer into him as he was going down. After what seemed an eternity we unloaded our bombs and got out of the hottest reception I've yet received from the enemy. Coming home we had to corkscrew nearly all the way. We seemed surrounded by fighters. Don brought us out nicely on track. ... Came at an average of 220 mph. Everyone in the crew admitted on landing that it was the most hair-raising affair they've been on. I'm not afraid to admit I was scared. ... That's 28 behind us and two to go.

6% of 348 aircraft attacking had been lost; two more crashed on return. Middlebrook & Everitt report the damage as widespread at the centre of Essen and in its western half.

In the morning came a break in my long association with Harry Wright. Most of Cook's crew had decided to go to Pathfinders; they, too, had been posted to 156 Squadron. The crew had done twenty-eight operations; Harry twenty-nine. Sorry though I was to lose his good company, I was consoled by the conviction that he would come through, however much he strained his luck. Even so, it was beyond all imagining that he would survive seventy-eight operations on heavy bombers. Blue Freeman alone remained on at Elsham, operating with crews needing a fill-in navigator or bombaimer.

The squadron's attention was now centred on us. Either we would show that thirty could be done from Elsham or give rise to strong superstition that 103 was indeed a hoodoo squadron. The day after Cook's crew left we were briefed for Kiel. Geoff wrote:

The girls waved us off the runway and waited until we came in at 1.20. Now that we are close to the end, everyone is taking a particular interest in the crew. ... It was a big effort of 570 machines. ... We've regained the blue riband and were first back tonight. The strain of the last few trips is beginning to tell – I'll be glad when it's all over. ... Where will the next one be, and what is to be the outcome?

Cloud over Kiel had been very thick. According to Middlebrook and Everitt, only a few bombs fell in the town area; no commercial premises were hit. For this poor result, over eighty aircrew were lost.

Before we could get away on our thirtieth, England was beset by gales. Down at Warboys Max wrote home:

The winds were sweeping across the country with fierce strength rising in gusts at ground level to 60 miles per hour ... Three belts of bad weather have passed during the day, and now that they have gone the night is perfect. The only sound I can hear is the faint crackle of my stove and the squeak of the pen. ... Now spring is really coming ... fruit trees are breaking into flower, pink and white and sweet-smelling. ... There is a new warm crispness in the air, the birth of a new season of rich promise. ...

He then wrote to me:

I hope you and the crew aren't getting too nervous about this thirtieth trip. It is natural, I suppose, for 29 trips all to appear as normal routine and for the 30th to assume gargantuan propor-tions. ... I know you will be careful, but for heavens sake don't keep going if something goes wrong simply because it is the 30th.

On April 8 we took off on the last of our many 'fun flights' which briefly put our thirtieth out of mind. Geoff was in his element on these occasions:

Did a wizard air test in B this morning. She's just been on a 50 hour inspection and is absolutely tops. They're a great ground crew – can't do enough for us. After trying the controls in steep turns, dives and climbs, we went over behind Scunthorpe and did a spot of low flying. One chappie nearly jumped from his truck when he saw us bearing down on him. Frank reckons he could have picked a fish out of the Trent.

By afternoon his mood had sobered:

We're on tonight – only the old crews. Heck, I'll be glad when it is over. It's the Valley; weather bloody awful, but still, the sooner it is over the better. ... Surprising the number of people who conveyed their hopes for this our last trip being a safe one.

So here it was. Tomorrow it might be possible to contemplate a reasonable future ...

In the room we had shared for the most unforgettable days of our lives, Geoff wrote on April 9:

Take off [for Duisburg] was not until 8.45 pm. It was Peg's night off, but still she came and drove us to our machine. Poor kid, she was on the verge of breaking down when she left us. ... The winds were terrific – 110mph from the northwest. It was all Don could do to keep us clear of Amsterdam. Quite a decent quantity of AA was hurled at us along the route in. Only by chance did we run across the sky markers. Saw no warning flares, so turned on ETA. After two minutes someone commented on the quantity of flak coming up, then, with a surprised voice Ted said, 'There's the flares dead beneath us in the cloud.' (We were in cloud at 21,000 feet) We were the only ones in the squadron to locate them. ... Were first back, and so ends a comparatively uneventful tour of operations. I can't realize that the seven of us are due to be separated any time now. ... I wonder how long it will be before we're longing to get back again?

'A comparatively uneventful tour of operations'! 'Longing to get back again'! The thoughts are very much Geoff's; I did not share them, but, on reflection, I recognized that it *was* a comparatively uneventful tour. After all, most men died and most of those who did complete a tour had experiences very

231

much worse than ours. And Geoff was right about himself; he *would* soon long to get back. But for now there was rejoicing and cables to be sent and phone calls made and a party in Scunthorpe with the groundcrew.

While we were celebrating at the 'Crosby', the squadron was out again to Duisburg, again in thick cloud. Ken Bickers,* a twenty-one year old friend of Max's, was attacked by two night fighters; his rear gunner was killed, his mid-upper gunner seriously wounded. Although the plane was badly damaged, he nursed it home and successfully landed, for which he received an immediate DFC. We went on leave with praise of him ringing in our ears. Ours had indeed been 'a comparatively uneventful tour', his nearer the norm

---

* K.G. Bickers, a Flying Officer at the time of this award, was killed on operations from 103 Squadron to Berlin on March 25, 1944. He was by then a Squadron Leader. It was the last raid by RAF heavy bombers on Berlin; 72 of the attacking force were lost – 8.9%.

21

End of the Crew

What a desolation is Coventry. The centre of the city is nothing but a barren waste. Outside the town stands a huge memorial over the communal grave of some 600 victims of one of the big raids. The drive through Stratford, Evesham, the Cotswolds and on to Wales is beautiful. It has been a glorious day. The roads were lined with fresh green hedges, the trees have their new spring foliage and the cherry and apple trees are in full blossom ... (Geoff Maddern, April 11 1943).

Geoff and I had left Elsham with Doug in the mid-afternoon of April 10 and were spending the night in Coventry. Its desolation was all the uglier after the beauty of the drive. Yet we had done worse than this, much worse. And had paid a much higher price in the doing of it.

At Burnham-on-Sea Nora and Stella greeted me with tears of relief. When I sat after dinner to write home, I felt stunned by stillness and homely sounds.

... No simile can quite catch this overwhelming calm of surroundings and mind after the past seven months. ...

Max had received my telegram giving our news; he wrote in his diary:

This is one relief; now only Bill [Charlton] to worry about. Harry [Wright] has also finished his first tour. ... That makes two finished a tour, seven missing. Not such a hot average.

He added later:

Don is lucky in that he foresaw all this. I was not quite so wise – somewhere there was the idea that people did get killed on operations. But it was all a game in Canada – just good work and grand fun. I couldn't visualize anything happening to the laughing twenty that made up our flight. I can remember prophesying that our flight would be lucky; but it does not seem to be working out that way. Maybe after the war we will be able to count heads and see just how the old crowd fared.

I might have foreseen the outcome, but I had certainly not expected my own survival.

I went down to Cornwall to see Jim Riddoch.* As Coastal Command demanded a longer tour than Bomber Command, he was operating still, but the squadron had fortunately converted from Whitleys to Halifaxes – an improved mark of Halifax to those that had plagued Elsham We looked back wryly on our expectations when we had volunteered in 1940; they had come to nothing; this, in fact, was to be the only day on which we actually flew together – a brief flight from St. Eval to Fowey for bombing practice. I wrote to Max while we flew low along the Cornish coast:

> *The little fields of England, green and ochre, come to these cliff edges and from there begins the ocean, today lazy and burnished by the sun.*
>
> *I intend leaving tomorrow for Exeter or thereabouts, and from there hope to walk northward through Devon.*

I finished with feelings of guilt; I was alive with all this beauty spread before me; he was operating still and faced by the daunting total of forty-five.

I decided on the Exe Valley because the map showed a stream descending between close contours and green splashes of woods; higher up were moorlands. Even so I was not

---

* Both Jim Riddoch and Claude Austin survived their Coastal Command tours.

prepared for the rich fare ahead. All these years later my diary bears me to two days that crowned my life in England, back to the feeling that nature was brimming with healing and sanity.

... I toiled up a lane and descended eventually on to Bampton, a sleepy little valley town. In soft light and the cool of the evening I walked on to Exebridge ... first uphill, then down, down again to the Exe. 'They'll do yerr well at the Hanchor.'

It was too late for dinner at the 'Anchor', but they fried ham and an egg for me. The inn lay beside the Exe; over the bridge was Somerset. In bed I studied the map and decided to walk in the morning to Dulverton, on the Barle, a tributary of the Exe, then on up the Barle to the moors around Winsford. I put the map aside, read T. E. Lawrence's letters awhile then fell asleep.

Frid. 16th April: Breakfast and then the road again, this time to Dulverton – a lovely town deep below the moors. I was delayed by a flock of sheep and followed them through the street. Though I had planned to reach Winsford, eight miles away, by midday, I now decided to walk with the shepherds ... Thus I continued for the whole morning, yarning to the two men and loitering pleasantly. All the morning I knew again the pungent odor of sheep, their silly leaping and bobbing gait, and saw again the play of bright sunlight across their backs. ... The [Barle] ran further and further below us as we climbed till eventually we came to the head of the valley where a number of springs formed the stream. The main spring flowed into a trough on which was inscribed, 'Freely have Ye received, freely give.' The water was clear and marvellously cold. The overflow ran down into the valley below. ... I followed the sheep until we were well up on the moors, a brown and silent place, devoid of all habitations.

Up there I came across an ancient, rough obelisk, on it the name 'CARACTACUS'. Whether it marked the site of one of his

235

battles, or was a memorial to him, I did not know, but I felt his presence in that lonely place, brief company as I passed.

Having descended steeply into Winsford I entered under the thatch of the 'Royal Oak', thinking it a beautiful place to stay the night, but when I phoned Nora and Stella it was to hear that our crew was recalled to Elsham for postings.

Surprisingly all seven of us arrived back on time. Geoff walked up from Barnetby with Lucette Edwards, the young intelligence officer who had so often interrogated us.

[She] gave me all the news about the boys. Lee-Brown is missing, Stoneman ditched and his machine floated for twelve hours. ... A number of the boys have been badly shot up. ... Methinks we got out just in time.

Johnnie Stoneman had run out of fuel over the North Sea after an operation to Spezia. The crew had been rescued after three and a half hours. Bomber Command had not finished with them; they were lost on operations three months later.

As far as we could ascertain, no 103 Squadrom crew had completed a tour since mid 1942 – over nine months back. But our good fortune was like the slight easing of a log jam; a trickle of crews began getting through. A trickle of survivors was all any Bomber Command squadron could claim for many a month yet.

To Geoff's chagrin his posting was to Lichfield, back onto Wellingtons; his heart had been set on Lindholme, where Lancasters were beginning to be used for training. Ironically, this was where Doug and Shag and I had been posted. Ted was posted to a bombing leader's course; Frank as a gunnery instructor to Finningley; Graham to Transport Command. There was little prospect of our ever getting together again, let alone flying together as a crew. We delayed our break-up so long that the adjutant threatened Geoff with a charge.

Despite all the moans and protests, it looks as though I'll have to go to Lichfield. Yesterday afternoon when I was packing the lads came in to say goodbye. Shag and Frank were both tight. At the time I was just in my U pants and shirt. They took me onto the road and bumped me thirty times. It was rotten seeing them going....

So ended the crew; only five of us ever got together again – and that was fourteen years later.

Lindholme was a permanent RAF station with two-storey brick buildings. After Elsham Wolds it seemed luxurious but I felt utterly lost without Geoff. Large numbers of Australians were in crews converting there before being allocated to squadrons. News at Lindholme of our Edmonton course of navigators was worse than ever. Two of the youngest had gone: Ron Wheatley, who had just turned twenty-two, and Ian Heatley. Close on this came Max's harshest blow:

This morning I heard from George [Loder] the worst news the war has brought me. Bill Charlton was missing from Stettin. It is unreal – I cannot grasp or believe it. I sent a telegram to 'Stiffy' just to make sure, and it was so. 460 [Squadron] has lost eleven crews in sixteen days. ... The news brought me a sense of weariness, of futility, of bitterness. In one breath I feel I must give it all up, must run away and hide before some new blow finds me. In the next I feel a surge of anger, something that drives me to want to operate ...

That is nine of the twenty. It is with a strange sense of detachment that one sees the list narrow, and wonder if you will be the next. Now and then I feel it is all a bad dream and that suddenly I shall wake up and find myself back in the canteen at Edmonton, with the juke box playing 'Concerto for Two' and all the boys lining up for toasted tomato sandwiches and hot choco-late. Bill, the gentlest, hardest working, and most loveable of all

– now a name. To some perhaps just that – a name in the casualty list. To those of us who knew him, a flame that will burn steadily in our memory while ever we hold on to life. Life goes on – if we did not have something to fill our minds we should go crackers ... We got as far as briefing; five minutes before it was due to start, the operation was cancelled. ... We have come back to the billet, and I am trying to think what to say if I write to Don. Maybe I'll just read some blood and thunder yarn and keep my mind from 'Stiffy's' brief telegram – 'Yes, that is correct.'

Bill was twenty-five, son of the Clerk of the Legislative Council of New South Wales. Like most of us, he had written a 'last letter' before the 'flaps' from Lichfield and had kept it among his belongings. After nearly fifty years, his words reflect a vanished era:

My dear Mum and Dad,

It is a year today since we sailed, and this naturally sets one reflecting on a number of matters – home, and all that it means; the past twelve months, and how packed with activity and new experiences they have been for me, and what may lie ahead.

Coming away has served to give me a fuller realization and appreciation of home, and this means primarily you. Living with different fellows, from all walks of life, and getting to know them well makes me understand more and more as time passes just how wonderful you have been, what your love and example have meant, what a grand start you have given me, and what I owe to you. Such things are beyond any repayment – I can only acknowledge this debt with gratitude too deep to express.

This last year has been an anxious and worrying one for you, and I feel rather ashamed when I consider how light-hearted and care-free I have been. But I want you to know that I am happy, although it is idle and untrue to say I do not miss you – happy when I consider all the wonderful blessings that I have received, – the fellowship of the chaps themselves, the new and magnificent sights I have seen, the kindness and hospitality of people everywhere, and the safety of my training, to mention but a few.

Now should anything untoward happen, please don't grieve and worry, for I am in the Lord's care and put my trust in Him. What I want of you is to be cheerful and continue to give thanks for all the blessings that have been mine. Stern tasks lie ahead, but when the time comes for them to be met and done I trust I shall prove worthy of the faith you have placed in me.

May God bless and protect you,

Your loving son,

Bill.

22
Return to Lichfield

On Sunday 27th June 1943, at Chequers, the Australian member of the British War Cabinet, Richard Casey, was among Churchill's guests. 'Tonight at Chequers,' he noted in his diary, 'in the course of a film showing the bombing of German towns from the air (made up from films taken during actual bombing raids) very well and dramatically done, WSC suddenly sat bolt upright and said to me, 'Are we beasts? Are we taking this too far?' (Churchill, a Photographic Portait, by Martin Gilbert, Heinemann, London, 1988)

Only a few days after I had settled at Lindholme I was told the posting ought to have been to Lichfield.

As I sat at dinner wondering how on earth I could get to Lichfield on time, a familiar voice said, 'Well, you might have a clean plate for me!' It was Max.

Of course, [this] solved transport difficulties. We swopped tunics and he dined in the sergeants mess, then we took off, my kit and bike aboard.

This turned out to be my last flight in a Lancaster – appropriately, with my flying partner of Edmonton days. We talked for some time of Bill Charlton, then began paying more attention to photography than to navigation. As a result we were soon lost over England in daylight – a Pathfinder and a tour-expired navigator! It was as if we had been back in Alberta, trying to find some elusive turning point. Late in the afternoon we landed, much chastened, at Fradley.

For Geoff, posted alone to Lichfield, the break-up of the crew had been desolating.

When I went into the mess tonight I felt absolutely lost and very miserable. As I walked in, a familiar voice from behind hailed, 'What are you doing here Maddern?' My heart jumped with joy when I saw it was Don. Gee it's great to have one of the boys down here. We're both in the same bunk and intend reforming and leading a sedate life – for how long I wonder.

Next day he was posted to Church Broughton, the new satellite aerodrome which had replaced Tatenhill. After this I saw him infrequently. I had refrained from passing on news I had heard of him: he was to be awarded a Distinguished Flying Medal. His first word of it came in a congratulatory cable from his family; the official notification arrived later the same day.

It's beyond my conception … I would much rather it had gone to Max [Burcher] – he was more deserving of it. And furthermore, why shouldn't the rest of the crew get one? I did nothing they didn't do.

I had no doubt that it was he who had shaped us and led us, and spared us heroic follies. The citation read:

Throughout his operational career this NCO has shown outstanding determination to press home his attacks with accuracy and bring back a record of his achievements … He is a keen and conscientious Captain of aircraft whose quiet confidence and courage have been an inspiration to the Squadron, and he is strongly recommended for the award of the Distinguished Flying Medal.

The Wing Commander had had the last words – and great words they proved. As an award the DFM was much less common than the Distinguished Flying Cross awarded to commissioned aircrew – this despite the fact that the great majority of aircrew were NCOs. Geoff particularly valued the words on the reverse: *For Courage.* There was no standardized procedure with either award. Many Dominions squadrons gave them as a matter of course when a crew survived a tour; RAF squadrons were generally more restrictive.

Geoff had begun instructing on Wellington IIIs. Although a great improvement on the worn-out ICs of our training days, he hankered still for Lancasters. Within days of leaving Elsham he was writing:

> *Whereas I had a restless feeling on the squadron, I now feel totally lost. It's an awful sensation ...*

And within a month:

> *The yearning to get back on ops is still with me. Frank wrote the other day. It seems that he too wants to get back. It's not heroics or anything like that. It's just that the life appeals so much to me ... I want the excitement and the thrills ...*

As the war swung in the Allies favour his yearning intensified.

> *Sometimes I wish it were all over, and then I feel that I want more excitement before it does conclude. Just a selfish lust.*

There were many tour-expired men like him, high still on their own adrenalin. Even the more sober men felt a compulsion to return. It was seldom patriotism, nor, for that matter, was there urgent need confronting us any longer – more aircrew were available than even Bomber Command could devour. It was a feeling close to guilt, a feeling that it was not decent to over-value one's life when so many friends had lost theirs, that to hold back was to be something less than a man. Only after a second tour of twenty ops was there tacit acceptance that death had been given chance enough; it was reasonable then to disengage.

But sometimes there were more rational reasons for returning. A few outstanding men recognized that the Command needed their leadership and expertise. Their presence on a squadron lifted morale enormously – provided they stayed alive. If they were killed, morale suffered proportionately. Epitomizing such men at Lichfield were two former Riverina farmers, Arthur Doubleday and Bill Brill. They were Squadron Leaders, each commanding a Lichfield training flight. In 1940 they had left Australia together, had trained together in Canada and had both been commissioned off course. They completed tours at the same time on 460 Squadron. Each was soon to return to operations from Lichfield as a Wing Commander of different squadrons; Bill Brill's second-tour navigator was to be our irrepressible Blue Freeman.

Both crews survived, Brill's even surviving the dropping on their plane of sixteen incendiary bombs. These set one wing on fire and started a fire internally. Brill ordered the crew to abandon aircraft, but on viewing Berlin burning below, they prevaricated and, astonishingly, the crisis passed. Arthur Doubleday was one of those men who 'wrote themselves off' as soon as they learned the Bomber Command odds; after that, each safe return was a bonus. He returned in all fifty-seven times. His attitude underlined the famous Micky Martin's contention that the greatest enemy of good morale was hope. For all that, I wonder still how many men were really able to surrender hope.

With ops over there was opportunity to view our role more clearly. How many of us pondered what Bomber Command was doing, I cannot guess. To have started a mess conversation on the morality of area bombing would have labelled one at least as odd. Most of us had accepted doing at a distance what we would probably have rebelled against face to face. Yet, if not by bombing, how else was this vast evil to be dislodged?

None of us then knew that the evil was more vast than anything claimed by British propagandists; we knew nothing of German extermination camps. For some reason Allied intelligence chose not to tell us. Had we known, it might have steeled our resolve; on the other hand we might have dismissed such enormities as propaganda less believable than the gross anti-German propaganda of the First World War.

Most Lichfield screens were Australians and most had completed tours in the Middle East. Living conditions there had been harsh, but survival rates generally much higher. The disproportion of Middle East instructors was not lost on the trainees. In class one day, as I lectured on operational navigation, the men pressed me to tell them what ops were 'really like'. One of them said, 'You've operated over Europe; most of the other instructors here operated in the Middle East.' This led another to interject, 'Just where *do* the men with experience over Germany get posted to?' Where indeed! A realist eyed me challengingly, 'I suppose most of them are dead!'

My answer could scarcely be convincing. I could only suggest how lives might be saved. To give them a chance of survival it was essential to give them operational hints and to keep up their morale; it would have worsened their chances to have preached doom. Anyway, the casualty rates were known month by month; any man could work out the odds for himself.

Because of delays in training I found men I had known as far back as Somers only now reaching Lichfield. One, Roy Clark, a young police constable, was a pilot commissioned off course. He typified the enthusiasm of hundreds. 'I want to do a tour on Lancasters, then switch over to Mosquitoes,' he told me.

I agreed that Mosquitoes were a good prospect, but urged him to think no further ahead than his first tour. I doubt that he heard me. Like most of the trainees, he did not complete a Lancaster tour.

We flew with each of these men on their first cross-country exercises, the screen navigator keeping an eye on whereabouts from the astro-dome, going forward from time to time to offer help with log and chart. At the end, the logs and charts had to be analyzed.

Bereft of a crew, my mind kept turning to the fortunes of the men I had trained with in Canada. Max I heard from regularly. His letters were often charged with the compelling insanity of the life we had left behind.

> *A couple of poor devils were shot down as we ran in. ... ... got back to base to find it fogged out. We were directed to Hamley, 58 miles west, on arrival there we found it was fogged out too, and we were re-diverted to High Ercall. ... We found kites everywhere – our turn to land was seven! ... When we finally got 'pancake' there was about 17 gallons in the last tank! ... When we had stopped taxying there was just five gallons!*

Like Bill Charlton, Wilf Burrows, Col Miller and a few others of our training course, Max had not touched alcohol when he left home. Once on a squadron his choice was company in the mess and local pubs, or solitariness; very few operational aircrew chose to be alone, besides, Max was a man closely drawn to his fellows. He wrote at Warboys:

> *Looking around the room, I knew a sudden fierce joy that my life had been cast with such grand company, especially with such as George and Harry ... just a sudden flare of love for my comrades which left as quickly as it came.*

On Anzac Day that year RAAF and RNZAF aircrew on his squadron got together for a celebratory evening.

> *... the usual thing – bags of beer, spirited if tuneless singing and hakas. By the end I was quite incapable, and remember scarcely anything of the trip home. When here I have recollections of George [Loder] holding me up while I became ill, uttering words of consolation and finally getting me to my site. George is undoubtedly one of the steadiest chaps of all. Next morning he*

seemed almost embarrassed at my thanks, so I cut them short. I reached the decision that being drunk is singularly unpleasant.

A couple of weeks later my leave co-incided with Max's, so I led him to the Exe valley and we went on up to Porlock, sharing a room at the 'Castle', intending to do a lot of walking. The weather was against us; we managed only one memorable day of scrambling about the coombes, glissading onto a deserted beach, finally reaching tiny Culbone church, shut in dripping woods. That evening we talked of the men we had known and tried to come to terms with loss of them. We read a long time from anthologies of poetry we had bought in Exeter, mostly pieces on the seasons, Max relishing, I remember, 'Sumer is icumen in.' Coming it indeed was, though we were seeing little of it. In the morning we had to return.

I wrote to him on May 26 telling him my commission had come through and that I was going to London the next weekend for 'kitting up', my plan being to stay at Charlwood rectory.

When I arrived at Charlwood I was flabbergasted to find Max here! He had had the day off, or had asked for it, and had found his way down here. It's great to see him anywhere. We went for a walk in the twilight ... Charlwood is hidden away in greenery now, its church, its pub and all its old, old cottages. Lupins are high in every cottage garden, chestnuts are blooming, roses climb every wall. What deep peace lies here.

In the morning Max had to leave early; the Rector was running him to the train at Horley. Our farewells over, I slept again. In a day or two I wore my new uniform in The Street, walking with the rector's wife, the peak of my new hat seeming to project into every scene. As we passed local people, caps and forelocks were tugged and I returned their salutations 'There's no need to salute,' said the rector's wife. 'Not with the villagers.' I would never understand.

I returned to Lichfield first class, as befitted my new estate; in my pocket was my first cheque book ever. A deferential batwoman woke me next morning; she bore a hotwater container like a small watering can. 'It's seven o'clock, sir. Which boots do you want cleaned?' It was a question easily answered since I still had only one pair. But, all in all, life became much more pleasant and coming summer was day-haunted with cuckoo calls. On June 12 a telegram came from Harry Wright. One word hit me at a glance 'Max', then 'missing'. The brightness drained from the day. 'Syd Cook looking after effects. ... '

I stood there, oblivious to my surroundings, feeling there was something urgent I must do, knowing there was nothing that could be done. George Loder wrote to me immediately:

After the lapse in our correspondence I'm sorry to have to reopen it with such bloody awful news, and only the fact that you may not hear from any other source prompts me to do so.

Max didn't return from ops on the 11th and, of course, so far we have heard no further news. Believe me, I know what a blow this is to you. I feel it perhaps just a little less myself, for although I wasn't associated with him as closely as you, I was tremendously fond of him – one couldn't help liking and admiring him.

Knowing the score about ops as you and I do, I can only say there should be some hope that the crew baled out. We were both on the same target – M – and, so far as I know, no kites were seen to go down over it.

I don't know whether there is anything I should or could to. Although Max and I knocked round a good deal since coming here, we never discussed unpleasant possibilities. If there is anything, will you please let me know.

'M' was Munster, a secondary target; only 72 aircraft had attacked it while over ten times that number had carried out a devastating raid on Dusseldorf. The Munster force had suffered 6.9% casualties. This was Lay's crew's twenty-fourth operation. I wrote at once to Nell, memories of our training days in Edmonton vivid in my mind. He had hoped for us – and we for him.

The rest I heard long after. The crew had been shot down over Holland; a Dutchman, Jan Rus, found Max's body by the Urk Dike, in Friesland. Rus himself perished in a concentration camp the following year. At the 1943 speech night at Cowra High School, where Max had been school captain four years earlier, a Max Bryant Memorial Prize was established; this has been continued in perpetuity by his only brother.

The letter I had received from George Loder was my first link with him since our course reunion in Doncaster. Only the abnormalities of Bomber Command life had led to such a lapse. Confronting the gap left by the loss of Max, my mind turned to George often. When I think of him today I realize to what a degree he epitomized the qualities – archaic qualities – inculcated in our generation: consideration of parents, reticence, duty, obedience, courage, endurance, frugality. He possessed, too, a great sense of humour and was well able to assert himself. To me he had remained 'the Imperturbable', though I never spoke the word to him.

In his crew were five Australians, one Englishman and the genial, rock-steady New Zealand pilot Mick Sullivan. When George wrote home of their experiences, his attitude was very different from mine – he spared his family to an extreme degree. He referred in a detached, half-amused way, to a terrifying episode over Cologne; it was more openly described by Eric Ritchie, their Australian W.Op.:

> ... we were hit by shellfire at the nose of our plane, which was thrown over on its back. We fell 7000 feet on our back and our captain gave us the order to 'abandon aircraft'. This, of course, was impossible as we were upside down and our parachutes had

been thrown in all directions. ... Then through the haze came the captain's voice to 'Hold everything', and slowly but surely we turned up on an even keel – we had completed an enormous loop-the-loop with a bomb load of 10,000 lbs. ...

We were certainly in His hands that night as we had lost all our navigator's maps which had fallen through a hole in the roof as we turned over. Then, as if we had not enough trouble, an enemy fighter attacked us while we were limping back ... Knowing that He was watching over us ... has given me much more confidence and I feel now that I will never be afraid again.

Even when Sullivan's crew was posted to the Pathfinder Force at the end of March 1943, George made little of it to his family; he did not so much as disclose his new duties, or even the requirement that their crew would now have a minimum of forty-five operations to do instead of thirty.

The crew's bombaimer was the Australian Vince Givney who had flown his first two operations with our crew from Lichfield as replacement for Ted Batten. By early July '43 the crew had been together a year – which in Bomber Command was a rarity. 'We have gained a pretty deep insight into each others' lives,' George told his parents. 'We face the future with quiet confidence. ... '

By the middle of August Vince had reached 32 ops, Mick 31, George 29. Early in September George was at last commissioned. I had often reflected on the unreasonableness of a system that had left such a man without a commission for so long. Even in Canadian days, we had viewed him as second only to Tib Barker.

When George went to London for kitting up, he bumped into Johnnie Gordon who had not long before flown on an operation to Friedrickshafen; the force had continued to North Africa instead of returning to England. George wrote home more freely of Johnnie's experiences than he ever did of his own:

They were so damaged by target defences that they couldn't get enough height to cross right over the Alps, so they mapread their way through the valleys. This nearly proved fatal. Suddenly a broad valley ended in a high peak which they could not possibly get over nor could they turn around. They spotted an off-shooting valley just in time. Anyway they eventually returned safely to England after a pleasant few days of sunshine and what must Jack do but get bowled over next night by a motorbike and have his leg broken. Poor Jack, he's an unlucky sort of bloke. I think he's the only one of our course still surviving that hasn't been commissioned and to my way of thinking he should have been one of the first. Unfortunately he has a manner which belies his real character and moreover won't speak up for himself.

The greatest blow George had so far suffered was loss of his flying partner of Canadian days, Harry Waddell. 'It's hard to realize – I looked on Harry as almost indestructible.' But I remembered from our days in Scotland that Harry had written himself off from the beginning. When my own tour ended George wrote to his parents:

I'm glad Don's finished for a while … curiously enough he always adopted the fatalistic attitude that once he started ops. his days would be numbered.

This was not quite so. In answer to Harry's conviction that he would not return, my reply had been that I hoped for everything but expected nothing.

George was as convinced as I was that Harry Wright and Blue Freeman would survive. His conviction remained even when, at fifty-two operations, Harry lost Syd Cook. Harry had been briefly in sickquarters; Syd, by then a triply-decorated Squadron Leader, had been obliged to operate without him and was killed on the eve of his twenty-second birthday.

By late October '43 George's crew was six operations short of the forty-five minimum demanded of Pathfinders.

... bad weather or not I suppose we shall finish by the end of the year. After being operational for twelve months, I wouldn't mind a change.

By his twenty-fifth birthday the crew had only three operations to do and was yearning for home.

I had a letter from Betty today enclosing a 'letter' from Elizabeth. It was rather hard to read but it seems Elizabeth was sending her love and hoping I would come home to see her soon.

Well, we are nearly through our second tour and I suppose by the end of the year our crew will be separating and its members going to different places ... – We've certainly been together a long time ... We're more like a family now. We're blunt and frank with each other. We've had time to see what each one is made of ... – we've had no quarrels and we're the best of friends. I know I could ask anything of any one of them and it would be done if it could be.

Although he allowed no emotion to creep into his letters, he was finding the last operations a great strain and began to suffer acutely from airsickness – something never mentioned to his family and played down with the crew. That November he and three others of the crew were decorated; this made six of them decorated in all.

Well – as you know – investitures are made as Buckingham Palace ... In our case I hope it will be delayed so long that we get home. I think it would be much nicer to be invested at Government House where you could all come along.

He went on to say that two more members of their crew had been commissioned; one was Vince Givney.

We had a night of celebration in the village and poor old Vince, riding back on a wagon, unfortunately fell off and broke his arm rather badly. Fortunately, being a couple ahead of the rest of us, he had finished his tour on our last sortie, but if he hadn't had the accident he'd have kept on with us. He was whisked off to hospital ... By the time he comes back we all should be finished ...

The weather deteriorated in December; fog closed in while they still had two operations to do. On the sixteenth they went to Berlin, a devastating raid by 483 Lancasters and ten Mosquitoes, but the costs were extremely high: twenty-five Lancasters were shot down; twenty-nine more either crashed or were abandoned when unable to get down through low cloud on their return. Mick Sullivan successfully returned to base.

The crew's forty-fifth operation was to Frankfurt. Middlebrook and Everett report that German control was able to plot the 647 heavy bombers all the way from the English coast to the target. There were many combats on the way in; in all, 6.3% of the force was lost. Damage in Frankfurt typified area bombing: 23,000 people were bombed out; various industrial premises were hit – so were the cathedral, the city hospital, the city library and sixty-nine schools.

At Warboys Vin Givney had the job of minding the drinks set aside for the crew's end-of-tour party. This time they did not return. They were shot down by night-fighters near Laubach, the aircraft exploding in mid-air, the wreckage falling over a wide area of forest. The Imperturbable's DFC was presented to his two-year-old daughter Elizabeth* at Government House, Sydney, on August 5 1944.

---

* In 1990 George Loder's daughter, Elizabeth Webby, was appointed Professor of Australian Literature at Sydney University.

23

Nineteen Forty-Four

The aircrew total [killed], 55,573, has special significance; in the First World War the officer losses of the British Empire included 38,834 killed, and this slaughter of the nation's elite was widely regarded as the most tragic and damaging aspect of that war. It was to avoid such a thing ever happening again that Britain turned her back on a Continental policy, and looked to the Air Force rather than the Army for salvation. Yet, ... by and large RAF aircrew were exactly the same type of men as the officers of 1914-18; it is salutary to see how the pursuit of a 'cheaper' policy brought in its train only a much higher cost, (The Right of the Line, by John Terraine, p. 682)

Most of our Edmonton course of navigators had been posted to squadrons in northern Lincolnshire; only Tib Barker and Johnnie Gordon had been sent further south, both of them to the Lancasters of the Australian 467 Squadron at Bottesford; up north we heard little of them. Tib completed a first tour of twenty-five then went to Pathfinder Mosquitoes. On these two-man aircraft he flew with two successive RAF pilots, flying forty-eight target-marking operations with the first, including fourteen trips to Berlin, then twenty-two as navigator to the master bomber, whose role was to direct the attack by radio-telephone. All of this work demanded navigation of the highest order. Both Tib and his pilot held Squadron Leader rank.

I met Tib in London when he had done over seventy operations; he was still the handsome, self-possessed man we had all regarded so well. As his first tour pilot said, 'When he came into a room, women's eyes turned to look at him.' When

I asked how long he aimed to continue operating, he replied, without hint of bravado, that he would like to reach a hundred, then operate in the Pacific. As Johnnie Gordon once remarked 'Tib isn't cursed with imagination.' But his aim was slightly less daunting than I realized at the time; ops on the Mosquito were statistically almost four times less lethal than on Lancasters, owing to the altitude and speed at which they flew. For all that, they were stressful enough for any mortal and as Tib neared his goal the strain began to tell even on him. Returning from his ninetieth, they were approaching to land when he saw his pilot's hand go mistakenly to the undercarriage lever, as if to retract the wheels. He knocked the hand away. As soon as they had taxied in he said, 'If I haven't a good enough grip on myself to speak instead of doing that, it's time I finished.' He finished that night and was soon afterwards awarded a bar to his DFC.

Johnnie Gordon also flew a first tour from Bottesford; his pilot, Squadron Leader Keith Sinclair, later became editor of the Melbourne *Age*. The only one of our old course who managed to visit him at Bottesford was George Loder. He wrote to me:

I found him perched up in the corner of the mess with his boots undone and the most dilapidated battle dress you ever saw. No buttons on the sleeves or pockets, half-faded and it looked as if it was just washed and not ironed. His skipper is always at him to get a new one but I suppose he has become so used to wearing it that he hates giving it up.

This is a yarn one of the chaps told me about him. The squadron commander asked his skipper what sort of a navigator he was. The skipper said, 'Bang on every time – never misses.' The chief said, 'He doesn't look too bloody bang on.' ... I thought you would like to know that he still has that old trait of doing things his way in spite of what the next bloke thinks.

That was Johnnie! As a crew member and a friend, few could touch him, but as far as authority was concerned he could be perverse and provoking, especially with those he regarded as 'born standing to attention'.

He once wrote home resignedly:

I just sit down and read till someone tells me what to do and if no one tells me what to do I don't do anything. Which is the procedure approved by the RAF. I get into trouble every time I try to think for myself – 'initiative' it's called and they don't like it over here – so now I don't ever think at all where the Air Force is concerned.

He had gone to war entirely out of a sense of duty and was one of the older men on our course – thirty-one by the time he got onto operations. When he enlisted he was a teacher at North Sydney Boys' High School; also he was a gifted violinist, a Country Week cricketer and a good middle-distance runner. He was a complex character – one of his sisters called him 'a wise, sad clown'. He carried on a love-hate relationship with England, the hate confined to the establishment and the obedient lower orders, the love to most else – countryside, theatre, scholarship, music. He wanted very much to go to Oxford at the end of the war to further his Greek.

During the latter half of 1943 I came to know him closely. I re-opened our correspondence soon after his crew's hair-raising flight to North Africa after bombing Friedrichshafen. They had had to leave their badly-damaged Lancaster down there and return with other crews.

She was a good kite was Z. Yesterday they gave us another (apparently they think we want to fly) but last night a new crew took it on a bullseye* and on return unofficially opened a new

---

* A night cross-country flight culminating in an infra-red photograph of a 'target'.

satellite drome about half a mile past the end of our runway. Unfortunately full preparations had not been made by the farmer for the reception of a bomber. (The careless bugger had even left a harvester on the 'runway') so now we ain't got no 'Willie'.

His jesting protected an inner man painfully sensitive to the insanity of war, in particular, to Bomber Command's relentlessly mounting attack. Even when he wrote of the most taxing experiences, he slipped into jest.

I see by the papers that the battle of the Ruhr has been won. The bloke who wrote that hasn't seen the place lately. At any rate, the Germans don't agree with him. The last couple of trips there have been hell, making Essen's previous displays (which were never pleasant) look like play. ... On our last trip we saw 6 kites go down to fighters in as many minutes in the North Sea. We saw one bloke bale out quite near us, took a fix, W/T-ed it home. ... Base got only the end of it and thought we had baled out in the drink. To add weight to that idea, we were late back, having gone practically all the way there and back on three engines. When finally we called up on R/T they got us down immediately and the welcome of the Prodigal Son was a very small affair in comparison. ...

Men seldom spoke about their fears, except in half-jocular vein. I had finished a tour knowing only how it had been for me, but I knew Johnnie well enough to ask him how he was finding it. He replied typically:

My reactions to ops are simply that I'm scared stiff. I get so scared that by the time we get to the target even all the fear has been dried up in me ... The only thing I like about ops is the fine solid feeling of the earth under my feet as I climb out of the kite. ... It all goes to prove what a bloke once told me, 'As soon as you leave the ground you're in danger, even if you only jump up in the air.'

He went on to compare our ways of spending leave:

My leaves, too, are spent mainly in rest. My last was spent in London and I can even say I enjoyed it. Much sleep, good food, a row on the Serpentine each day in the sun. Plays and concerts …

The Gordon children had lost their father when Johnnie was nineteen; he, as eldest of five, had watched over his siblings' upbringing. From England he had tried to dissuade his youngest brother, George, from going into aircrew, but the day came when George, then twenty-one, was posted to Coastal Command, to 461 Squadron, Pembroke Dock, as a wireless operator on Sunderlands.

… he was wild because they didn't send him to Lancs. Three of his friends came to this squadron, but two of them are already missing. That ought to convince him.

Despite the long tours demanded on Sunderlands, their survival rate was relatively high.

When Johnnie was knocked over by a motorbike and sent to hospital, he lost Sinclair's crew and had to finish at Bottesford with whatever crew happened to need a navigator. This was often prescription for death, especially on their squadron at this time – they had lost eleven crews in seven weeks. A story reached me of his fathering of a crew who were on their first operation. On the final leg of the attack the bewildered pilot called, 'What's this going on ahead of us? Could you have a look?' Emerging from behind the navigator's curtain Johnnie pronounced, 'That's the target. They've spent a lot of money putting on that show for us. The sooner you get in there the better.' They came safely back and eventually he completed his tour and was awarded 'a routine DFC'. He was then a Warrant Officer, but had been interviewed for a commission.

I had an argument with both the Wingco and the Groupy at the interview. Still, they didn't tell me I wouldn't get one so I suppose I can presume to hope.

Three months after the interview, on October 28, he came to see me at Lichfield, still a Warrant Officer. We walked along the beautiful stretch of the Trent and Mersey canal by Ravenshaw Wood. It was familiar territory to both of us. I remembered Johnnie coming from it in our training days, telling me, 'I met an old bloke fishing and I asked him if there is a book on fishing in these parts. He said, 'Well there be un called "The Compleat Angler".' To return there with him now was foretaste of company to come; I fully expected him to be posted to Lichfield as an instructor.

We talked of England and ops and the ways in which we had spent leaves. It is well over a year since we parted. The scene was tranquil and full of colours. The canal on these autumn days is a place of perfect reflections and frail, floating leaves of many hues.

As I was starting a forty-eight hour leave next day, we went to London together and got a room at the 'Imperial' in Russell Square and talked far into the night. He admitted to deep loneliness. 'I've made no friends since the old flight broke up.' In the morning we wandered along Charing Cross Road, lingering in bookshops, then bought tickets for 'The Marriage of Figaro.' The choice of opera was mine. The performance enchanted me, but I was conscious of Johnnie's restlessness. During the interval he confessed he was not a Mozart man; his loves were Bach, Beethoven and Wagner; Wagner above all. Wagner bore me into Gothic gloom, nor could I understand any mortal not being swept away by Mozart.

It was, I suppose, less than realistic of me to expect Johnnie to come to Lichfield. The mixture of hilarity and frankness he would have brought to the classroom could have landed him in endless trouble. An instructor could not be specific about the havoc of area bombing, nor about crews' slim prospects of survival. I well knew Johnnie's feelings about the 'blind mass murdering of the main force'. I think he shunned responsibility for leading others into it. I ought not have been surprised when he decided to go straight to 617 Squadron – the Dambusters – on Special Duties. The highly-trained 617 specialized in pinpoint bombing of military objectives; this involved precise, low-level flying after long training.

His close company lost, he carried on my education at a distance. I at last read the *Oedipus* he had sent me and wrote to him while still under its spell. 'Sophocles knows the game a bit, doesn't he?' he replied:

> *Anyway, hang you, didn't I recommend* Antigone *(Sophocles) to you ages ago and didn't you ignore it? Well, try it now. And the* Medea *of Euripides and the* Agamemnon *of Aeschylus ... And if you like comedy try the* Frogs *of Aristophanes.*

Deprived of Johnnie's company, I was more inclined to heed Geoff's importunings to return to operations. Tib Barker, Harry Wright, and Blue Freeman were 'pressing on regardless'; I felt ashamed. As soon as I expressed willingness, Geoff was off for an interview with Gp Capt Dickens at Elsham. Shag we counted out, for Hilda had borne a baby daughter who had lived only an hour, as much a victim of Bomber Command as all those others; Graham had already done a second tour. The rest were willing to come.

Although Geoff returned from Elsham confident we would soon be back, the RAF had different intentions; we would stay where we were. Frank Holmes was dismayed. He said in a letter to me, 'I'd rather do two tours with you and Geoff than one with another crew.' As he feared, he was sent back with another crew; soon afterwards he was killed – our lively poacher, our brother whom we hoped might join us in Australia 'after the war.'

Although Geoff and I settled back into life at 27 OTU, Geoff never really gave up his attempts to get back onto ops until he became engaged in 1944 to a Burton girl.

All through these months pupils were killed, mostly in crews of five on cross-country exercises; one in May, two in June, one in July. It was not as bad as our own training days, but bad enough. And there were bizarre accidents: '11 Aug., propeller fell off, pilot and rear gunner killed'; '10 Sept., attempted overshoot, aircraft hit house, all killed' and, on November 6, two separate collisions on one night, taking thirteen Lichfield staff and pupils. The only survivor was Gp Capt Paddy Heffernan, our Australian commanding officer. He was found in a ditch suffering multiple fractures, shock and exposure.

The remains of crews killed away from Lichfield were buried away; the thirty-one Air Force graves then in Fradley churchyard represented only part of our total losses. As well as these training losses, there was always news reaching us from the insatiable squadrons of men killed on second tours and former Lichfield pupils killed. There was a navigator trainee named Keith Bradbury with whom I had gone to school at Frankston, who wrote to me of a crash in which he had lost nearly all of his crew. Having read his letter I could not get out of mind boyhood images of him on long, lunchtime chases through the miles of bush near our school. Then he was gone; killed with a second crew.

14 Nov: Each day gets progressively colder. Wet winds moan all day about the buildings; the leaves have gone and the very grass is perishing; everywhere there is mud underfoot; always the skies are sombre and devoid of any promise of better days to come. The tannoy gives warning after warning of storms, gales, squalls or snow. As we face into the pitiless wind our tempers become short and we tell ourselves that we can't possibly stand the pain any longer. The old cry goes up, 'Let them give the Jerries the bloody country!'

Yet, strangely, we had become part of the 'bloody country'; we wore our Englishness as a cloak over our Australian selves.

Totally unexpected postings began taking place – postings home. Our minds could scarcely take it in. Selection seemed to depend upon how long one had been away from Australia. Time passed and we began to receive letters from the repatriated men. Don't come, they advised; the RAAF look on us as outsiders; the real war is here; we have been 'tourists'; our experience counts for little. It was bewildering. There had been no war 'out there' when these men had left home. 'They reckon we even speak like Poms,' wrote one. Men began making excuses to delay their departure. Kodak House became annoyed; henceforth nominated men would go without option.

Late in November I had wholly unexpected news from Johnnie Gordon: he was to be married:

You see, you don't know it all. I haven't known [Mary] long but we're engaged and in not long we'll be spliced, (if she doesn't realize her mistake in time.) Hell, when you're lonely and in such times as these, it doesn't take long to form friendships and from there the disease spreads like leprosy. We have just about everything in common – even religion.

I knew 'the disease' well. Letters between Nell and me had diminished. I was confident still that all would be the same if we could see each other, but it was a remote 'if', and more and more I was finding the thought of marrying in England appealing.

For a month or so Johnnie sounded 'like a kid with a new toy', as he put it. He did not mention wedding arrangements, but I assumed his brother George would be his best man. Then, on Christmas Eve, George's Sunderland failed to return from operations. It had been shadowing eleven German destroyers in conditions of low cloud and had been shot down. Within a few days it was known there was no hope for the crew. Johnnie went to Pembroke Dock to find out what he could. The only consolation was that he now had someone close to him in his grief.

A week after this, I was stunned to find myself one of the Lichfield screens posted home. By now marriage was about the only acceptable reason for delay.

> ... the uppermost feeling in my mind is that this English world of mine with its happiness and tragedy and its many people who have come to mean much, is breaking up about me, as all one's worlds sooner or later must break. That I will be seeing those at home is as yet a fantastic dream. ... I wish above everything that Geoff were coming.

There was no prospect of that; he was to be retained at Church Broughton until the end of the war, converting 108 pilots in all onto Wellingtons and being awarded an Air Force Cross. He married his Burton girl.

On January 31st I was to go to Johnnie Gordon's wedding. (At last he was Pilot Officer Gordon.) I went to London the preceding evening and he met me at Paddington. We stayed together at the 'Great Western', talking late about his brother and about Mary, whom I had not yet met. I met her at the church in Northfield next morning when I took George's place as best man.

Twelve days after this Johnnie's crew went on a difficult raid, led by Wing Commander Leonard Cheshire. They were to bomb the Antheor Viaduct near Cannes. The viaduct, which lay in a steep valley, carried a rail link between France and Italy. Cheshire and Sqn Ldr 'Micky' Martin made low runs along the valley, but the heavy defences and difficult location denied the attackers any real success; Martin's bombaimer was killed. After the long flight back, all the aircraft landed at Ford, on the south coast, and refuelled.

Johnnie's pilot, Sq Ldr Bill Suggett, was a Canadian. A RCAF friend of Suggett's, Flg Off Don Bell, wrote later to the Gordon family:

> ... *the boys had a meal and a wash up. Then they took off to return to base. There was a layer of cloud which hung pretty low in spots. All the planes climbed up through the cloud to go back except one. Suggett was a wonderful pilot and had had intensive low flying training and experience, so set course for base below the cloud. Two minutes later they crashed into the top of a 150 foot hill ...*

After all their experience – one hundred and fifty feet! I felt as much outraged as bereaved.

> ...*'tis enough, 't will serve.*

24

The Long Way Back

Bomber Command was consigned to obscurity. Churchill did not mention it in his victory broadcast. No campaign medal was struck for it. Alone among the successful war leaders, Sir Arthur Harris was not elevated to the House of Lords. Yet indiscriminate bombing had been for four years the British achievement most prized by both public opinion and statesmen. (The Second World War, by A.J.P. Taylor, Penguin Books, 1976.*)

On Sunday 20 February 1944 we left London, a contingent of tour-expired Australians, most from the Middle East and Coastal Command, a handful from Bomber Command. Our port of departure was not disclosed to us.

> *At about 2 o'clock we set off in an ancient train, six to a cold third class compartment. ... Darkness closed over English fields, I wondered if I would ... see them again. York, Newcastle ... attempts to sleep.*

> *Mon. 21: 'Rise and shine, we're there!' 'Where?' 'Gourock.' I felt sleepy, nostalgic and indifferent to my company. The name Gourock brought vividly to mind our arrival and my first impressions of the Home Country, memories, too, of the boys I set*

---

* A.J.P. Taylor equated area bombing with indiscriminate bombing; yet thousands of aircrew lost their lives while striving to bomb the Pathfinder markers, and the Pathfinders were themselves established to reduce inaccuracy. Nevertheless, precision bombing proved unachievable by night. The options open to Britain were to accept the inevitable spread of bombs – i.e. area bombing – or cease night bombing. The bomber chiefs not only accepted the inevitable; they capitalised on it.

out with one spring day nearly two years ago. We stepped off
Scottish soil onto a ferry.

... The sky was flushed, throwing into dark relief the eastern
hills. There was much activity on the water, a bustling to and fro
of disembodied lights, but there were no sounds and not a breath
of wind. On the far shore subdued lights of various colours were
growing wan. We cast off and throbbed through the fresh morn-
ing, a glassy wave falling back from our prow. ... We crowded to
the port side, for our ship lay there, a most beautiful shape. We
swept under her stern, like a rider passing below a mountain and,
looking up, read her name, Queen Mary ...

She was carrying very few troops. I found I was to share a
cabin with a quiet, impressive youth, a wireless operator, Bob
Kellow DFM, formerly of 617 Squadron. He had been in the
crew of Flt Lt L.G. Knight, a Melburnian, and had taken part
in the Ruhr Dams raid of May 16 1943 – it was Knight's bomb
that had breached the Eder Dam. On that operation eight of
nineteen Lancasters had failed to return. Four months later, on
September 15, Knight's crew was one of eight from 617 Squadron briefed to breach the Dortmund Ems-Canal at low level.
By the time the Lancasters reached the canal, ground fog had
greatly reduced visibility. The raid failed and five of the
Lancasters were lost – 62.5% of the attacking force. Knight
himself clipped the tops of trees, choking his engines. He had
only power enough climb to 1500 feet to enable his crew to bale
out; he could not escape himself. Kellow, in a long, adventurous
saga, evaded capture. Soon after his return to England, he was
posted home.

There in our cabin, listening to this mildly-related tale, I felt
a surge of admiration and joy; here was one at least who had
dared everything and still lived. Bob, calm, even serene, was
oblivious, I am sure, to the impact of his words. Later we went
up together on deck; by then it was 4 o'clock, the sun low in the
west, softening bold contours of mountains about Loch Lo-

mond. We had not yet moved. I noticed again the startlingly clear Scottish air and the wonderful pageantry of skies, a combination that formed our last picture of Britain. We began moving slowly seaward under our own power; Gourock and Greenock with their dour, straight houses, their kirks and open uplands, began slipping into the past.

As we watched the shore scenes change, Bob spoke of his plans when we reached New York. He had gained permission to go to Winnipeg to marry the girl to whom he had become engaged in his training days. He had no notion of the effect of his words on me. I did not know if such an option were open to me, but even if it were, could I positively say I wished to go to Edmonton to marry? After more than two years, could Nell say it? We needed time to talk; time, too, for me to put a viewpoint to her differing greatly from her father's. But time seemed beyond attaining. Added to this, I was conscious of being a man without a job to go to even if I survived the war. I could never return to Nareen, love it though I did; there, too, I had been an observer rather than a farmer.

I walked alone to the bows, thinking futilely over these things. In wartime one was a chip of wood borne on floods. It was now near dusk; I could just make out the boom across the entrance of the Clyde. A passing sailor remarked, 'Once we pass that we go like hell.'

It was so; there was a great surge of power and the land of our adventures and sorrows began shrinking astern. Our whole time there – for me just twenty-one months – began to seem like a bizarre play. Was it really possible that so many of those I had started with were dead? I had not seen them die, not one of them. I had not seen our victims die. Surely the curtain would go up soon on the reassembled cast.

This notion of a play – a long, tragic play – was to persist for years in my mind till I put words to it.

It was the last act but not yet the last scene. Warriors killed in battle lay so thickly on stage that they distracted the less assured of us from our parts. The play had been running continuously in the northeastern counties for four years; there were even actors who had been on stage since 1940.

Most of us were graduates of the Empire School of Drama. Month after month, all over the Empire, large groups of us had presented ourselves for auditioning, but relatively few had been chosen. Then, during rehearsals hundreds who had been accepted were rejected as unsuitable by the producers, or were given lesser roles.

When Bomber Offensive *opened it received enthusiastic notices in the Empire press and great acclaim from audiences. In part this was so because it released feelings of revenge the British public had harboured, but had lacked means of expressing. It must be admitted, too, that no other play of consequence was being produced just then in the British theatre.*

When our cue came, Bomber Offensive *had been running for two years, but a newly-appointed producer, being dissatisfied with past performances, had introduced revolutionary new techniques; added to this, the play had gathered momentum and direction of its own. In our initial confusion we had to* ad lib *quickly and listen for the prompter. There turned out to be several prompters, their scripts seemingly at variance. Some of the more seasoned actors – men distinguishable by brightly-coloured ribbons stitched to their jackets – willingly gave us advice, but too often they disconcerted us by pitching over among those playing Warriors killed in Battle. We were distracted, too, by the extraordinary set designs, the use of powerful spotlights, the deafening sound effects. Gradually we managed to pick up words and actions appropriate to our parts. These we repeated over and over until now, the moment of our exit ...*

We were beckoned off stage and told there were young actors waiting to replace us. We could pack our belongings now and return to our places of origin. Many of the actors had come from Canada, others from New Zealand, ourselves from Australia. As we prepared to leave we noticed several distinguished-looking critics also leaving, their expressions displeased, some declaring that the press had over-praised Bomber Offensive, *that there was no real precision in our performance, others that the play was morally reprehensible and ought never have been staged. Some of this latter group had applauded the earlier performances wildly.*

The director's assistants shook hands with us and wished us well. We lingered in the wings, reluctant to leave those of our countrymen still playing roles of Warriors killed in Battle. There were so many more of them than of us. We hoped they might soon get up and make their exit with us. It was taking the play too far to leave them lying there forsaken. A few of our countrymen who had gone on stage with us, were still playing active roles, striking defiant attitudes, declaiming brave lines against the overwhelming din. Reluctantly we left.

I did not imagine that all my life I would look back on the play, questioning myself about it, reading critics' opinions of it. Nor would I have believed that the Empire School of Drama would soon close its doors forever, much less have believed that Australian generations would arise who would scorn our loyalty to the Empire.

To make an end: in New York we of the *Queen Mary* contingent were told we were not yet to go home; for three months we must do a conversion course in Tennessee onto Liberators, the 'B24 four-engined combat bombardment ship', as the Americans called her. These we would fly to Brisbane.

It was a flight I was never to make. I completed the course, but did the long flying exercises in considerable pain – I had slipped a disc in my spine. To make matters worse, the Liberator lacked a proper seat for the navigator; only a wide, webbing belt stretched before his table, without a back rest. At our point of departure, near San Francisco, I was told I must return home by sea. A ship was to leave in two days, another a week later; I could go by either.

I recognized that a point of decision was presenting itself. I chose the second departure and sought permission to go to Edmonton, then telegraphed Nell. On May 17 I left by train, travelling the same route to Vancouver that our *Monterey* contingent had travelled over two and a half years earlier. Of the twenty men who had trained in Edmonton and gone to heavy bombers, six now remained alive, one of them a prisoner of war. On the return journey, I felt at once solitary and physically vulnerable, yet buoyed by the hope that in Edmonton all might yet work out.

In Vancouver I phoned the parents of Roly Newitt, that sergeant of Elsham Wolds, now a Squadron Leader on his second tour. They whisked me from my hotel, put me in Roly's room, reminded me, as they might have reminded him, of the permanent nature of marriage.

A day and a half later the train drew in at the station we had disembarked at in 1941. No curious crowd of Edmontonians now. I walked as fast as I could manage along the platform, glancing into faces.

Then I saw Nell and the moment I saw her I knew that all could be as before ... I was almost completely dumb and all Nell seemed able to say was, I can't believe it's true!' and 'You're exactly the same!'

Her parents were no longer in Edmonton; they were living in Victoria, B.C. We talked uninterrupted for seventeen hours and, at the end phoned our decision to them. I telegraphed my unit in the U.S. for permission to marry.

We went out to Victoria, with us Billie Willson as Nell's bridesmaid – that other girl who had looked from the stair landing on two Australians at the door, the girl who had partnered Max on so many of our outings.

269

We married on June 8, Max much in all our minds; nine days later I was admitted to hospital; I remained there six months.

Early in 1945, while I convalesced after surgery, RAAF Ottawa offered something we had neither sought nor imagined possible: a 'nurse' could share my cabin on the Swedish freighter *Kookaburra* Sydney-bound. It was an outcome beyond all imagining.

And so Nell came to her mother's country. We arrived at the beginning of March; not long afterwards we made the extraordinary discovery that our grandfathers – dead before we were born – had been friends in the Melbourne of the 1860s.

On July 31 I was discharged from the RAAF and next day started with air traffic control. Less than a month later aerial bombing – that development of my lifetime – had its full flowering over Hiroshima and Nagasaki.

Personal matters seem of small consequence in such a context. Enough to say that war gave me everything: a marriage happier than I could have imagined; children; a career; recognition of a first book; a home built for us by that intimidating pacifist, Neil East, in his 76th year – all this in ironic contrast with what it had taken from so many who had hoped only to 'grow old, As we that are left grow old.'

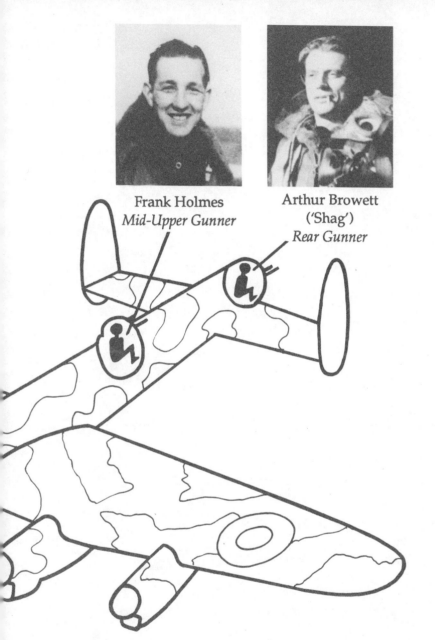

Frank Holmes
Mid-Upper Gunner

Arthur Browett
('Shag')
Rear Gunner

LANCASTER B-BEER
103 SQUADRON, RAF
BOMBER COMMAND